DIAMONDS IN THE MUD

A working-class hero is something to me

—◆—

BRIAN READE

MIRROR BOOKS

MIRROR BOOKS

1

Published in Great Britain and Ireland in 2021 by
Mirror Books, a Reach PLC business,
5 St Paul's Square, Liverpool, L3 9SJ.

www.mirrorbooks.co.uk
@TheMirrorBooks

Hardback ISBN: 9781913406639
eBook ISBN: 9781913406622

Photographic acknowledgements:
Tony Woolliscroft, Mirrorpix, PA Images, Blink Films.

Design and production by Mirror Books.

Printed and bound by CPI Group (UK) Ltd,
Croydon, CR0 4YY.

To everyone born with nothing who
chose to fight for something.

CONTENTS

PROLOGUE

SOLDIERS who fight in wars tend to keep battlefield memories to themselves.

Which is why I was surprised when, in my early 20s, a former Japanese POW indulged me with explicit details of his time in the Burmese jungle. He had watched that morning's televised Cenotaph event and the sight of certain dignitaries sporting rows of gleaming medals on their chests, despite never seeing action, had given him the urge to ram them up their regal jacksies.

He compared their absence from the theatre of war with young comrades who had fought heroically in abysmal conditions, many of whom never came home, and others who, when they returned, emaciated and broken, were given no recognition or reward. Indeed, they were treated as an embarrassment. "Heroes come cheap in this country, son, never forget it," he told me.

I thought of that old soldier in 2002 when the BBC compiled a definitive list of the 100 Greatest Britons.

Amid the ten monarchs (and the current one's fetishised mother, Gawd bless 'er) plus the many dukes and knights, was The Unknown Soldier. The ultimate national symbol of selflessness and sacrifice. Which you may think would make it a shoo-in for the number one spot. It actually came in at 76.

One place ahead of Robbie Williams. Well, he has got a decent collection of tattoos, to be fair.

In the Spring of 2021 I thought of that old soldier's advice again, when the government announced that the reward for NHS workers who had suffered physical and mental exhaustion fighting the Covid pandemic in which colleagues had died, would be an effective pay cut.

What a contrast to a year earlier, when every Thursday, from concrete tower block balconies to blossom-strewn millionaire rows, Britons went blinking into the sunset to bang pans and applaud those same workers. Back then a commonly-held view emerged that the notion of heroism was being turned on its head.

That traditional idols were now bit-part extras compared with the stars who turned up for work in disease-ravaged hospitals and care homes, those delivering letters and food, supermarket staff, bus drivers, cleaners and every other low-paid worker who risked their life, often with pitiful protection, for the common good.

When Prime Minister Boris Johnson was taken into intensive care he made his own Damascene conversion very public. He gushed about the expert treatment he had received, much of it from migrant workers who were doing 14-hour shifts in the grimmest of circumstances. And many people, even those who had voted for successive public-sector slashing Tory governments, questioned why these world-class assets had been treated so shabbily?

As spring turned to summer and the Black Lives Matter movement took to British streets following the murder in the USA of George Floyd, the heroic status afforded to men from past generations began to be questioned. The statue of Bristol slave trader Edward Colston was dragged down and Oxford's Oriel College agreed to remove the one of imperialist Cecil Rhodes.

Might this be a turning point for a country happy to ignore its historic failures and encourage an air of exceptionalism? A moment of hope for a nation whose history had become a vehicle for self-glorification rather than something to learn from?

Some felt that Britain was finally re-evaluating who was important in its past and present, and the country would never be the same again. But many like myself, who had long mocked the accepted view of heroism, were more sceptical.

We sensed that once the crisis was over and the economy needed dragging back from the brink, those warm words from on high would seem nothing more than empty platitudes. That the needs of those at the bottom who had kept the country going would once again be sacrificed, as the onus switched to helping the "wealth creators" create more wealth.

That there would be wage freezes in the care industry, or below-inflation pay rises for the lucky few; that knighthoods and lordships would be handed to favoured businessmen, party donors, and cronies, with a handful of minor trinkets tossed at the heroes of the pandemic.

And that is what happened in the New Year Honours List and the 2021 public sector pay awards. The old, established order was safely back in place. The life-savers had to make do with a clap.

One man who basked in far, far more than a clap was the Queen's husband, when he died in April 2021, sparking a staged outpouring of grief from the British media which made North Korea's state propagandists look like amateurs.

On the day after his death eight national newspapers ran 302 pages on the story. The following day eight Sunday papers devoted another 223 pages and the orgy of sycophancy continued to dominate editions for more than a week. All this for a half Greek/half Danish man who had served in World War Two but had held no constitutional role, had no hereditary link with previous monarchs, had lived a privileged lifestyle off the back of British taxpayers for three-quarters of a century and had done little to change the country for the better.

There had been no eight days of mourning four years earlier for the 72 people burned alive a few miles away from Buckingham Palace in Grenfell Tower. No compulsory black tie wearing of newsreaders for them.

Contrast the newspaper coverage with that given to another public servant called Philip who died the previous May in the line of duty. Phil Rennie, a 60-year-old ambulance driver from Rochdale, described by his bosses as a "dedicated" care worker who had "touched many people's lives" died after contracting Covid while transporting patients to hospital. The day after his death the national media coverage he received amounted to three paragraphs in a down-page story in *The i* newspaper.

The lack of any semblance of honesty about Prince Philip, whom many regarded as an arrogant, racist reactionary, was summed up by this front page headline from a right-wing tabloid: 'We're All Weeping With You Ma'am.'

The truth was that more people were weeping at the state broadcaster wiping out the BBC One and Two schedules for 24 hours to air quasi-religious tributes to a man whose greatest achievement was to keep walking two steps behind the Queen for 73 years without throwing himself into one of their castle moats. A record 110,000 people complained to the BBC about its over-the-top coverage, baiting it for sacrificing editorial freedom for fear of upsetting the Establishment. Many millions more nodded in agreement.

It took me back to a January day 56 years earlier, to the funeral of supposedly the greatest hero Britain had ever known.

Legend had decreed Winston Churchill to be a God-like figure who had saved the world from being subjugated by the most evil of regimes. But from where my seven-year-old head was lying, that wasn't how it looked.

It was resting on my palms, crouched on a rug in front of my nana's roaring hearth, staring at the blurred, crackling images of men with plumed helmets bobbing up and down on horses on a tiny black-and-white telly, listening to an alien voice solemnly describe the procession through central London.

It was bleak, grey and sombre. The only sound, when Richard Dimbleby stopped talking, was the thumping of muffled drums and the clomping of soldiers' boots.

Huddled in the back terraced room in the Wavertree district of Liverpool were aunts, uncles and my mum, looking on intently, saying nothing. At first, all these adults who had lived through a war that ended only 20 years earlier, kept a respectful silence.

But when Dimbleby told us this was the first time for a century that a state funeral had been afforded to a common man, my 68-year-old Irish nana sitting in her rocking chair in the corner, could take no more: "A common man? Him? All he did was kill the common man. Good riddance, you oul' whoremaster."

I was gone. In bits. Rolling round the rug squealing with laughter, despite not having a clue what a whoremaster was.

Which only encouraged my nan to spout even more vitriol in the direction of Churchill's coffin.

"He sent the Black and Tans to Ireland to rape all the nuns and turned the troops on the miners. Which is why he got his arse tanned by the common feckin' man in the election after the war," she continued, to a room now buzzing with laughter, while on the small telly the bleakness of London made the faces of the mourners – who doffed their caps and rubbed moisture from their National Health specs – look even more ashen.

We always had different heroes in our family and as I grew older I realised there were many other families like ours.

Almost half a century after Churchill's 1965 funeral, a few miles down the road from my nan's old house, I was at an event in Garston where locals are known as Mud Men because they used to collect coal from the mudbanks. It was a celebration of the centenary of the birth of Spanish Civil War veteran and trade union leader Jack Jones.

As I stared at a mural of Jack, a man in his 80s sidled up and asked what I thought of him. When I told him he was one of the finest men I'd ever met, he replied, "You're right, lad. He's Garston's finest. A true diamond in the mud."

A phrase that perfectly describes Jack, and every other working-class hero who never fully had their praises sung. Or who, like the low-paid frontline workers of the pandemic, were quickly forgotten.

As the old Japanese POW told me back in the 1970s, heroes come cheap and we should never forget it.

That's why I wanted to write about the diamonds I have been lucky enough to meet. The ones who rose from humble backgrounds to transform the world.

Some changed it in a huge way, others in a smaller way, but all made the people they came from immensely proud.

In an age when being worshipped for doing nothing comes easy, these ordinary working-class people who ended up doing extraordinary things are, to me, humanity's real heroes.

Let me tell you why.

THE —◆—
INSPIRATION

SALFORD — March 2019

FOR more than 40 years, Mike Leigh has been writing and directing films that give a voice to the British working-class.

Brilliant, uncompromising screenplays anchored in reality, such as Secrets and Lies, Vera Drake, All Or Nothing and Life Is Sweet.

When his home town of Salford made him a Freeman of the City, its mayor, Paul Dennett, said, "With our magazines, our books, our televisions so regularly filled with images of the successful, the rich and the powerful, Mike's work is a refreshing and straightforward reminder of the world in which the majority of people live."

Leigh picked up that accolade in July 2019, months after the release of Peterloo, his film about the 1819 massacre in St Peter's Field, Manchester, when sabre-waving cavalrymen from the 15th Regiment of Hussars and the Manchester and Salford yeomanry, surged into a crowd of 60,000 men, women and children who were peacefully campaigning for parliamentary reform, killing 18 and injuring more than 500. It was the 19th Century's Bloody Sunday. The deadliest political clash in British history.

So sensitive to the ruling class were the unprovoked killings that James Wroe, the editor who coined the phrase The Peterloo Massacre, which referenced the Battle of Waterloo four years earlier, was jailed for a year for seditious libel. And his liberal newspaper, *The Manchester Observer*, which carried first-hand, critical reports of the slaughter, was closed down.

It sent a wave of revulsion across liberal Britain. Percy Bysshe Shelley wrote a poem about it called The Masque of Anarchy and

The Manchester Guardian, today called just *The Guardian*, was set up in the aftermath as a left-leaning newspaper campaigning for voting rights for the masses. At its launch the publishers proclaimed it would "zealously enforce the principles of civil and religious liberty, warmly advocate the cause of reform and endeavour to assist in the diffusion of just principles of political economy."

Hannah Barker, professor of British history at Manchester University, said, "Peterloo became a national event almost immediately, commemorated in vivid cartoons, on plates and teapots and even on handkerchiefs. It was a symbol of the struggle for democracy against state suppression and the fight of ordinary people for civil rights and liberties."

Author R. J. White, in his 1963 book Waterloo to Peterloo, called it a watershed moment in British history as the working-classes of provincial England realised their moment had come: 'The ship which had tacked and lain for so long among the shoals and shallows of Luddism, hunger-marching, strikes and sabotage, was coming to port,' he wrote. 'Henceforth, the people were to stand with ever greater fortitude behind that great movement, which, stage by stage throughout the 19th century, was to impose a new political order upon society. With Peterloo, parliamentary reform had come of age.'

Yet, despite growing up 15 minutes away from St Peter's Field, Mike Leigh was never taught at school about Peterloo and it has never been widely studied as part of the national curriculum. Generations of children who had facts about kings and queens beaten into them know little or nothing of a pivotal moment in their history which focused attention on the fact that only two per cent of Britons had the vote.

"What is remarkable for me is that people in Manchester and the northwest are proud of our socialist history and yet Peterloo wasn't really talked about," said Leigh in an interview at the time of the film's release.

"Henry VIII had six wives. For a school kid, that's simple. He had six wives, he bumped them off and blah, blah, blah. You don't have to extract from it any particular resonance. You could have a serious discussion about sexual politics.

"You could also have a very healthy discussion about the redundancy and stupidity of monarchies. But they don't, because it's a safe subject. To try and teach the Peterloo Massacre, how can you talk about it without talking about what it meant?"

I'm sure people in most British towns and cities have a similar story to Mike Leigh's. In the seven years I was at Liverpool's De La Salle, a Christian Brothers' school attended by mostly working-class boys, history teachers taught me the names of many murdered figures from Richard the Lionheart to Archduke Franz Ferdinand. But I never once heard about Liverpool's Bloody Tuesday. The day that John Sutcliffe and Michael Prendergast were killed by the state a few hundred yards from where my dad had lived as a boy.

They met their end during the 1911 Liverpool Transport Strike, when 250,000 workers across the city struck for better pay, conditions and union recognition, which employers and government were determined to resist at all costs.

To quell discontent, Home Secretary Winston Churchill sent in thousands of police from other forces and stationed a gunboat on the River Mersey, with troops primed to act.

During an overwhelmingly peaceful 80,000-strong meeting at St George's Plateau, a few scuffles prompted a local magistrate to read the Riot Act and mounted police waded into the crowd, batons drawn, hospitalising 186 people. As the workers fought back, 96 protestors were arrested, summarily tried and sent to Walton Gaol.

The prison vans that took the men to prison, on August 15, were escorted by cavalry from the 18th Hussars, and when they met resistance from a crowd on Vauxhall Road the soldiers opened fire. John Sutcliffe, a 19-year-old carter who was putting shutters up on a house he was about to move into, was shot twice in the head. Michael Prendergast, a 30-year-old docker, was hit in the chest. Both died and a dozen others were seriously injured.

There was an outcry, and fearing the worst, concessions were made, and the transport strike ended. It meant, as some small compensation, that their appalling and unnecessary deaths may not have been totally in vain. A point recognised by the city's working-class people.

When Prendergast was laid to rest at Ford Cemetery, his burial reportedly drew the biggest crowd ever, at the time, to attend a funeral in Liverpool as 800 people made the four-and-a-half mile walk from Vauxhall Road to Litherland. Amazingly, at a time of acute sectarian division in the city, 250 mourners from the Netherfield Road Protestant Reformers Crusade attended the Roman Catholic funeral.

The following month at a workers' rally in East London, Sutcliffe and Prendergast were hailed and remembered as being "killed in the interests of capitalism."

There is a memorial plaque to the men on the wall of a derelict pub in Vauxhall Road, but you won't see any organised school trips heading there. Maybe if there were, they would have to teach them about St Winston's bloody-minded contempt for the working-class whose demands for better treatment were met with a hail of bullets from the 18th Hussars. The same regiment Churchill sent to Wales the previous year to fire on miners at Tonypandy as they struck for better pay.

Is it any wonder the British have such a slanted version of their history? Obsessing on aristocrats like Churchill and monarchs like Victoria, seeing them as the heroes who shaped our destiny, when for the ordinary man and woman it was those from humbler backgrounds whose actions changed countless lives.

Charles Spencer, 9th Earl Spencer, has spoken of his pride at his own children learning about the death of his sister, Princess Diana "as part of British history at school." Why? How could the life of a not very bright, rich woman brought in by the Windsors to provide heirs because she was an eligible Protestant virgin, then cast aside when her job was done, be worthy of so many billions of words?

It does not happen in most other countries. Ireland educates its people on its long struggle to be free from its colonial oppressors with the working-class heroes involved given due status. The USA, which has a public holiday in honour of civil rights activist Martin Luther King, teaches its children to sing God Bless America. We tell our national tale through the narrow prism of monarchs, Eton-educated prime ministers and gallant dukes leading men to war, ordering our kids to sing God Save The Queen.

Is learning about the life of a celebrity princess like Diana more crucial to children's understanding of modern British history than learning about women such as Doreen Lawrence, whose unstinting demand for a judicial inquiry into her son's murder led to an overhaul of our race relations legislation, which created the strongest battery of anti-discrimination powers in Europe? Or Donna Marie McGillion who was burnt so horrendously by the Omagh bomb she was given a one in five chance of living, yet defied the bombers without an ounce of self-pity, her stoicism helping to convince her people never to accept a return to the days of The Troubles? Or the Hillsborough mothers, who battled heroically for decades to overturn one of this country's worst injustices without any help from above?

Why don't our schools put these stories on the national curriculum along with the ones about coronations and empire builders? Maybe if children in state schools were taught about the achievements of those from the same class as them they would have a fraction of the confidence enjoyed by public school pupils and realise that they too have the capability to change the world. Maybe Britain would become less of a cap-doffing nation that teaches ordinary people the main thing they need to know is their place.

A ten-minute walk from St Peter's Field, now the area surro- unding St Peter's Square, stands The People's History Museum, which across two floors attempts to tell the story of the organised working-class fight for rights, democracy and justice.

I took my then 15-year-old daughter, Lucy, there in the week before the 200th anniversary of Peterloo. She marvelled at the exhibits and banners, the newspaper cuttings and speeches about the Chartists, the secret societies, the birth of unions, the anti-fascist movements, the fight for shorter hours and the establishment of the welfare state. When we left I asked her if she'd learned anything about that in school and she replied, "None of it."

What about through literature or TV drama I asked, and she said that apart from documentaries she'd watched with me, and the odd Charles Dickens book, nothing. And this is a bright, politically-aware girl, then a year away from her GCSEs at an excellent state school in a radical city like Liverpool.

But it came as no surprise. The adaptations of classic literature that make it to our screens seem to be set in country mansions inhabited by bored rich folk, usually men in britches, whose only worry appears to be finding a well-bred filly to impregnate so they have offspring to leave their land and titles to.

Untold working-class heroes with inspirational stories were rising up to demand their stake in the wealth their labour produced during the industrial revolution and beyond, yet all we get are aristocrats dancing at balls while those in the sculleries, factories, fields and hovels are kept out of sight like demented royals. In case they spoil the fairy tale.

My parents were born within a year of the first talking movie, The Jazz Singer, which hit the screens in 1927, and like most working-class people before the advent of television, they were obsessed with the cinema. It was where they spent their wages, fell in love, had their first fumbling sex, lived out their fantasies via the Hollywood stars and were given a window on the world through Pathé newsreels.

British towns and cities were teeming with picture houses and their audiences were overwhelmingly drawn from the working class. But it wasn't until I was born in the late 1950s that there was any sign of British working-class heroes up on the big screen. Previously, most working-class lead roles were written for clowns or baddies, or a twist in the plot would reveal that they were in fact born further up the societal chain. In 1956,

THE INSPIRATION

John Osborne's play Look Back in Anger revolutionised English drama by focusing on a new kind of hero. Jimmy Porter was a working-class man who believed he had more intelligence and talent than his so-called betters who looked down on him, and refused to accept his pigeon-holing.

Osborne was part of a group categorised as Angry Young Men who produced plays, novels and screenplays depicting proudly working-class characters trying to better themselves while remaining true to their roots.

It was hailed as the British New Wave and landmark films which looked at the harsh realism of working-class life such as Room at the Top, Saturday Night and Sunday Morning, A Kind of Loving, The Loneliness of the Long-Distance Runner and This Sporting Life, were critically acclaimed.

Here, the majority of the country's population who lived in terraced houses with outside loos finally had their stories told through the mass media of cinema. Those films had a toughness and an anti-Establishment attitude, portraying the working-classes as individuals, not as faceless hordes belonging to a cheap labour pool who only existed to ensure that those above prospered. Taking the lead roles were working-class actors like Tom Bell, Albert Finney, Tom Courtenay and Richard Harris, none of whom would have had a sniff of landing the top parts in the drawing-room and Empire-fixated British films of the 1930s and 40s.

Yet despite the breakthrough of writers, actors and directors focusing on the struggles of people at the bottom, British cinema rarely devoted its attention to landmark events in working-class history. One of the few exceptions being Bill Douglas's film Comrades about the Tolpuddle Martyrs.

The Angry Young Men phase was over by 1963, sunk in part by a movie industry desire to refocus its cameras on the more profitable notions of glamour, make-believe and wealth. Nothing summed this move away from realism better than the elevation to the big screen of Ian Fleming's 007 spy books. Working-class heroes like Jimmy Porter were blown out of the water by a character drawn to portray the archetypal upper-class British male, James Bond.

Sean Connery, whose mother was a domestic cleaner and whose father a factory worker, was plucked from obscurity to play an arrogant, Eton-educated, ski-loving, culture-swerving, Royal Navy commander, full of Christmas cracker one-liners who treats low-paid waiters like dirt if they don't stir and shake his Martini to his exact requirements.

A colonial throwback who permanently jets off to exotic tax havens where he mixes with shady characters and lounges around at night in a dinner jacket schmoozing the local women before retiring to a master bedroom to moan about "the things I do for England". Think Prince Andrew with charisma.

How apt that in real life former Edinburgh milkman Connery ended up a tax exile drinking coconut milk from trees on his estate in the Bahamas.

British television, though, was picking up the New Wave mantle with left-wing writers like Ken Loach, Mike Leigh, Alan Plater, Dennis Potter, Alan Bleasdale, Jimmy McGovern and Shane Meadows shining an authentic light on the struggles of the working-class.

And then there was Coronation Street, a phenomenon that steered the nation's attention away from Home Counties middle-class parlours and into two-up, two-down, cobbled streets filled with northern accents and no-nonsense attitudes. The undoubted stars of Tony Warren's soap were the magnificent women: Annie Walker, Ena Sharples, Hilda Ogden and Elsie Tanner. In the early 1960s these larger-than-life battle-axes, caustic wits, inverted snobs, inveterate gossips and tarts with hearts were an inspiration to working-class women still largely marginalised by a male-dominated world and a middle-class culture.

In many ways Elsie Tanner, played by the superb Pat Phoenix, was the first feminist of British popular culture. Her sexual allure, refusal to be stigmatised as a single mother and her fuck-you attitude to moralisers told millions of watching women they didn't have to stand by their man, take crap off their boss or lectures from snobs. That a woman could walk into the pub, that bastion of maleness, and drink, smoke, have sex with whoever she chose, and hold court as the genuine centre of attention.

In truth, most British working-class families knew that women ruled the roost. It harked back to the two World Wars when females kept the home going for years on end, working in factories, finding dodgy ways to make ends meet, raising the family, while the men fought in foreign lands.

These fearsome, indomitable matriarchs, with a wicked ability to take the piss out of themselves, their men and the wider world, set the rules.

Which is exactly how I remember my Irish nan and her five daughters. They were the engine of the family. My nan would slaughter the Tories, the Royals and the British Empire. She'd tell of watching the 1916 Easter Rising at Dublin's GPO, from behind a fruit cart in O'Connell Street during her lunch break from work, before launching into long lectures about the bastard, nun-raping Black and Tans.

Because she told it in such a casual way, and because she nearly always exaggerated for effect, I never knew whether to believe her. It seemed like a Dallas waitress claiming to be on the grassy knoll when JFK took the bullet.

I've often regretted not having conversations with her to establish if she was a first-hand witness to a pivotal moment in history. But I wasn't alone in my ignorance of the past. How often do you see working-class celebrities on the BBC's Who Do You Think You Are? programme displaying total shock when the fascinating lives of their most recent ancestors are revealed?

The further you go up the class system the more they know about where they came from and the people who made them. The aristocracy has country estates with portraits on the walls, and family trees mapping their lineage, mainly because they had titles and wealth to pass down.

The further we move down the class system the fewer photographs and belongings are exchanged between generations. We had a joke during the 1980s and 90s that the only thing that got passed down in our family, apart from wedding and engagement rings, was the 'cancer telly'. That white portable TV someone had given the dying relative so they had something to watch as they spent their final weeks spluttering out the remainder of their lives in bed.

What a revelation it must have been in the early 1960s to see working-class characters transfixing TV and cinema audiences, played by people from the same stock. While Pat Phoenix, a socialist who campaigned for the Labour Party throughout her life, was smashing it on Coronation Street, Salford lad Albert

Finney – who turned down a knighthood in 2000 saying "the Sir thing perpetuates an English disease called snobbery" – was winning rave reviews in Alan Sillitoe's Saturday Night and Sunday Morning.

As four working-class lads from Liverpool were changing the world forever with their talent, their accents and their look, to quote the American folk singer who took his name from Dylan Thomas, the times were a changing. But they never changed for good. In the decade leading up to the mid-60s, Britain had three Prime Ministers all educated at Eton. In 2010, 45 years later, the first of two more Old Etonians, David Cameron and Boris Johnson, were back in Downing Street.

Normal class service had resumed.

Acting had been reclaimed for the public schoolkids. The working-class found it increasingly hard to enter the upper echelons of the profession due to cash-starved councils cutting subsidies to local theatre groups, tuition fees excluding the poorest students, and the top theatre schools situated in London, a city outsiders without money had no chance of moving to. Meanwhile, Old Etonians like Damian Lewis, Dominic West, Tom Hiddleston and Eddie Redmayne and Old Harrovian Benedict Cumberbatch were dominating the acting scene.

In 2013 Dominic Dromgoole, then artistic director of Shakespeare's Globe Theatre in London, claimed the dominance of privately-educated actors was a "real worry" and teenagers "without means" were finding it "harder and harder" to break into the profession.

Those fears that all the world was a stage but if you wanted to get on it you'd need an old school tie, were being backed up by working-class actors. When Stephen McGann, the youngest of four acting brothers from inner-city Liverpool, was interviewed in 2014 by *The Independent* he claimed the working-class had a better chance of getting decent acting jobs during the middle of the last century than they did in the second decade of this one.

"If you're a messy kid from a council estate today, I think the chances of you making it as a successful actor are a lot worse than they were," he said.

"When I was growing up, we had theatres open that aren't open now. We had opportunities in adverts that aren't open now. We had films that don't get made. We had television pumping out of all kinds of studios that aren't there any more."

Salford-born actor Christopher Eccleston claimed in 2015 that "you need to be white, you need to be male, and you need to be middle class," to secure the top roles in contemporary British theatre while Liverpudlian David Morrissey decried what he called the slow "economic excision of working-class actors."

Another Scouse thespian, double Golden Globes winner Jodie Comer, said in 2020, "Coming from a working-class background there is the notion that you are going to have to work much harder to be successful. People are continuously being surprised by your capabilities."

And Smethwick-born Julie Walters told *The Sunday Times*: "I look at almost all the up-and-coming names and they're all from posh schools. Don't get me wrong, they're wonderful. It's just a shame those working-class kids aren't coming through. When I started, 30 years ago, it was the complete opposite.

"Back then, it was still possible for a working-class kid like me to study drama because I got a grant, but the way things are now, there aren't going to be any working-class actors."

The facts backed up those claims. In 2016, educational

charity The Sutton Trust published research showing that 42 per cent of British Bafta winners went to a fee-paying school. And data from the Great British Class Survey, a huge social study compiled over two years, found that the most privileged could afford to attend the best acting schools, avoid taking dead-end roles and were least likely to be typecast because of their accent.

One working-class actress told the study's authors: "In an audition someone asked me whether I could speak 'properly' if I wanted to. They actually said that to my face."

An actor claimed one of his lecturers said to him, "Have you ever considered going back to being a plumber?" Others felt that if you were working-class you tended to get the most menial of roles. "I've played more nurses than there are in the whole of St George's Hospital," complained one black actress in her 40s. "I started to get bored of that and I wouldn't take the role if all she was saying was 'the doctor will see you in a few minutes.'"

In the austerity years that followed the 2008 banking crisis it wasn't just the acting profession that saw the pendulum swing back heavily in favour of those with money and connections. Smart, creative kids from council estates were struggling to get access to the best jobs.

Even in that most working-class of activities, singing pop songs, the likes of Coldplay's Chris Martin, James Blunt, Florence Welsh and Marcus Mumford and Ben Lovett from Mumford & Sons were flying the public school flag high.

In 2010, music magazine *The Word* estimated that more than 60 per cent of that year's successful pop and rock acts were former public school pupils compared with just one per cent in 1990.

With David Cameron's Cabinet brimming with more Old Etonians than at any time since the late 1950s, those heady days of the state-educated classes changing the cultural dynamic of Britain were a distant memory. The glass ceiling had been repaired and reinforced with steel.

One picture perfectly summed up that re-configuration of the class system. A black-and-white 1987 photograph of ten tailcoat-clad sons of aristocrats and millionaires looking down at the world with the sullen air of arrogance and entitlement we thought had died out with Brideshead Revisited.

It was Oxford University's Bullingdon Club about to embark on a typical night of alcohol-fuelled debauchery, toasting Thatcher with the finest champagne, trashing the restaurant, humiliating the staff and burning £50 notes in front of rough sleepers.

Among the ten Bully Boys were David Cameron and Boris Johnson, who went on to become the pivotal political figures of the 2010s. Also at Oxford around that time were future Tory Cabinet power players George Osborne, Jeremy Hunt, Michael Gove and Jacob Rees-Mogg.

It was an astonishing coincidence that made you wonder if Oxford was some secret Willy Wonka-type factory that handed out golden tickets to run the country.

When in 2019, Johnson was elected Tory leader and thus Prime Minister by 92,153 mainly white, rich, southern, male Conservative Party members, it felt as though, a century on from the Representation of the People Act, which extended votes to most men and some women, we had never been less genuinely represented.

So much of that goes back to Britain's pyramid-shaped education system. At the bottom are state schools so skint they need to beg parents to pay for books and teachers to dip into their pay to feed hungry kids.

Very close to the top is the public school system and at the pinnacle is Eton, which costs roughly £300,000 to put a boy through, and buys privilege par excellence.

In the past few years alone, the country has been run by politicians like Cameron, Johnson, Rees-Mogg, Rory Stewart and Oliver Letwin who went there. It's been informed by influential journalists like Dominic Lawson, Charles Moore and Geordie Greig who are Old Etonians. The Archbishop of Canterbury and the next-king-but-one got their education there alongside thousands of mandarins, moguls, judges, generals, ambassadors, investment bankers and key civil servants.

That 2016 Sutton Trust report showed how public schools had a stranglehold on every key profession in Britain. Despite only 6.7 per cent of the population being educated privately, 71 per cent of top military officers, 74 per cent of top judges, 61 per cent of the country's top doctors, 42 per cent of top actors and 32 per cent of MPs received a paid-for education.

The research showed that it gets even worse when you look at how many Oxford and Cambridge graduates hold key positions: They educate less than one per cent of the population, but 74 per cent of the top judiciary, 54 per cent of the country's leading journalists and 47 per cent of the Cabinet got their degrees there. The trust's chairman, Sir Peter Lampl, concluded that private schools were providing a massive leg-up in the world and "the key to improving social mobility is to open up independent schools to all pupils based on merit, not money."

Which is a nice sentiment but unlikely to happen any time soon in Britain where the big attraction of public schools to those with money is not merely the advantage it gives their kids in reaching the top universities but that they keep out the riff-raff. It allows their offspring to mix with equally wealthy professional families thus cultivating crucial contacts.

It's a huge masonic club working on unspoken rules such as "you get my son an internship in your law practice and I'll get your daughter one in my publishing firm." Meanwhile, kids without contacts or money, and from outside London, no matter how bright, are effectively excluded because they can't afford £1,000-a-month to survive in unpaid internships in one of the dearest cities on Earth. And so the grip tightens.

David Cameron knew this better than anyone. He secured his first political job at Tory Central Office after an anonymous call from a family friend in Buckingham Palace. And the minute he left Downing Street he stopped the pretence that he'd like his children educated in state schools.

When his successor Theresa May held a major Cabinet reshuffle in January 2018 she claimed to have created a government that "looked more like the country it serves." In reality it looked like a Belgravia gentleman's club with a few of the chaps thinking it was Bring Your Wife To Work Day. Out of 23 Cabinet members only one was non-white, six were women and 34 per cent attended fee-paying schools, which was five times more than the general population. And half of them went to Oxford or Cambridge.

Any wonder that in the month before that re-shuffle the entire board of The Social Mobility Commission resigned in protest at the lack of progress towards a "fairer Britain."

One of the tricks the Establishment pulls to convince the masses that we are all equal under God and The Queen is the honours system. As a journalist of 40 years I've witnessed the twice-yearly bestowing of titles on sports stars, actors and musicians which guarantees a Saturday splash and two inside spreads praising the Establishment for recognising down-to-earth National Treasures.

But they merely serve to distract attention from the political kick-backs being handed out to party donors, political lackeys, Downing Street and Palace mandarins.

Which is why the bestowing of National Treasure status is the most pain-inducing condition in the English language. And I say that as someone who's had a major organ removed only to be kicked out of hospital two days later with a handful of paracetamol.

I'm talking about it being given to the likes of Dame Shirley Bassey for services to armpit exposure and screeching, Sir Ken Dodd (Diddymen and tax evasion) Sir Trevor McDonald (autocue reading) and Sir Bruce Forsyth (catchphrases and celebrity golf). We didn't elect them. We just woke up one day to find their saintly gobs looking down on us from a high altar, demanding worship.

I've never held it against working-class people who take these honours and I get why justice campaigners accept them on behalf of voiceless people who have been let down by the system.

But I have always had an undying admiration for those who don't accept knighthoods, damehoods, lordships or hereditary peerages, such as Alan Bennett, Albert Finney, David Bowie, Dawn French, Geraldine McEwan, Jack Jones, Michael Foot, Tony Benn etc. Most of whom turned them down because, despite being hugely talented in their specific field, they didn't believe they were better than anybody else.

It's not just in the twice-yearly honours system where celebrity stooges are used to convince people that Britain recognises heroes across all classes. In 2013, Royal Mail issued a set of stamps to commemorate the lives of ten great Britons who would have been 100 years old that year.

Among them were viscount's granddaughter Elizabeth David, CBE, a food writer, and royal photographer Norman Parkinson, CBE. Not included was honours refusenik trade union leader Jack Jones whose achievements include fighting the fascists in the Spanish Civil War, organising supply ships to feed the starving of Barcelona, giving workers shorter days, weekends, paid holidays and ACAS, and single-handedly pushing pensioners' rights to the top of the political agenda.

But clearly that didn't make him good enough to merit a Royal Mail stamp. If only Jack had told us how, in the Sorbonne, they teach one how to make the perfect crème brûlée, or managed to make Princess Anne look less like Red Rum than normal on her wedding snaps. Maybe then he'd have been a great British hero.

I mentioned in the introduction to this book that in 2002 The BBC carried out an exhaustive exercise to compile a list of the 100 Greatest Britons, the results of which were dubious at best and comical at worst.

Celebrity aristocrat Princess Diana was named the third greatest person to come from these islands. Which surely insults every war veteran, teacher, priest or charity worker who's ever inspired you, or the doctor, nurse, firefighter and paramedic who saved the life of someone you love. Everyday heroes who never allowed injustice, fear or low pay to crush their spirit, just quietly carried on serving others.

Unsurprisingly, Winston Churchill was voted by a landslide

as the greatest Briton of all time. And due to his heroism in facing up to the Nazis he's certainly worthy of a shout. But try to say there was another side to him, as many working-class people have, and you're labelled a traitor.

In 2019 Labour's Shadow Chancellor John McDonnell felt the full force of an enraged nation after calling Churchill a villain.

Or rather, when asked in a quick-fire Q&A if he was a hero or a villain, he answered, "Tonypandy – villain." As in, it was far from heroic behaviour to set the Army on striking miners, killing one of them and injuring 500. As it was dismissing hunger marchers as shirkers, sending the Black and Tans to murder the Irish as Colonial Secretary in the 1920s, claiming no wrong was done to American Red Indians or Australian aborigines by the white man and that British imperialism was a good and natural thing as "a higher-grade race" could lead the "primitive" and "subject" races.

Heroic in defeating the Nazis? Undoubtedly. But villainous at times elsewhere? No question.

The Queen Mother was deified by the entire British media throughout her long and privileged life but few questioned her racist views. She supported apartheid, refused to call Rhodesia "Zimbabwe" and claimed that the EU wouldn't work because, "Huns, wops and dagos" never get on.

Say anything against our 20th-century Cleopatra (who apparently also saved Britain during the Second World War by participating in East End photoshoots after the Luftwaffe had dropped by) and you're a commie, or a "Poundland Lenin" as Churchill's grandson Nicholas Soames called McDonnell.

Almost by definition we are conditioned to believe that the ruling class are heroic and everyone else is incidental. The Queen made her sons, Andrew and Edward, Knights of the

Most Noble Order of the Garter, despite one weeping like a homesick nursery toddler after five minutes in the Marines and the other spending eight hours a day on the golf course. Even longer now he's been ordered to drop his royal duties after being linked to convicted paedophile Jeffrey Epstein.

They say history is written by the winners but in Britain's case it appears to be written by, and about, the economic winners. Our heroic narrative flows through King Alfred The Great, Henry VIII, Queen Elizabeth I, Sir Frances Drake, Viscount Nelson, The Duke of Wellington, Queen Victoria, Sir Winston Churchill, Queen Elizabeth II and Baroness Thatcher with a bit of Shakespeare thrown in for creative balance. And any deviation from that narrative is denounced as left-wing heresy.

In November 2020, when the nation was embroiled in a heated debate about which historic figures should be placed on statues and in museums, Eton-educated Jacob Rees-Mogg gave this tub-thumping put-down in the Commons to those who dared question the established British order: "Of all the world's great heroes there's none that can compare with Boadicea, Alfred the Great, Richard the Lionheart, the Black Prince, Henry V, Francis Drake, Prince Rupert, the Duke of Marlborough, Wolfe, Nelson, Moore, Wellington, Gordon and Montgomery – amongst others. These are our great heroes and we should celebrate them. And I haven't even mentioned Caractacus. We should be proud of our history, and proud of Caractacus."

This from an upper-class bluffer who, the previous year, authored a book called The Victorians: Twelve Titans Who Forged Britain which was slaughtered for its banality, with esteemed historian A.N. Wilson describing it as "anathema to anyone with an ounce of historical, or simply common sense."

Referring to a chapter about General Charles Napier's conquest of Sindh in Pakistan, Wilson wrote, 'At this point in the book you start to think that the author is worse than a twit. By all means let us celebrate what was great about the Victorians, but there is something morally repellent about a book that can gloss over massacres and pillage on the scale perpetrated by Napier.'

Kim Wagner, a senior lecturer in British imperial history at Queen Mary University of London, also stuck the critical boot in: "At best, it can be seen as a curious artefact of the kind of sentimental jingoism and empire-nostalgia currently afflicting our country."

Yet Rees-Mogg was the Leader of the House of Commons at the time. A man of mediocre talent and intelligence who rose to the top of British government on the back of schooling, cast-iron connections and the way he speaks.

Sentimental jingoism was undoubtedly the tone the Tory government hoped for as the opening ceremony of the 2012 London Olympics was being put together.

However, creative director Danny Boyle had other ideas, preferring to tell the story of modern Britain through the NHS, the Jarrow March, The Windrush Generation, The Sex Pistols, Dizzee Rascal, The Beatles, Trainspotting, Brookside's lesbian kiss and the solidarity of mining communities.

One of the ceremony's most senior production figures told me that when they showed it to Culture Secretary Jeremy Hunt his face resembled George Bush's as he was told the Twin Towers were under attack. He wanted to know why the NHS was celebrated when winning the Second World War, and Shakespeare, weren't.

To which a stunned creative team pointed out the Olympics

isn't supposed to be a celebration of bombing guest nations and, as for Shakespeare, he'd just witnessed the ceremony open with The Tempest. But that reference to the Bard's work had gone straight over the Culture Secretary's head.

Other Tories were apoplectic. Bloggers railed against what they believed to be "socialist brain-washing," and Aidan Burley MP called it "leftie, multicultural crap."

Minister Damien Green tried to claim the liberal high ground by writing a *Daily Telegraph* piece claiming Tories needed to pass the "Danny Boyle Test" to prove their modernity. To which the first of 800 angry comments underneath the online article read: "We don't want Danny Boyle's Marxist tripe vision of Britain."

Yet the nation, and the wider world, took Boyle's opening ceremony to its heart, hailing it an uplifting masterpiece which showcased this multi-cultural, multi-faceted country in a new and modern light.

Finally Britain was telling its national story and it wasn't a jingoistic flaunting of colonial supremacy but a heartfelt celebration of the genius that its people, many of whom had risen from below, had given to the world.

Maybe, after all, a working-class hero was something to be.

2

THE
INCORRUPTIBLE

CLASS
WARRIOR

DENNIS
—•— SKINNER

THE HOUSE OF COMMONS — January 1997

I WAS starting to convince myself I'd have a better chance trying to secure an audience with the Archbishop of Canterbury in the back room of a brothel.

Three times I'd phoned his House of Commons number before the Christmas recess to ask for an interview, and three times Dennis Skinner had declined.

Occasion number one consisted of me telling the man I had admired since he was elected to parliament in 1970 that it had always been my ambition to interview him. Which was not going too badly (as in the impatient sighs at the other end of the line were becoming less pronounced) until I blew it by saying it would be a tribute to him as he approached his 65th birthday.

"Ah, right, so you want to do a piece about Skinner the pensioner taking someone else's job when he should be retired?"

"Well, no. Of course not. I hope you stay there until you're 90," I told him nervously.

"That's as may be. But that's how the Tories will spin it. Sorry. Bye." Click.

So I tried again, and was met with a bark when I'd finished my pitch: "Look, what's your angle?"

"There isn't one," I replied. "I just want to tell the story about the man behind the Commons character."

"Yes, but I took a socialist pledge with my wife never to speak about our private life. I've never used my family politically so I don't see why I should have to talk about them. I'm not David Mellor you know."

"And I don't want to talk about your family, just you."

"Sorry. No can do. Bye." Click.

When I called back two days later he was in a better mood, complimenting me on my doggedness, but saying he didn't know why I was so determined to interview him as he wasn't really that interesting and if I wanted to know his thoughts I should study the Commons record book *Hansard*. When I joked about it being far too boring to wade through, he caved in and agreed to meet me.

Then he rang back and cancelled. Then he rang back again and said, "I'll do it. I've sat here the past 15 minutes feeling like shit. I promised you, and I don't break promises. I don't want to do it, mind. I hate interviews. Hate them. They're just elitist crap. But go on then. I'll be back in work the first week of the New Year." Click.

It was still the Christmas recess when I walked into a cold and empty Palace of Westminster to be greeted by a squat figure with the build of a middleweight boxer, in grey sports jacket and red tie, looking me up and down suspiciously with his hands on his hips like Jimmy Cagney in White Heat. He was the only MP in Westminster two days after New Year's Day, there, he tells me, so he can be alongside the porters, security guards, postal staff and cleaners, to "establish my working-class credentials."

To Skinner, the Palace of Westminster should be a temple for the common good. The place where Britain is put right.

"I'm always taken aback how beautiful this building is when I come and you appreciate it even more when there's no-one around," I said awkwardly, trying to break the ice.

"Aye, it's alright. But to me, it's just a place of work. It's like the pit I worked down for 20-odd years. And no more important. That's why I'm in today dealing with letters in my office because most of the workers are back in the factories and shops. MPs are no different to them, just better paid. We should just come here to do our bit as honestly as we can. Shame most of them don't though," he said, the echoes from the empty, cavernous building accentuating his point.

"By the way, before we start, are you in a union?" he asked, and I nodded and gave a look that said as if I wouldn't be. "Good. Because if you weren't there'd be no interview."

Skinner was immensely proud of the fact that he turned up at Westminster, spent more hours in the chamber, and voted more often, than any other MP. And also of the fact that most years, despite his Bolsover constituency being 150 miles away, he came in at the bottom of the expense claim list.

The Beast of Bolsover spent 49 years in parliament battling against the Cult of Personality. But with a personality that ensured cult status, he never stood a chance.

Even the Tories, not known for their imagination, noticed that. The week the interview appeared in the *Mirror*, one of their backbench stooges asked a question about retirement incomes at Question Time just so John Major could bring up the fact that Skinner was about to hit 65, and pretend to congratulate him on becoming a pensioner.

Skinner's response: "God knows how much time they spent planting the question and planting the answer. But that's the embodiment of the Tory Party. They're only here to play public school games."

He may have fired off more one-liners during his time in the Commons than you'd hear in an Audience With Bob Hope but he never played games. He would rather have cut his hand off than accept a favour. I asked him if the tea-room was open so I could get him some breakfast, but he declined on the grounds that he had never taken so much as a cup of tea off a journalist as it could be seen as a bribe. He even refused a cuppa from a reporter on *The Morning Star*. He's that incorruptible.

As we walked to his office I anticipated an hour spent with an unreconstructed Stalinist reciting iron ore production figures and threatening me with a miners' pickaxe if I asked a personal question. But I was pleasantly surprised. He let me see the gentle man behind the class warrior, a glimpse of the pussycat within the beast.

I was reminded of something my old boss at the Greater London Council, Ken Livingstone, had said of him: "I was worried about Dennis because of all the aggression. But, in fact, he's a really cuddly person. Although he'll probably sue me for saying so."

It turned out Dennis was an Only Fools And Horses addict who thought Trigger the funniest man to draw breath. A film buff whose favourite movies are Woody Allen's Hannah and Her Sisters, Play It Again, Sam and Annie Hall. A Coronation Street fan who couldn't get his head around Jack and Vera Duckworth running The Rovers Return: "Here's two people who didn't have two ha'pennies to rub together becoming entrepreneurs with pigeons in their backyard. No bloody way."

He even sang. In a strong voice that needed no microphone, honed from years of doing Frankie Laine and Al Jolson impressions in Derbyshire pubs. He treats me by belting out a song he composed and crooned a few years earlier for a Labour conference revue, to the tune of I Wonder Why:

I hear Thatcher but there's no-one there,
I smell Tebbit and his greasy hair.
All the time they said she walked on air.
I wonder why,
I wonder why.
Leon's tossing in his sleep at night, Heseltine has lost his appetite.
Stars, they used to twinkle in her eyes.
And now they're telling lies,
And we know why.

The Maverick's Maverick, who manoeuvred his way to a prime seat in the front row of the Labour benches, next to the gangway and just below a microphone, for maximum exposure in the TV age, is a born showman. And what a show he put on for a year shy of five decades for those of us who despise the corrupt and chummy Westminster gentlemen's club.

Dennis Edward Skinner was the third of nine children born in 1932 to Edward and Lucy in the Derbyshire pit village of Clay Cross. In his Who's Who entry he proudly states that he was born into "good working-class stock."

His father was a miner and staunch trade unionist, who was sacked after the 1926 General Strike and blacklisted by bosses who barred him from working until the late 1930s when war was looming and they were desperate for labour.

Reinstatement didn't change Edward's ways and he was sacked again in the 1950s, when, as the miners' delegate, he tore a strip off management about the dreadful pay and conditions down the pit. They invited him to apologise or lose his job. His response: "Apologise? It would be like putting my head in the oven." Then walked.

"Because of my dad, ours was a very political household. We had politics for breakfast, dinner and tea. And I knew at a very young age which side of the struggle I was on," Dennis told me.

Two of his brothers went into local politics and sat on the Clay Cross council that held out alone against the Heath government in 1971, when it tried to impose housing rent increases on local authorities. The two Skinners along with the rest of the council refused to back down and were consequently banned from working in local government and made bankrupt.

Dennis would later tell of how, when his brother Graham heard they were after his car, he took the wheels off and put it up on bricks. But they took it anyway.

However, when Dennis was growing up, the house wasn't all Marxism over bread and dripping. His mother, a cleaner who took in washing to make ends meet, had a sweet voice and would sing old musical hall songs to the nine kids she doted on. Many years later Lucy was asked by a reporter how proud she was of Dennis, and let him know that she had seven sons and was equally proud of all of them.

The politics of the father and the singing of the mother would form two-thirds of Skinner's personality. The other third was his love for nature, which was nurtured in the wild Derbyshire countryside where he roamed for much of his time outside of school.

It was a passion that stayed with him when he was elected to the House of Commons and would spend his lunch-hours strolling through the parks near Westminster studying the fauna and flora and, as he put it, "getting to know every blade of grass."

He was a very bright schoolboy who could reel off his times tables backwards when he was aged six, just to prove how easy memorising is, and could recite poems in full after the shortest of time reading them. He passed the 11-plus at nine-and-a-half and went to Tupton Hall Grammar School at 10.

At 16 he had a choice to make which would define his life. Did he follow the advice of his teachers and parents and go into sixth form and on to university, or did he follow his mates, and his father, down the coal mine? Very much against his mother's wishes he chose the latter. It was higher education's loss.

His biographer, political journalist Kevin Maguire, told me: "Dennis would have been one of those working-class people who, if he'd gone to university, would have excelled. He confided in me that he'd have loved to have been an actor. But I thought he'd have made a brilliant QC or professor.

"The way he used his wit was a brilliant political weapon but being seen as a joker distracted from his huge intellect. I learned more from him about politics than I did for three years studying the subject under professors at York University."

Skinner worked first at Parkhouse colliery, near Clay Cross, until its closure in 1962, then at Glapwell colliery, near Bolsover. In 1964, at the age of 32, he became the youngest-ever president of the Derbyshire region of the National Union of Mineworkers and a councillor in Clay Cross. He also attended the Labour trade union Ruskin College in Oxford after completing a course run by the NUM at Sheffield University.

He was well on his way to being rescued from the pit by politics and when the Bolsover seat became vacant in 1969, after another former pit-worker Harold Neal stood down, the miners decided they wanted Skinner to be their candidate. "I never put my name forward. It was the miners," he reminds anyone who asks.

Proof of how psychologically entwined he still was with the mines, on the Monday following his landslide 1970 election win, he turned up at the pit to work. "I didn't know when Parliament started to pay my wages," he would later admit.

His father gave him some advice before he boarded the London-bound train. "It's just like going to the pit, lad. Examine the workplace and keep an eye on them that's down there." He did. During his first week at the coalface, he began studying the Mines and Quarries Act. On his first day in the House of Commons, he started to learn Erskine May, the bible of parliamentary procedure.

I asked him how he felt when he arrived as a paid member of the Establishment after 21 years down the pit.

"Well, I knew it would be a different place to anything I'd ever been in before and I knew there would be attempts to re-shape me. But I was determined I would not change an inch. I would stay the same and represent the people I came from."

To retain his working-class identity he made himself three vows that he would stick to religiously over the following 49 years as an MP.

"I refused to pair. I realised Tory MPs needed to be away to make money on the side, or to swan off to Royal Ascot, so I decided there was no way I was joining in what was effectively organised truancy," he told me, eyes blazing with pride.

"Secondly, no foreign junkets. I've never used a passport for extra-parliamentary visits. Some MPs go on these so-called 'fact-finding' trips with each other and get pally-wally. Even if I could find it in myself to be like that with a Tory, it's not what I'm here for.

"And thirdly, no socialising in the Westminster bars. No-one can work in the pit and drink at the same time so why should they do it here? Besides, I don't want to get into a room where there's an atmosphere of 'we're all mates together' because we're not.

"My philosophy is contrary to theirs. I don't want to spend my life laughing with people who just want to look after number one."

I asked if, over the years, he had come across a Tory he was quite fond of, and he took a millisecond to reply: "Never. How could I when I've never had a friendly conversation with one? I'd never discuss policy with them because we come at every subject from a completely different angle. Imagine me talking to one of them about education when they no doubt send their kids to some posh private school. There's no common ground. Not for me anyhow."

Another reason for his refusal to become chummy with the enemy might be that a thawing of hostilities could lead him to tone down the ferocity of his attacks. He disagrees when you tell him his quips and heckles are what he'll be remembered for. But they just are. Because it's a magnificent body of work, which has resulted in virtually every Speaker he's had the pleasure of disobeying, throwing him out of the Chamber.

The month before we met, in the aftermath of Prince Charles's messy divorce from Diana, when the government announced the nation was buying a new Royal Yacht, he yelled "why don't you call it Camilla."

After John Redwood challenged John Major for the Tory leadership he said to the PM, "Do you remember saying you had three bastards in your Cabinet, well you can't count. You've just found out you've got 89."

He told the Commons that the last words of John Major's trapeze artist father were "oops" and christened the diminutive

Tory Sports Minister Colin Moynihan "The Miniature For Sport." When Paddy Ashdown was outed for having an extra-marital affair he referred to him as "Paddy Pantsdown" and one of his finest to Margaret Thatcher was "Madame Ceaușescu."

He was thrown out for calling David Cameron "Dodgy Dave," John Gummer "a slimy wart on Thatcher's nose" and Labour defector and SDP leader, David Owen, a "pompous sod." He told the Speaker he'd be as conciliatory as he could and withdraw the pompous bit but not the sod, but was still given an early bath.

He was also given his marching orders for accusing the Tories of conducting a crooked deal to sell off coal mines, alleging the deputy speaker, Sir Alan Haselhurst, was biased towards the Conservatives and calling Jim Prior, then secretary of state for employment, the "minister of unemployment."

His finest moment of unrestrained comic savagery came in 2005 when he brought up tabloid allegations from a prostitute that she had taken cocaine at a party with George Osborne before he became an MP. It resulted in an undisputed sending-off from the Speaker.

This is how he described it to me afterwards: "Osborne was attacking Gordon Brown for having only 1.75 per cent growth. I'd read in the Sunday papers about his party habits so I said, 'When the Tories were closing the pits in the 1980s they'd have been glad of 1.75 per cent growth but the only things growing were the lines of coke under Boy George's nose.'

"There was uproar, but I said, 'I can't withdraw it, because it's the truth.' To be honest, I was more worried I'd upset the real Boy George. But he sent me a copy of Karma Chameleon as a thank-you."

He tells me that he thinks up his one-liners and subtle turns of phrase when he's out walking in London parks. Being at one with nature relaxes his mind, reminds him of who he is and where he's from.

"As soon as I came up from the pit in the summer I'd go walking in the fields breathing in the fresh air and I began to learn about nature. When I came to Westminster I went walking in my free time and came across St James's Park, which is a wonderful park. And also Hyde Park which has a magnolia tree, which, when it's in full bloom is one of the most magnificent things you'll ever see."

He also used his solitude in the parks to reflect, like a football manager, on the things that went wrong with his game, concentrating on the lines that got away. He has never written any speech down beyond a couple of notes. It's all in his head. But in his park post-mortems he would often kick himself that he didn't improve an insult by twisting the knife even further into his prey. He is a man in search of the perfect insult. And it's fair to say that over the years he's had a good go.

His sketches involving Black Rod during the State Opening of Parliament became as hotly-anticipated as The Morecambe and Wise Christmas Show.

"Ayup, here comes Puss In Boots," he shouted in 1988, starting a British tradition up there with, well, pantomime. The following year as Black Rod thumped on the door he yelled, "I bet he drinks Carling Black Label," re-creating a popular beer advert of the time, which led to an explosion of laughter from MPs. When the bell went in 1990 not long before Thatcher was ousted by her own, he remarked, "It tolls for thee, Maggie."

"Tell her to pay her taxes!" he yelled when the Queen was

mired in controversy over Royal funding in 1992. "Any Tory moles at the Palace?" he joked in 2008 after Conservative Damian Green MP was arrested. Following a series of break-ins at Buckingham Palace in 2003, Skinner asked: "Did she lock the door behind her?" And three years later, he used a recent film about the Queen for inspiration: "Have you got Helen Mirren on standby?"

The following year, when Prince Harry had been questioned after two hen harriers were shot dead at Sandringham he joked, "Who shot the harriers?" In 2009 as Black Rod arrived in the Commons, Skinner barked, "Royal expenses are on the way." In 2012 he shouted, "Jubilee Year, double-dip recession, what a start!" A year later it was, "Royal Mail for sale. Queen's head privatised." And in 2017, when the Queen's speech clashed with Royal Ascot he yelled, "Get your skates on, first race is half-past two."

When I asked what the motivation is for grabbing the headlines with his humour he said, "You have to take your audience with you. I realised over the years that you could get into trouble with a dull speech. But if you can keep them laughing, you can get away with murder.

"When I was a young lad, my dad would take me to hear people speak. After one meeting I said to him, "Well that man could talk, Dad." And he said, 'Make 'em laugh, make 'em cry, make 'em think, and send them home happy.' That's always stuck with me, has that."

A lot of research goes into those insults though. As well as spending more time in the Chamber than any other MP, few spent more hours in the library than him, gathering ammunition for the next assault.

Usually, such an intelligent, charismatic firebrand entering the House at 38 in a rock-solid seat, would have built alliances that allowed them to climb the greasy pole into Cabinet. But Skinner was never interested in seeking power, believing that the nature of acquiring it corrupts the soul.

Jim Callaghan once sounded him out but was given short shrift, telling him he didn't agree with patronage. As his years became more advanced he told the Commons authorities not to contemplate making him Father of The House, because the only position he would take up was one he was elected to.

If Skinner had an ambition for power, it was for Labour Party power. The height of his political career was in the 1980s, when he was a key member of Labour's National Executive Committee, fighting a long, losing battle against the drift to the right.

I ask if he's enjoyed his working life, and if so, the biggest lesson it has taught him.

"Oh yes. Dame Fortune has shined her light on me. I could have finished up on the scrapheap. Instead, I landed on my feet. If life has taught me anything, it's that we all need to stick together. You can't live by yourself, you know. Robinson Crusoe only lasted until Friday."

Which in any other interview would have been a cue for me to ask about his divorce, but the metaphorical pickaxe was dangling over my head so I steered clear. For the record, he married his wife of 29 years, Mary Parker, in 1960, and they had three children, a son and two daughters who all attended his old school and went to university. In 1989 they separated amicably and he later set up home in London with his researcher Lois Blasenheim.

For a 39-year-old, like me, who had lived under Tory rule for 18 years there was optimism in the air that January day in 1997. There was a General Election coming within months which Labour were heavily fancied to win. What, I asked, were his hopes?

"Unemployment is our biggest problem which I tell Tony Blair all the time. It's breaking the social fabric. When I was elected to parliament there were houses in my constituency where the doors would be unlocked at night. Now they're locked three and four times over.

"That is the reality of Thatcher's legacy. The idea that the highest calling in this life is to look after yourself. It's a crazy concept. I'm amazed the British people have swallowed it for so long.

"You couldn't allow market forces to win the war could you? It was won by planning, intervention and people pulling together.

"Imagine Churchill saying to Montgomery, 'I hear you're going to start the El Alamein offensive. Don't do it. I've just heard the price of oil is going to fall next month, so hang on old boy, we can win the war cheaper.'"

I asked what he would say to critics who argue that his old school socialist politics are dated and everyone on the left needs to embrace New Labour?

"Well, I address 200 meetings a year. Most of them packed. When I tell people that over the past 17 years the richest 10 per cent in Britain have accumulated an extra £50 billion and that we should take it back and give it to the health service, education, housing and pensions, I don't get people challenging me."

I told him that in a matter of months he could be sitting on the government benches and asked if he plans to aim his savage put-downs at his own party if he smells a sell-out? He thought for a few seconds and chose his words carefully.

"Well, if they get unemployment down, reduce health service waiting lists, build houses, reduce class sizes, redistribute wealth and power to give us a more egalitarian system. If they do all that, well, no, I can't see a problem.

"Can you see a problem?"

"Yes," I told him. "And I'm looking at him." He liked that.

I stayed in touch with Dennis after that January day in 1997 when Labour were still in opposition. We'd see each other at conferences or around Westminster and he would refer constituents on to me, with issues they wanted to see highlighted in the national press.

He rang me out of the blue one day in 2005 after a bad run of form for my football team, Liverpool, which cheered me up no end and made me realise he sees everything in terms of socialism.

"Ariyt son, Dennis Skinner here."

I mentally trawled back through my recent columns to try to work out what I'd written that could offend him. Everything was the option that sprang to mind.

"What the bloody hell is happening to our football team. I can't fathom it."

"OUR football team. I didn't know you were a Red?"

"Oh aye. I have been since Shankly made them a good socialist side." He ran through all the old stars of the 60s like Hunt, Yeats, St John, then onto Keegan, Clemence and Heighway, espousing the collective will to win that saw them steamroller other teams. But not Emlyn Hughes as he "were obviously a bloody Thatcher fanboy. Have you seen him on Question of Sport drooling all over Princess Anne?"

He said he had another team, Derby County, because Brian Clough was also a good socialist. "Funny how the best managers were socialists isn't it? Alex Ferguson's another. It's the only way to get success," he said. "That's why most of the southern teams like Chelsea are crap. They're all Tory teams, run by Tories, supported by Tories."

I didn't have the heart to tell him a big Red called Roman Abramovich was about to make them great. Although, if I had, he'd probably have gone off on one and told me to never confuse a wealth-stealing oligarch with a socialist.

Not long after the MPs expenses scandal broke in 2009 I had a coffee with him (he paid for his own) and congratulated him on being 657th on the list, taking £121,000 less than the biggest claim.

"And you think that's something to celebrate then? Why? I was only second to bottom. There were a Tory below me. I'm ashamed," he said.

As his 80th birthday approached in early 2012 I requested another interview for the *Mirror* to mark the milestone. This time, he ummed and ahhed, and asked, "is it really that interesting?" but agreed. The Beast was clearly mellowing with age. I met him again in his workplace, the Commons, while he was putting in a shift, and this time, with the recess over, there were actually other MPs there. As we walked to his office I asked what he had planned for the big day. He stopped in his tracks and looked at me as though I'd just said I'd left my union and was a happy scab.

There was nothing of a celebratory nature planned. No party, drinks, or dinner with his three children and four grandchildren. Just a morning spent listening to his Bolsover constituents' worries, a brisk afternoon walk and a train back to London. "It's only a date. Why would I have a party? Parties are organised happiness but happiness is accidental. You can't legislate for it," he says.

I remarked that he should try telling that to newspapers, the BBC and the wider nation who were gearing up for a gushing orgy to celebrate the Queen's 60th year on the throne.

"I can't bear it. Just another way of keeping the working-class in their place," he said before telling a story about receiving an invitation to a Buckingham Palace garden party when he was a Clay Cross councillor in the 1960s. "It came with a parking pass which I chucked straight in the bin. But when I told a mate called Joe, who was a big racing fan, he begged me to dig it out of the bin, which I did. And Joe used it to sail into Royal Ascot for years to come", he said with a grin of satisfaction at helping to strike a blow in the class war.

Dennis had suffered a few serious health issues since the 1997 interview. He was diagnosed with advanced bladder cancer the following year which left him feeling "like everything was ebbing away." Until NHS doctors in Chelsea operated on him.

"As they were wheeling me back to the ward I could see blood dripping into a bag at the side of the bed and the surgeon leaned in and whispered: 'I think we got it all.' He was right. I saw him a fortnight later and he put the camera into my bladder and gave me the all-clear."

Skinner's face lit up as he recalled that moment. "You just can't buy that feeling," he said. "It was May time and there was all this blossom on those cherry trees outside the Chelsea hospital and it was absolutely the blossomest blossom I had ever seen. I can still smell it. I was on such a high I walked straight past the underground station. I was flying, floating. I just kept going and skipped all the way to Westminster thinking, 'I'm so lucky. I got away with it. Millions don't.'"

The news was a turning-point. "I was going to finish after that parliament, and I thought, 'no, carry on, carry on.' I realised I was a lucky bugger who had landed on his feet by getting into politics and out of the pit.

"I sucked in the cherry blossom and thought, 'I'm not finished yet. Life's for the living.' Now that was happiness. You can't organise that."

He had also had a heart by-pass and a hip replacement but with his thick General Custer mane, taut skin and trim body, the former cross-country runner and toe-to-heel walking champion looked fitter than a butcher's dog.

"David Cameron called me a dinosaur the other week, you know? Well, I'm the only dinosaur who can ride a bike 12 miles a day," he said. "That comment showed him up for what he is. I hate to say it because I voted against everything Thatcher did, but she had principles she believed in. This bloke is nowt but a shallow spinner, who hops from twig to twig directed mainly by Gideon Osborne.

"When they were at the age I was running cross-country for my county, they were in the Bullingdon Club, rampaging through hotels, causing mayhem, treating working people like dirt, and getting away with paying for it because they came from money.

"That's where all this nonsense about the Big Society comes from. They see no problem in getting an army of volunteers to clean everything up while they swan off to their country homes because that's how they were brought up.

"I keep hearing that class no longer exists but the difference between the top and the bottom today is greater than when I started down the pit in 1948. By a mile."

I took him back to his 65th birthday, on the eve of Labour returning to power, and reminded him that he seemed optimistic that great things would happen. He believed they did, citing the tripling of NHS funding, and the rebuilding of most state schools as examples. But he admitted that Iraq left Labour looking like a shower of dishonest warmongers and all the good work they had done had been forgotten.

He lamented the financial crash of 2009 which effectively did for Labour and argued that now, more than ever, his brand of socialist thinking, not Tory austerity policies which strangled growth, were needed.

"Look back to 1945. The world, well Europe, were skint. Every major country hit with the equivalent of the biggest recession you can imagine. We had no money but Nye Bevan said 'we're going to build a national health service.' And Stafford Cripps said, 'where the hell do you think the money is coming from?'

"And Nye said, 'we're gonna borrow it, just like they do in the private sector.' Do you think when Tesco expands they tell a staff member to go and get some money out of the till or the safe? No.

"When private companies expand they get it out of someone else's safe. Borrowing to expand is not some left-wing Marxist fantasy, it's capitalism. Keynesian capitalism.

"So in 1945 we built hospitals and council houses in every

city, we found jobs for the hundreds of thousands coming out of the army and the women who had worked in the factories during the war.

"We had free education and pensions for all. And all done in five years. And at the end of it, unemployment stood at just over two per cent. This Thatcherite mantra that you can't borrow is nonsense. The idea that you keep on letting the rich get richer and they will put it into charities or back into the economy is an illusion.

"They put it into Swiss banks. The only way to see the economy work for everyone and to flourish is to give everyone a decent living wage and let them spend it. It's simple economics. But not the type that the rich want to hear. Because they want to keep the lion's share of the wealth for themselves."

I've met many incorruptible class warriors in my time. Tony Mulhearn, the former President of Liverpool Labour District Party and a key member of the city council that took on Thatcher in the mid-80s, was a great man whose funeral I was so pleased I attended as I've never been to one so uplifting.

It was a humanist send-off, held in a Unitarian Church in Liverpool which supports left-wing causes, and was attended by hundreds of mourners. There were no hymns or prayers, just personal music and lovely tributes from friends, colleagues and family in a peaceful, dignified setting. Tony's proud socialist spirit shone throughout, with tales of generosity and solidarity greeted with laughter and tears. He was a great man who never stopped fighting until he died aged 80.

Harry Leslie Smith was another radical maverick who battled against injustice right up to his death at 95. I met him at a Labour Party Conference in 2014 when he brought the house down with a speech about the need to protect the NHS that drew two standing ovations.

He spoke of life in Barnsley in the 1920s being "a barbarous time" when public healthcare didn't exist. "Back then hospitals, doctors and medicine were for the privileged few because they were run for profit rather than as a vital state service that keeps a nation's citizens fit and healthy." Meanwhile, he said, in the dusky tenement streets that oozed poverty where he lived "common diseases trolled our neighbourhoods and snuffed out life like a cold breath on a warm candle flame."

When I chatted to the writer, activist, war veteran and self-proclaimed "world's oldest rebel," he drew me under his spell with tales of his remarkable life.

He spoke so eloquently and honestly about the horrors of Great Depression poverty he endured as a child, the Nazis he fought as a young man and the refugees he was trying to save in his old age, that he left me in awe.

When Harry spoke of his life going full circle under the Tories' austerity drive and warned, "don't let my past be your future," it left a lump in the throat.

But there was something about Dennis Skinner that set him apart. His wit and his torpedo-like ability to score direct hits on Tories resonated more deeply with me than any other socialist I've met.

Tony Benn was a left-wing giant I interviewed a couple of times at his Holland Park home and admired immensely. He had a towering intellect and was a mesmeric orator who could tie his opponents in knots with his knowledge and insight.

But I always felt that, due to his privileged upbringing, unlike Skinner, much of his socialism was theory. Indeed, Skinner once summed up the difference between the pair when he confided: "Tony Benn used to talk to me romantically about the pits. I'd tell him I did 20-odd years down them and there wasn't much romantic about it. It was no way to work. It was modern slavery."

Kevin Maguire sees Skinner as the ultimate class warrior. "With Dennis it was all about the people he came from. His motivating force every day was to represent his class. He would say anyone who's wealthy and successful has stood on other people's shoulders to gain that wealth and success. Because no-one gets anywhere on their own.

"If you're an MP you have to work hard to remain working class because of your lifestyle and earnings but he gave away so much of his salary. During the 1980s miners' strike he gave it all to the strike fund," said Maguire.

The more I spoke to Dennis the clearer it became that he was totally shaped by two things: The poverty he saw all around him in his mining town and the Second World War. Even his famous moniker, The Beast of Bolsover, is linked to the pit. He was christened it by Labour MP Andrew Faulds, after Skinner accused him of lobbying for the Middle Eastern oil companies which threatened coal production.

But when I asked him what he was most proud of in his long years in the Commons, neither of those issues, nor any of his legendary quips, got a mention. Instead, it was killing off Enoch Powell's attempt to ban stem cell treatment in 1987.

"Powell's bill had floundered in committee but he'd been given a second chance to get it through in the Commons. I did my research about protocol by re-reading sections of Erskine and May, and realised I could stop him even talking about his Bill if I moved a writ before he was due to start.

"So I filibustered by talking about the Brecon and Radnor by-election for three-and-a-half hours, and by half-past two Powell hadn't been able to open his mouth.

"He came up to me afterwards and said, 'I reckoned without you, Skinner.' Now whenever I hear of another life saved by stem cell treatment, I know that I had a big hand in that. Which is something that is very important."

When I was interviewing him for his 80th birthday, I asked if he had any plans to retire and expected to be thrown out of the room. Instead, I got a philosophical answer: "You can't go on forever, can you, but I love doing this job, and it's one that needs doing. My job is to look after the people who haven't got two ha'pennies to rub together. And there will always be the need to fight for them because there will always be people at the bottom.

"When I look at the Tories and the House of Lords I see people protecting their class interests. So it's a war. And I'm here fighting for my class. And I want to win."

When the interview finished he asked how my family was and I told him that my dad had been suffering from Alzheimer's Disease for a while and was going downhill.

"Do you sing to him?" he asked me.

"Not really, no. Should I?" I asked.

"Familiar songs are the way to unblock the brain. I discovered this with my mum when she got dementia so bad she couldn't remember my name.

"I'd read that people with a stutter never stutter when they sing. I realised the memory of songs must come from a different part of the brain. So one day when I was in a park with her I started singing an old song that she used to sing to us when we were kids, called If Those Lips Could Only Speak and by the time I got to the second line, she'd joined in.

"When I told the family, one of my brothers said I was talking rubbish so I told them to sit at her bedside with the radio on when I did Desert Island Discs. I asked Sue Lawley to play that song, and guess what? My mum joined in. After that I went to sing in the care home in Bolsover and they started an early dementia singing class. And now it's spread like wildfire around Britain. So the next time you see your dad, sing one of his favourite songs to him," he said.

Which I did. I put a Frank Sinatra DVD on in the car and started singing along, and he joined in. I was chuffed. In fact, I thought I was on the way to curing his dementia. Until he remarked: "What a voice she had, eh?"

I bumped into Dennis a few years later and asked if he was going to run in the 2015 General Election, despite being 83, and he harked back to that dinosaur moment in the house: "Yes I am. Mainly because Cameron told me to retire.

"People seem to forget he told me three times in parliament. If I'd have finished, it would have looked as if he'd scored a victory. He would have talked about it. The moment he said that, I knew I'd have to keep on running."

He was victorious again, although the 18,437 majority he'd won a decade earlier was now down to 11,778. At the General Election two years later that majority was cut to 5,288, and in December 2019, Skinner was beaten by more than 5,000 votes, a victim of a backlash against Labour in traditional Red Wall seats over the party's confused Brexit message.

The irony being that he was one of the few pro-Brexit Labour MPs who had voted consistently against EU membership throughout his time in the Commons because he saw it as a cosy capitalist club that threatened the supremacy of the UK parliament and could thus be a barrier to socialist change.

For those of us who love Dennis, the sadness of his loss was deepened by the fact that he was now quite ill. He'd gone into hospital for a routine operation and caught an infection which ruled him out of canvassing during the run-up to polling day or being present at the count.

According to Kevin Maguire, he was wavering on whether he should stand but felt he had to because if he didn't, he'd be letting down the left-wing of the party in its hour of need. Kevin has been unable to speak to him since.

"He won't have a mobile phone so if I need him I have to go through his partner Lois, who is incredibly protective of him. In the year after his defeat she said he had become disengaged from British politics and didn't want to pass comment on it. Not even Jeremy Corbyn's deselection by the Labour Party. Lois reckoned he'd become more interested in American politics, watching the downfall of Trump."

So we don't even know how he reacted to losing the Bolsover seat he had held for a few months short of half-a-century.

"I think he will have been devastated and taken it personally, even though he couldn't have done anything to stop it because in many of those traditional Labour strongholds in the North and Midlands the tide was going out. But he will have been gutted losing that constituency because he truly loved it and he'll have felt he'd let his people down," said Maguire.

Insult was added to injury by the man who took the Bolsover seat off Labour for the first time since 1950. Mark Fletcher, was not just a Tory but a former communications director for Synergix which was part of the privatised NHS sector. But even Fletcher paid tribute to Skinner, calling him a "wonderful constituency MP" before generously stating, "I haven't found a street where Dennis hasn't helped somebody."

When Bolsover fell you knew Boris Johnson's Tories would not be caught. They went on to record a landslide 80-seat majority, their biggest win since the 1980s. It was a mauling. The feeling of anger and desolation took me back to the 1983 General Election and a Henley-on-Thames nightclub with a girlfriend who had a set of mates, some of whom no doubt went on to become very rich on the back of what happened at the polling stations.

At 1.30am I rang home to ask how it was going and heard my mum close to tears, as she told me that Tony Benn had lost his seat.

When I returned, stunned, to my girlfriend, news of the Tory landslide had reached her mates who were mwah-mwahing each other's cheeks and toasting "Good old Maggie" for once again keeping their families' wealth out of socialist clutches.

The pain in the pit of my stomach that night was the same one I felt hearing Dennis Skinner would no longer be seated on his front-row bench waging war on the party opposite. Or anywhere else in Westminster.

Most veteran Labour politicians who put in a fraction of his service believe it's their divine right, on leaving the Commons, to be handed a seat in the Lords, where they can carry on sucking on the taxpayers' teats while giving off a whiff of power. There was never any chance Dennis would go there.

He was as straight as an arrow and never strayed a millimetre from the miner who donned a suit and walked into the Houses of Parliament in 1970. Over the following five decades he retained a certainty about his beliefs that made him more like an evangelical preacher than a politician.

I doubt there has ever been an MP more devoted to turning up for work every day to put their beliefs into practice for the sake of the people they came from.

The ultimate class warrior was the ultimate one-off. And there is little chance that Westminster will see his like again.

3

THE RELENTLESS
MATRIARCHS

MARGARET
ASPINALL

ANNE
WILLIAMS

PORTCULLIS HOUSE, WESTMINSTER — *May 2016*

I'D run this scene through my head so many times that the sense of déjà vu was numbing.

For 27 years I'd dreamt of watching a parent who lost a child at Hillsborough stand up in parliament and slaughter the political class for their gross dereliction of duty.

And there she was. Margaret Aspinall, 18 years after being told in a different part of Westminster that a Labour government was refusing to hold a judicial inquiry into the disaster, raining shame down on them.

Back in 1998, I'd watched families storm out of Westminster Hall, many in tears, after Home Secretary Jack Straw offered only a meaningless scrutiny of evidence, despite Labour promising in the previous year's General Election manifesto to get to the bottom of the 1989 disaster.

On that painful day, Margaret, who lost her 18-year-old son at Hillsborough, described her feelings about the betrayal as worse than anger. "It makes me feel ashamed to come from a country that could let people down so badly and leave them nowhere to turn for justice."

I'd known Margaret since the early 90s when there was no sign of justice in sight for the victims of Britain's worst sporting disaster. Back then few, even inside her own city, were fighting to get their voices heard about the criminal negligence that killed her son James, and 95 others, at Hillsborough, and the despicable cover-up that followed.

The mother-of-five from a Huyton council estate was licking stamps on letters for the Hillsborough Family Support Group alongside its chair Phil Hammond, and had an air of cheery optimism about her that disguised the pain that was eating away inside.

I bonded with Margaret, and all the other families whose loved ones went to that FA Cup semi-final never to return, because I walked through those Leppings Lane gates on that beautiful spring day and only the luck of being allocated a ticket for a seat saved me from turning into the tunnel of death.

I had vowed, from the day after the disaster when I wrote an article for the *Liverpool Daily Post* about 96 lives being lost because to the authorities they didn't count, that I would campaign as a journalist until the wall of lies about Hillsborough was brought down.

Over the long years I'd stood outside courts and grey civic buildings trying to pick up devastated mothers after the system delivered another kick to their teeth by assuring them their day would come. Even though a big part of me doubted that it ever would. That's what I'd said to Margaret Aspinall as she wept tears of anger in Westminster Hall in 1998 after Straw's refusal to hold an inquiry.

And there she was, in 2016, in another stuffy parliamentary room, a fortnight after jurors at fresh inquests had returned Unlawful Killing verdicts on the 96, having that day. And she used it to ensure that the assembled MPs, Lords, and current and former party leaders felt the same disgust she had 16 years earlier.

"The politicians of this country ought to be ashamed of themselves for what's happened in their name. We as a nation should be ashamed that our families had to fight for almost 30 years to get to the truth," she told them in her trademark slow, smoky voice.

"I personally am ashamed of the past governments. I am ashamed of the government I believed in at the time. The one that was supposed to stand up for working-class people like me. Labour politicians in the 90s gave us fancy promises but they didn't listen." Her powerful, unscripted words left the likes of Labour leader Jeremy Corbyn and ex-Tory leader Lord Howard gobsmacked.

On she spoke, for more than 20 minutes, demanding the law-makers level the playing field for bereaved families who lack money but who are thrown into a legal fight not of their making: "You have to change things in this country for the good of the ordinary people because if they can cover up 96 deaths what can they do to individuals? No-one should have to beg for information about the loss of their loved ones and everyone should be entitled to legal aid."

This doughty, then 69-year-old, next told a story which left many in the audience, including actress Sue Johnston and the Bishop of Liverpool, close to tears.

"When James died I had four other children; the youngest was six, the eldest was 15. We didn't have money but my house was rich with love. I didn't realise I had to pay for my own son's inquest but Trevor Hicks, who lost his two lovely girls that day, asked 42 families for £3,000 to pay for a barrister.

"I thought 'my God how am I going to raise £3,000?'" She then remembered that she had been sent an official letter from the authorities offering her £1,226.35 in compensation for James' death, which she almost binned in rage, before placing in a drawer to remind herself how little value the state had put on her son's life.

"I'd have dearly loved to have told them to shove that cheque where the sun don't shine. But we had to raise £150,000 to get a barrister. So I took it. Then I got to the inquests and saw the police had ten barristers, paid for by the government, against our one. We were the innocents but they got funded. How on God's earth can that be right?

"We saw the matchday commander at Hillsborough, Chief Superintendent David Duckenfield, retire on ill health grounds with a full pension, while he was still under investigation. He got another job afterwards, too. That's how ill he was.

"That's why I'm calling on all of you, today, the law-makers, on all sides, to introduce The Hillsborough Law which says if police officers are found guilty of charges they should pay all their pensions back, the time limits on retired police officers being investigated for misconduct should be dropped and equal funding given to legal representation of bereaved families."

She told them there was a "disease in this country" citing South Yorkshire Police's role in Hillsborough, the Battle of Orgreave and Rotherham sex abuse scandal, and argued, "Hillsborough was bigger than the police. It was political. It went right to the top. So it's up to you politicians to unite and never let the likes of it happen again."

Watching this pocket battleship passionately and articulately lay down the law to the law-makers, with some of them grimacing at her every word, was truly life-affirming. When she'd finished, the five-minute standing ovation she received felt like a thunderclap being released in the airless, beige room.

I felt so proud of her. How did that shy woman I'd first met in a Liverpool City Council room in those bleak years that followed the disaster grow into a self-assured orator? A working-class mother who cleaned floors to raise money to keep the fight going when most people willed her to accept that her son had died in a tragic accident and move on.

Where did that confidence come from to speak truth to power so articulately inside the walls where the Hillsborough conspiracy was perpetrated?

Britain's worst sporting disaster was all about working-class heroism, beginning on the afternoon itself, when the only people trying to save lives were fans who turned advertising hoardings into makeshift stretchers. The three-decade long fight for justice was about ordinary people refusing to be cowed by the weight of denial from on high.

It was the love of these bereaved family members, especially the mothers, who heroically refused to back down in the face of overwhelming odds, that brought the truth of that disaster to light.

There were so many heroes among the families, too many to name-check. But the two mothers whose names became synonymous with this Herculean fight to reveal the truth about the deaths of their sons were Margaret Aspinall and Anne Williams. And I had the honour to be with them from the start.

FORMBY — October 1991

When I first met Anne there was no Hillsborough justice campaign and little appetite for it.

The families were still raw from grieving and bruised by the blows inflicted on them by a system that refused to buckle. Most felt beaten by a cocktail of lies and apathy.

Anne was different though. The events of the previous couple of years had left her looking pale, weak and in a permanent state of mourning the beloved son she had lost. But inside, as the banner that now flutters on the Kop testifies, beat the heart of an Iron Lady.

I'd been told of her one-woman struggle to get to the truth of 15-year-old Kevin's death on the Leppings Lane terraces by two women from Liverpool City Council's Hillsborough Working Party, Ann Adlington and Sheila Coleman. Two women whose work, especially in the years when few wanted to hear about Hillsborough, was brave and inspirational. They had read a few columns that I'd written in the *Liverpool Echo* about the injustice of Hillsborough and asked if I'd like to run Anne's story. It was an easy decision.

So there I sat in Anne's neat Formby semi, sipping tea, and listening to a tale that became the first to chip away at the wall of lies. A heart-wrenching story which so contradicted the police narrative of what happened that day, and so blew apart the inquest verdicts, it still remains the most compelling evidence of a cover-up.

It began on Friday April 14, 1989, with an excited Kevin telling his 38-year-old mum he had a ticket to see his idols, Liverpool, play in the next day's FA Cup semi-final.

She puts her foot down, telling him he's too young to go to Sheffield without an adult. The lad fills up and sidles back to his room in a sulk. But Anne's husband, Kevin's step-dad Steve, tells her, "The poor little bugger. All he does is study for his GCSEs. Let him go. Reward him for all his hard work."

Kevin is called back downstairs and told he can go to his first away game so long as he travels on a train with a police escort. He leaps around the room, punching the air and singing the name of his beloved Reds. He's off to Hillsborough.

The next morning he calls into the newsagent's shop where Anne worked to get snacks for the journey. She pats him on the head, tells him to have a good time and says she hopes they win for him. He turns round at the shop door, beaming, and says "No problem Mum. Three nil. Don't save any of your moussaka for tea, I'll have beans on toast instead."

And those were the last words she heard her son utter.

"I don't remember much about the first months of Kevin's death," she told me in a matter-of-fact way staring at his framed photo on the sideboard. "My oldest son Michael was ill and my little girl Sara was sent to a specialist because she thought she was dying. I was out of my mind worrying in case I lost another one. I kept having nervous spasms."

Her tale then moves to the Sheffield inquests which opened in November 1990, where, like the rest of the bereaved, she was told that Kevin had died of traumatic asphyxia and that he, like all the victims, were dead, or brain dead, by 3.15pm. That was the official version which enabled the police, ambulance services and Sheffield Wednesday FC to say that nothing could have been done for the dying fans.

It closed down questions such as why were more than 40 ambulances not allowed into the ground, and why did the police not activate the major accident plan until 3.55pm? Unsurprisingly, the Sheffield jury directed by a coroner employed by Sheffield Council who were themselves culpable for not issuing Hillsborough with a valid safety certificate, returned a 9-2 majority verdict of Accidental Death on all the fans.

But before Anne went into the court she was told something. That Kevin had spoken a word at 3.57pm in the makeshift mortuary to a Special WPC: "I said straight away, 'It was Mum, wasn't it?'" said Anne. "The policeman nodded and I broke down in tears. I was inconsolable. That word shattered my heart. I felt I had lost Kevin all over again," she told me. "I couldn't stop thinking why didn't they tell me about him saying 'Mum' before we went to Sheffield?"

Anne then went on a mission to track down the WPC, which took a few months, and when she did, SWPC Debra Martin travelled from Sheffield to Formby to meet her. It was the only thing that had happened in more than two years since Kevin's death that brought her any joy.

"Debra said she held him in her arms like a baby. She gave Kevin heart massage, and his ribs were moving. She told me how she could never forget his eyes opening because he had lovely long lashes. She said he opened his mouth, said 'Mum', then died.

"I can't begin to tell you what an emotional moment it was when she told me. We just held each other and cried. But it was such a weight off my mind. I was so happy that Kevin had died in the arms of such a lovely woman and that he wasn't just dumped somewhere to die, as the inquest said he was. It made such a difference to me. Suddenly, after hearing the truth I felt at peace."

SWPC Martin also told Anne how she'd been pressurised by South Yorkshire Police to make a fresh statement, denying Kevin had spoken. How they made her write the following about her attempts to revive him: "My head had gone. I wasn't aware of what was happening or what I was doing. I felt like a zombie."

It was a light-bulb moment for Anne. The callous motives behind that revelation forced her to dedicate her life to over-turning the false official version of her son's death.

In her Formby living room back in 1991 I asked Anne why she was so determined to overturn Kevin's inquest verdict, and in the decades to come, whenever the Hillsborough campaign hit a wall I'd draw on her answer: "While I have breath in my body I'll fight that wicked verdict because when you bring a child into this world the words on the birth certificate are accurate. When they leave, the least they deserve is the right ones on their death certificate."

As I found out, that was the mantra of so many of these mothers who, when they arrived in Sheffield on the night of the disaster, were told they weren't allowed to touch their children who lay behind a pane of glass because they were "property of the coroner."

Anne went to a top pathologist who established that Kevin hadn't died of traumatic asphyxia but of neck injuries which closed down his airways. She hired a succession of barristers in her one-woman fight against an Establishment that had closed ranks and frustrated her at every turn.

Three times she applied to the Attorney General to have the inquest verdict overturned, even taking it to the European Court of Human Rights, but each time she was turned down. Yet as I was discovering, the apathy towards the families didn't just come from above.

Astonishingly, I struggled to get Anne's story into the *Liverpool Echo*, despite having a copy of the letter her local Tory MP Malcolm Thornton had written to the Attorney General stating, "there is now the most powerful case to re-open these inquests."

Back in 1991, even in Liverpool, there were many who groaned at the word Hillsborough, and asked, "Why don't those people let it lie?" It would be said a million times over the following decades. And the answer was always the same: Because these people were made of different stuff.

It had looked promising four months after the disaster when Lord Justice Taylor published an interim report, which completely contradicted the lies being peddled by the police in Yorkshire, Margaret Thatcher's press secretary Bernard Ingham and their journalist allies in Wapping, who all agreed the deaths had been caused by a ticketless, tanked-up mob.

A story that had gone around the world as quickly as the lie put out that day by the policeman in charge, David Duckenfield, that Liverpool fans had stormed a gate he had given permission to open.

Taylor ruled that drunkenness, late arrivals and fans turning up without tickets were red herrings. That there was no evidence of any kind of hooliganism and that fans were not to blame for the crush. He even described their role in trying to save the dying as "magnificent."

Instead, Lord Taylor laid the blame squarely at the door of the police. He highlighted their planning failure which allowed "dangerous congestion at the turnstiles" and ruled that "the immediate cause of the disaster was gross overcrowding, namely the failure, when the exit gate was opened, to cut off access to the central pens which were already overfull.

"Pens that were overfull because no safe maximum capacities had been laid down, no attempt was made to control entry to individual pens numerically and there was no effective visual monitoring of crowd density."

He hit out at the police's "sluggish reaction and response when the crush occurred" and put to bed the ticketless fans theory by announcing that the total number of fans who entered the Leppings Lane terrace "did not exceed the capacity of the standing area".

Most importantly he said Duckenfield "froze" after ordering the exit gate to be opened. "A blunder of the first magnitude," he called it.

Taylor's report not only vindicated the fans but gave hope to the families that justice would be coming soon. That the people into whose care they had entrusted their loved ones would face up to their responsibilities for allowing a wholly avoidable disaster to happen. But their hope was short-lived.

The sham Sheffield inquests hauled the emergency services off the hook. The Director of Public Prosecutions threw out all charges against the police on grounds of insufficient evidence. No senior officer was prosecuted and a disciplinary case against Duckenfield was stopped when he took early retirement, aged 46, on medical grounds, with a full pension.

No legal, moral or financial compensation came the families' way. The majority receiving little more than funeral expenses. In contrast, 14 police officers who were "traumatised" by what they saw that day picked up £1.2million. To add insult to injury their claims for compensation were based on the insurers accepting that their superiors had been negligent.

However, by the mid-90s there was a momentum gathering behind the belief that a major miscarriage of justice had taken place. Screenwriter Jimmy McGovern was commissioned by Granada TV to tell the families' stories in a two-hour drama-documentary.

Researchers unearthed new evidence which undermined the police case, crucially that the CCTV camera trained on the

Leppings Lane end, which they said had not been in operation, was working.

The ground engineer swore an affidavit to that effect which proved South Yorkshire Police had been lying when they told the inquest they couldn't see the extent of the crush from the control box. This could not have been challenged at the inquests because, mysteriously, the CCTV tapes from the day were "stolen" and never found.

On December 5 1996, Hillsborough was back on the front pages of a national newspaper. This time *The Mirror* splashed with a headline THE REAL TRUTH above a story I'd written urging every reader to watch McGovern's drama.

The Mirror's phone lines were swamped with angry readers demanding justice – 25,695 adding their names to the paper's petition calling on the Attorney General to launch a new inquiry. We lobbied the Labour Party, which was gearing up for a General Election months later and they pledged to consider holding an inquiry into the disaster.

Yet, when Labour were elected, they bottled it. Jack Straw set up a token Scrutiny of Evidence under Lord Justice Stuart-Smith whose opening line to the families was "are you like the Liverpool fans, turning up at the last minute?" After that, it was obvious the retired judge was going to take the Establishment line that those 96 deaths were at best accidental and at worst self-inflicted.

Especially when *The Sun's* publisher Rupert Murdoch had played such a part in electing Tony Blair. Especially after a handwritten note was discovered, written by Blair, which questioned calls for a new inquiry with the words: "Why? What is the point?"

Stuart-Smith cross-examined nobody and studied the evidence in private. And despite discovering that 183 police statements had been edited to remove criticism of senior police management, he ruled there was not enough evidence to merit a fresh inquiry.

By now the families were running short of stamina and options but still they fought on. A sell-out pop concert at Anfield featuring The Lightning Seeds, Stereophonics and The Manic Street Preachers, raised enough money to take out private prosecutions against Duckenfield and his deputy on the day, Supt Bernard Murray, who went on trial at Leeds Crown Court in July 2000, charged with manslaughter and wilful neglect of duty.

But once again justice eluded them. Under a judge, Justice Hooper, who was openly contemptuous of the families having the audacity to bring two senior policemen to court, Murray was cleared of all charges and the jury failed to reach a verdict on Duckenfield. Hooper halted the trial, cleared him, and ruled he could never be retried.

It ended in tears again, this time with eight armed police officers escorting the families out of the court building. Presumably in case they caused trouble. Speaking to the mentally exhausted and financially broken families on the streets of Leeds after that trial, it felt as though the fight was over.

That they would do what most of the nation had been begging them to do for 11 years, shut up and turn it in. But these iron ladies were not for turning.

DAILY Mirror

Thursday, December 5, 1996   30p

9PM, ITV, TONIGHT
All Britain must watch the most harrowing TV programme ever made

HILLSBOROUGH

1 ORDER: Chief Superintendent David Duckenfield, played by Maurice Roeves, takes the fatal decision to open the Leppings Lane gate

2 RUSH: The gate is unlocked, letting 2,000 fans into the ground and funnelling them towards the stadium's two already-packed pens

3 DESPERATE: Trevor Hicks, played by Chris Eccleston, stands in an empty pen pleading to police that his crushed daughters are dying

4 DISASTER: Police on the pitch realise their mistake too late as 96 fans begin to die in front of their eyes .. and the cover-up begins

THE REAL TRUTH

By Mirror man BRIAN READE who was there

TONIGHT at 9pm, a TV programme will at last tell the truth about the Hillsborough disaster. You must watch it.

The searing two-hour drama will haunt you and hurt you. But do not miss it.

New evidence about the football-crowd horror in 1989 in which 96 young Liverpool fans died may help to right one of the most grievous wrongs in British legal history. The lie is that the fans themselves — and not the incompetence of the authorities — were to blame.

Cracker writer Jimmy McGovern is the maker of Hillsborough, the man who unmasks the official cover-up.

He says: "Surely you have the right to know the truth about how your child died."

I believe his story is the true one, because I was there that sunny April day in Sheffield.

Thank God, and Jimmy McGovern, that someone had the guts and the talent, all those years on, to expose the lies. To tell it like it was.

● TURN TO PAGES 6 and 7

ANFIELD — *April 2009*

The one event that pricked the nation's conscience about the unanswered questions surrounding Hillsborough was the annual memorial service at Anfield.

Sitting at the front of a packed Kop, the families and supporters, Liverpool players and staff, would hear speeches and hymns as the 96 names were read out by local clergy.

It was an understated, dignified occasion that allowed those who had remained in the Hillsborough Family Support Group (HFSG) to have a focal point for their grief. Other families who had split into the Hillsborough Justice Campaign, of which Anne Williams was then a member, held their own event outside the ground.

I was honoured to receive an invite every year to meet with the HFSG families beforehand for a cup of tea in an Anfield hospitality room before walking on to the Kop and sitting alongside them. Then struggling to keep my emotions in check throughout the moving service.

As the 20th anniversary approached, change was in the air. Phil Hammond who had led the group since the early 90s, suffered a brain haemorrhage the previous Christmas, and although he pulled through, was severely disabled and incapable of leading the fight.

Their choice to take up the reins was Phil's deputy, Margaret Aspinall, who had attended every HFSG meeting since its inception. She wanted something different for the 20th anniversary. Conscious that there would be more attention on Anfield that day, and that the ground with possibly triple the number of usual mourners would be far more boisterous, she ditched the etiquette that said politics should be kept out of the occasion.

Despite being warned by Trevor Hicks that this had always been a non-political platform, she asked Culture Secretary Andy Burnham, who had been supportive of the families, to speak.

It was a decision that turbo-charged the fight for justice. Just as Anne Williams hearing Kevin had said "Mum" pushed her into action, so another word, chanted repeatedly from the Kop to drown out Burnham, had a seismic effect: "Justice."

Andy Burnham is a decent politician, Scouse-born and Evertonian, his desire to pay tribute to the 96 and support the families, was genuine. But if you enter an emotion-soaked Anfield, with 28,000 people contemptuous of an Establishment cover-up, bringing words of goodwill from the top of that Establishment, then you should expect to hear what resides in their hearts. And that was a sense of betrayal that a Labour government which had been in power for 12 of the 20 years since the disaster had done nothing to facilitate calls to unearth the truth.

Which was why, when Burnham said he brought a message from Prime Minister Gordon Brown that the Hillsborough victims would never be forgotten, pockets of the crowd booed, jeered and chanted, "Justice for the 96".

The message was simple. Words are easy, actions hard. Don't patronise us with easy soundbites. Because, when you have the power to right this terrible wrong but do nothing, you not only insult the living but the dead.

As Trevor Hicks, who lost his two teenage daughters Victoria and Sarah at Hillsborough, told Burnham, "If ever the Government needed proof that the families have not had justice just look around this stadium today. We refer to them as the 96. But they were real people, our kin, our flesh and blood. Real people who did not come home from a football game. And no-one has paid the price."

The hostile reaction rocked Burnham, and the government too, when they saw the footage dominate news schedules that night and read the *Daily Mirror* the next day, with our front page demand for a proper inquiry. The sight of a Labour hotbed like Liverpool and a Labour paper like *The Mirror*, turning on a Labour government did not sit well with Gordon Brown whose support was crumbling, especially in the heartlands, where the party was about to suffer its worst local council results in 40 years.

Action was swift. Home Secretary Jacqui Smith announced she would break the 30-year rule and release all relevant documents, including secret files about Hillsborough, into the public domain.

Her successor at the Home Office, Alan Johnson, set up a Hillsborough Independent Panel, with a remit to oversee "full public disclosure of relevant government and local information" and "consult with the Hillsborough families to ensure that the views of those most affected by the disaster are taken into account." The aim was to produce a definitive report, under the chairmanship of Bishop of Liverpool, James Jones. But the families, fearing it could turn into another Establishment whitewash, demanded Phil Scraton, an academic who had written extensively about the disaster, be a part of the panel. Thankfully he was allowed to, and led the research team that got to the heart of the facts.

The panel's work took almost three years to complete, but when their report was released, the narrative of Hillsborough changed forever.

LIVERPOOL ANGLICAN CATHEDRAL — *September 2012*

It was a judgement day they had been pining for, yet dreading. Judgement on how and why their loved ones died. Judgement on the fans they had been so protective of and judgement on whether or not they had been wasting their time and energy for most of their adult lives in a quest to find the truth.

The families were taken into a large room in the cathedral and handed the 1,400-page report with the headline findings explained to them by members of the panel. We, the media, were put in a different room, unable to hear what had been said until the families had digested the report. Standing outside the vast cathedral, it felt like waiting for white smoke to rise from the Vatican.

I received a one-word text from inside, strictly against the rules. It said "brilliant." Which made me guess we were on to a winner, even though I didn't know the score. When we were led into a makeshift media room and handed the report it felt as though life's lottery was paying out a jackpot.

The British Establishment, after the most catastrophic of failures, had been found guilty of the most heinous of cover-ups.

The headline conclusions were that no Liverpool fans were responsible in any way for the disaster and that its main cause was a "lack of police control." It said crowd safety was "compromised at every level" and that as many as 41 of the 96 who perished might have survived had the emergency services' reactions been better.

It said 164 witness statements had been altered, with 116

amended to remove or change negative comments about South Yorkshire Police.

It said South Yorkshire Police had performed blood alcohol tests on the victims, even the children, and ran computer checks on the national police database in an attempt to "impugn their reputation."

It said the then Conservative MP for Sheffield Hallam, Irvine Patnick, had passed inaccurate and untrue information from the police to the press. Information that led *The Sun* to run its infamous "The Truth" headline, above a story which claimed Liverpool fans had urinated on the police as they attempted to resuscitate victims and stolen from the dead.

Finally, The Real Truth was out. And we were about to watch on a live link from the House of Commons, Prime Minister David Cameron, offer a profound apology to the families seated in another part of the cathedral, for the way they had been treated and tell the world that they were right all along. While those who sought to discredit them, or block their path to justice, were branded corrupt liars.

"With the weight of the new evidence in the report, it's right for me today as prime minister to make a proper apology to the families of the 96. On behalf of the government, and indeed of our country, I am profoundly sorry that this double injustice has been left uncorrected for so long," said Cameron to a hushed Commons.

It was a speech I'd waited 23 years to hear and it came at a hugely emotional time. Five days earlier I'd watched my dad, Reg, die a slow death in Whiston Hospital after suffering dementia. Sat in that hospital room with him for long hours my mind had drifted back to the first football game I ever went to, aged seven, at Bolton in 1965, when I sat on Reg's shoulders throughout, putting so much stress on his back he was off work for the next fortnight.

I thought of others I'd lost in the 54 years I'd been alive. Especially my brother Vic, who had died in 1983 from a heart attack when he was only 29, and my mate Billy, who was taken by cancer when he was 40.

Conscious that the Hillsborough Report was due out in days I thought of how I too could easily have died young, aged only 31, if my ticket for that semi-final had been for my usual standing spec behind the goal.

It could have been Reg, along with my mum Sheila, and sisters Karen and Cathie, who would spend the next 23 years of their lives waiting for someone in authority to say they were sorry for the sadistic torture dished out to families by the British state for simply having had a loved one go to a football game.

They were the emotions swirling through my mind when I gave my reaction to this historic day in *The Mirror*, under the headline: Kicked To Hell And Back – The Mothers Who Refused To Let Their Lost Children Down.

'WE'RE taught from childhood to always believe that the truth will out. That however bad a deed or lie, justice will eventually be seen to be done. Because that is how life works.

For 23 years and 150 days, almost 100 bereaved families, hundreds of mentally-scarred survivors and thousands of fans who witnessed what happened at Hillsborough stadium on April 15, 1989, have scorned such a notion.

They played by the book, trying every point of authority to get that truth out. They pleaded with the Establishment's conscience to cease looking away and finally admit why 96 people, half of whom were 21 or younger, never came back from a football game.

Yet they got nothing back but rants about whining and kicks in the teeth from size 10 boots.

Until yesterday when the house of lies came tumbling down. When the sheer force of love and dedication and refusal to be beaten forced out that truth.

Like a few thousand others at Hillsborough that fateful day who looked on as men, women and children were killed for simply being football fans, it felt like the heaviest burden I'd ever carried had been lifted.

It felt like a machine-gun was hosing down all the myths and lies that led to the grotesque fiction that said we killed our own.

The inquest verdicts of Accidental Death, the defence that there was no cover-up, that the disaster was caused by a 'tanked-up ticketless mob,' The Sun's front page, the accuracy of the police and ambulance statements, the notion that the stadium was safe and that victims could not have been saved.

All shot down as cruel and calculated lies.

A few months back, David Cameron compared the families' quest for justice to "a blind man, in a dark room, looking for a black cat that isn't there".

When he read yesterday's report he clearly changed his mind and I thank him for his apology, and the tone of horror in his voice. But so staggering was the cover-up and so steeped in criminality that he had no other option.

This is how it felt after 23 years of campaigning to hear that Prime Ministerial apology: Like you'd been scratching at a concrete dam with your fingernails for half a lifetime hoping to see a chink of light, and then it came, and it grew, until a tide of truth surged through to reveal a blue sky, with a blinding sun and a single cloud in the shape of a question mark. Asking why it took so long.

However, the sense of triumph and relief that the families had finally been vindicated was laced with anger. A deep, simmering anger that it had taken an eternity for the full picture to emerge. That the bereaved and the survivors had been kicked to hell and back, leaving a soul-numbing trail of broken marriages, suicides and deaths through broken hearts.

'I always knew we'd get there,' said Margaret Aspinall, her expression an intense mix of ecstasy and pain. 'You fans have all been exonerated and the 96 can rest in peace.'

'We did it,' said Trevor Hicks. 'But this morning in there was bloody hard. When we realised that half of the 96 could have been saved, it blew me away. Three people fainted.'

When I read how some of the young victims had blood samples taken and their names cross-checked with the police computer to see if they had criminal records, I almost fainted myself. That got to me. As did the harrowing prospect that 41 victims could have been saved.

But it was the look on the mothers' faces that got to me most. Women I'd seen age from being in their 30s and 40s into near pensioners, dragged down by it all, but never dragged under.

The likes of Margaret and Anne Williams, Jenni Hicks, Doreen Jones, Hilda Hammond, Mary Corrigan, Dolores Steele, and all the others who fought on with every breath in their body for their babies, who had not only been killed but viciously neglected by those who were supposed to be in their place in their hour of need.

The Establishment reckoned it would eventually wear down the opposition but never realised it was dealing with the most potent *force of all – a mother's love. As Margaret Aspinall said yesterday: 'We were our children's eyes, their ears. We were their voices. And we were never going to be silenced.'*

The families never thought as one. How could they. Hillsborough and the aftermath ripped the hearts out of 96 different families, who all coped without it in different ways.

Indeed, what I call the third Hillsborough tragedy came when the families could not agree on the best way to achieve justice and split into two groups, each decrying the others' methods. Yesterday the Family Support Group (HFSG) and the Justice Campaign (HJC) wouldn't share the same press conference.

I reminded Margaret Aspinall how, many years ago, when we walked out of the House of Commons after the failed public inquiry, I told her that one day she would walk out of a big old building with the word justice ringing in their ears. And a nation left in no doubt of the truth of that terrible day.

'You're jumping the gun,' said Margaret. 'We've got the truth but we still haven't got the justice.' Margaret said all she'd ever wanted was to remove the blanket of lies that had been thrown over her son James and Hillsborough.

All she'd been given, for 23 years, she said, was the crumbs off the table. Yesterday she got a few slices short of the full loaf. But did it feel like that? 'No,' she said. 'We're still the losers in all this. All I've got today is a better quality of grieving.'

Maybe when the families get those final few slices, closure from this horrendous nightmare, the biggest cover-up in British history as Mike Mansfield called it yesterday, can begin.'

Immediately after the publication of the report, the families called for new inquests for the victims as well as prosecutions of South Yorkshire Police for unlawful killing, corporate manslaughter and perverting the course of justice. They also demanded Sheffield Wednesday, Sheffield City Council and The FA be investigated for their roles in providing, certifying and selecting the stadium.

This time the government had nowhere to hide. Home Secretary Theresa May ordered a criminal investigation, under the name Operation Resolve; the Independent Police Complaints Commission launched an investigation into an alleged cover-up, and the High Court quashed the original inquest verdicts of Accidental Death and ordered fresh inquests.

It was six days before Christmas when more than 40 families made the trip down to London for the hearing, while many more watched by video-link in Liverpool. When giving the ruling, The Lord Chief Justice Lord Judge expressed his "admiration and respect for their determined search for the truth" and his regret that the process the families had gone through had been "so unbearably dispiriting and prolonged".

Afterwards, as they stood on the steps of the Royal Courts of Justice, there was unbridled joy on the faces of the families.

Anne Williams said she was delighted for her son Kevin and relieved for the fans who helped the likes of him on the pitch back in 1989, saying "they should have medals." She spoke of how the authorities had gone out of their way to lie just to secure the accidental death verdict, and now "it's their turn to pay for what they have done."

She burst into a smile when she said, "We made history didn't we? Everyone will know now that Hillsborough was not an accident. If only they'd held their hands up and admitted what they'd done, but they wouldn't. But I knew they were lies because I knew what happened to my son and I wasn't going to let it lie. I'd like a corporate manslaughter verdict after the new inquests and God willing, I will still be here to see it."

Those last few words were laden with poignancy because despite Anne's smile, her gaunt and hollow face told of another tragic twist to the tale. The 61-year-old, who arrived at The Strand being pushed by her brother Danny in a wheelchair, had been diagnosed with terminal bowel cancer weeks after the publication of the report.

She had finally achieved part of what she had always sought: To have the wrong words removed from her son's death certificate. But now, it was almost certain she would not live to see the correct ones written on it.

Her daughter Sara, then 33, later told me of the moment Anne was given the news in the Countess of Chester Hospital. She was clutching her mum's hand when a doctor said to her, "I'm so sorry, Anne. After everything you've done, you've got cancer and there's nothing we can do."

It jolted Sara sideways but Anne did not flinch. She had no questions for the doctor, only words for her daughter. Words that in the shadow of death defined her life. "Right then," she said. "You'll have to carry on Kevin's case for me now."

On the 24th anniversary of Hillsborough in April 2013, against all medical advice, Anne attended the memorial service at Anfield.

As Everton chairman Bill Kenwright told the packed Kop that the two greatest words in the English language were "my mum", an extremely frail Anne, watching quietly from her wheelchair, choked with emotion at the aptness of that phrase. When Kenwright added, "Not only did they pick on the wrong city, they picked on the wrong mums" he summed up these women to perfection.

Over the years people were intimidated by Anne, some even questioned her state of mind. Her daughter more than anyone identified with that. "Mum had this tunnel vision. She'd get so frustrated with people she felt were holding her back. She could be hard to deal with because she was so focused," said Sara, who wrote a book about Anne's quest for justice called With Hope In Her Heart.

"The amazing thing was she was so shy and quiet. When people hinted that she should shut up and go away, it only made her more determined. She could never be silenced.

"But although Hillsborough defined her, she had two separate lives. One minute you were with a mum and a nan, the next you were with this fiercely determined woman who wanted to take on the world.

"The really sad thing is that in the end Mum was tired of Hillsborough and looking forward to a life without it. She would have loved to just sit back after all the hard work she'd done and enjoy the justice coming."

Three days after the memorial service, Anne died.

I heard of her death hours after covering a virtual state funeral at Westminster Abbey for someone hailed as the ultimate inspiration to womankind, Margaret Thatcher. But I knew, as did the Kopite who made the Iron Lady flag dedicated to her, who the real inspiration was.

In Liverpool, they lowered the flags to half-mast and beamed a moving tribute to her on to huge city centre screens. In Formby, locals lined the streets to get a glimpse of her coffin, while inside Our Lady Of Compassion Church, MPs and local dignitaries swelled the pews, mourners stood four deep in the side aisles and many dozens more looked on from the back.

It was as though a war hero was being laid to rest, and in a way it was. A hero of a 24-year battle against lies and subterfuge. A hero who never flinched in her fight against injustice right to the very end.

How apt it was that her life was celebrated on a beautiful April day, the same as it was when she last saw Kevin racing out of that newsagents' shop telling her not to save any moussaka for his tea.

I sat next to Andy Burnham in the packed church and watched her coffin being carried in to the sound of the football hymn Abide With Me.

Stevie Hart, who carried Kevin from the pitch, recited a poem called The Farewell, by Armagh writer Peter Makem, penned in memory of "a heroic life, a great citizen of the city and the world". It read:

Farewell good Anne, earth and sky are calling,
Farewell fair and noble friend,
the parting hour has tolled its bell,
the parting hour is come,
when we must turn and set you free into the arms of eternity.

Farewell good friend, farewell.
Your deeds have changed us, your days have lived in us.
That we must speak the flame they lit,
our fullest thought, our fullest sigh.

What beat that heart will live forever,
what filled those veins can never die.

Farewell again, farewell,
and even though our heads are down,
even though our grief is full,
the stirrings in us stir again.
No dark will fall upon you, no dark can come upon your way
as you journey, on and on,
Into the water of sunset, Into the milk of dawn.

As her cortege slowly headed off for Southport crematorium, the crowd on the pavements burst into spontaneous applause for the petite, shy local woman who never tired of kicking down seemingly overwhelming obstacles.

One woman threw a rose at the hearse. And, as her coffin moved slowly past his eye-line, a middle-aged man next to her simply mouthed, "What a bloody inspiration."

Nothing else needed saying.

BIRCHWOOD PARK, WARRINGTON — *March 2014*

After what felt like an eternity, the families finally walked back into a coroner's court with hope in their hearts.

It had been 23 years and three days since they left Sheffield Town Hall's Victorian oak-lined council chamber engulfed in grief and anger at the accidental death verdicts on their loved ones. How it contrasted with the vast brand-spanking new courtroom, in an office building at Birchwood Park, Warrington, which was purpose-built for the fresh inquests.

As 150 family members filed in, some clutching photos of those who died, Margaret Aspinall, who was 44 when the last inquests ended and was now 67, looked around and said, "I know it's what we've been fighting for all these years but it brings the horror back. When this started I was a young woman with a young family. Now I'm an old woman with grandchildren my son didn't get to see. I just hope this time it really is the beginning of the end and they get the job done."

They took their seats one-and-a-half hours before the coroner, Lord Justice Goldring, began jury selection. And although there was busy, optimistic chatter between them, there was also sadness behind the eyes. Not just for their lost loved ones and the lost years of brutal knock-backs, but for the kindred spirits they lost along the way.

Fathers like Eddie Spearritt and John Glover who went to their graves early, thinking justice would never be seen. Mothers like Joan Traynor and Anne Williams and all the brothers and grandmothers, sisters and aunts, the numerous guilt-ridden survivors who committed suicide and those like long-time campaigner Phil Hammond, too ill to attend.

The rows in front of the families were packed with 86 legal staff from 21 different teams, two-thirds of them representing "interested parties" such as South Yorkshire Police, The FA and Sheffield Wednesday.

The judge warned the jury that the inquest could take up to a year but he was being optimistic. It lasted more than two years, making it the longest inquest in British legal history.

It started poignantly, with loving pen portraits of all 96 victims, written by family members, being read to the jury to give a sense of the individuals who had died. It moved on to recreating the experience of all 96 victims based on CCTV footage, eyewitness accounts and press photographs, with pathologists revealing in gruesome detail what happened to their bodies and the causes of death.

Old wounds were painfully re-opened, distress levels went off the scale as their personal agony, as distinct from the collective one of not having justice, was piled on to them again. They were literally forced to re-live their worst nightmare.

The day the jury came to consider the case of James Aspinall, his mother Margaret felt such a deep sense of guilt, it made her want to crash her car on the way home.

As she watched, for the first time, close-up video footage of the 18-year-old, happily playing with an inflatable ball on the sun-drenched Sheffield terrace six minutes before the 3pm kick-off, her heart sank.

When she next saw him lying on his back on the pitch, arms outstretched, his face to one side, alone, untended and not even placed in a recovery position as a policeman stepped over him, feelings of betrayal overwhelmed her.

"I felt guilty because I felt I'd neglected him. I was working on behalf of other people. I should have delved more deeply into James' case but I didn't," she told me.

"Whenever I was on support group business I'd quietly say, 'forgive me, son, I'm putting you to one side for the moment' because I never wanted to let the other victims down.

"I'd never missed a family meeting in all those years. I'd always thought, 'I'm doing this for 95 other people'. If I'd put James into the equation I couldn't have done my job because I'd have been broken. But then, when it came to his individual inquest, it was like a ton of bricks hitting me. I was broken.

"The reality of what I'd done came crashing down on my head. I felt I'd let him down badly and I wanted to drive my car off the road on the way home. I just wanted to die."

Margaret had been told, following the 2012 Panel report, that James was one of the victims who could have been saved had he received proper medical assistance after he was lifted from the pen. As she watched footage of him in Warrington being carried across the Sheffield Wednesday pitch by other fans, the agony deepened.

"I couldn't see his face as it had a coat over it, so I couldn't tell if he was still alive. Was he asking for his mum as he lay there? I'll never know the answer, and that's my nightmare. I'll have to live with that torture for the rest of my life," she said.

It also made her revisit the last time she saw James, behind a glass screen on a trolley in a dark room in Sheffield, on the day after the disaster, and the inhumane treatment she received as she tried to give her beloved first-born child a final cuddle.

James had only been to see Liverpool play half-a-dozen times and was, in truth, a bigger fan of Chris de Burgh. Like Anne Williams's son Kevin, it was his first away game, and like him his last words to his mum were that Liverpool would win easily and he would be home late. But James was more worried about missing Saturday evening mass than what he wanted for his tea, telling his mum that he'd go to church the following day instead.

"I watched him walk up the road and a strange feeling came into my head as I thought 'that's my beautiful son.' I remember thinking that I wanted everyone to know I was his mum because he was so kind, so generous, so good," said Margaret.

That afternoon as she was ironing she heard on the radio that there had been deaths at Hillsborough and the toll was rising. She tried calling the emergency numbers but couldn't get through. Her husband Jimmy was also at the game but he'd driven over by car, separate from James.

When he got home, she shoved him back into the car and told him they were driving to Lime Street to meet James off the bus. They waited agonizingly for every coach to come in until 11 pm when one of the drivers told her his was the last coach and no more were returning.

Jimmy drove back across the Pennines to look for James while Margaret waited at home in case he turned up. He toured all the Sheffield hospitals and phoned her every hour on the hour as he'd promised. When he did so at 3am, Margaret told him not to come back without her son.

When Jimmy didn't call at four, or five or six she began to fear the worst and was struggling to breathe, so went outside for some air. That's when she saw her husband being driven down the road with his head in his hands.

She ran away from him, down the street, screaming "please don't catch me up," as she was terrified that if he did he would tell her that James was dead. When she eventually turned around, Jimmy was on his knees, sobbing. She broke down.

Eventually, that morning she and Jimmy drove back to Sheffield, her last words as she left the house being "get James' coat. He'll be cold and he doesn't like the cold." She can't recall anything about the journey as her mind had gone blank.

"When we got to Sheffield we were taken into a big room where lots of people sat crying. I said to Jim, 'Why are they all crying for my James? They don't know him.' I was in such a state I didn't realise these poor people were crying for their own loved ones.

"After a while this person asked if I was ready and I thought 'ready for what?' He took us to a dark room with curtains and a glass screen. When he opened the curtains I could see James on a trolley and I just wanted to go in and give him a cuddle. But they wouldn't let me. I begged him, saying 'but I love him so much. I have to let him know his mum's here and I want to put his coat on before I take him home.'

"And I was told that he didn't belong to me any more. He belonged to the coroner. I just started screaming and screaming until I passed out. Then got carried out.

"Telling a mother that her son doesn't belong to her any more is the most awful thing to say. I'll never forgive them for not letting me give James a final cuddle."

Her first instinct, even though she was a Catholic who'd maintained her faith, was to blame God for her son's death but days later when she heard stories being spread about drunken, ticketless fans, she knew where the real responsibility lay.

"They were telling lies. Somebody wasn't doing their job and that's how I knew there was going to be a cover-up.

"I was even more certain when the West Midlands Police came to our house and the first question to Jimmy was, 'did you have a drink?' We knew they were trying to build a picture. James didn't have any drink in him and Jimmy hardly touches a drop but he got questioned as if he was a drunkard.

"They took the blood alcohol levels of all the deceased as they lay on the concrete floor and searched the criminal records to see if there were any matches. That's how low they were stooping.

"They kept asking me if I had James' ticket stub. Right away, my brain kicked into gear. They were trying to say he was ticketless.

"We knew from the very beginning that they were going to try to blame the fans and they did a good job didn't they, but they didn't count on us never stopping fighting to get to the real truth. My mother always used to say 'give me a thief before a liar' and I didn't get it at the time. But when Hillsborough happened, I knew what she meant. You can get an honest thief because you know they're a thief. But you don't know a liar when they come through your door."

Margaret made the 40-mile round trip from her Huyton home to Warrington on most of the days during those two years of the inquests and called it the hardest two years since the aftermath of the disaster.

"I felt so angry sitting in that court every day, having to go through it all again after 26 years. It was a holy disgrace. For families to see video footage after all that time, of how their loved ones were so appallingly treated, was the worst kind of torture.

"We went through every legal avenue possible even knowing that vital evidence was being held back. To then see it, knowing they knew it was there all along, was sickening in the extreme."

It also angered her to hear the old accusations about the fans being partly to blame for the disaster. "When I heard the police defence barrister say they were turning up with carafes of wine and bottles of champagne I felt like jumping up and saying to the coroner, 'are you listening to this shit?'

"We know all the fans weren't angels with wings, but we also know and have found out in court they were all innocent people who did nothing wrong but go to a football game."

The hardest part for Margaret and the other family members was not being able to comment on police evidence because she would have been in contempt of court.

The worst day came in March 2015 when David Duckenfield took the stand, claiming it had haunted him to think of mothers staring at their dead children on a dirty concrete floor. He said it on James' birthday.

"None of us needed to hear that. It was evil. It was as though he was toying with us. He said it to make himself look decent, but he's been indecent for all this time. He retired on ill health grounds, on a full pension, then got another job at a golf course, and the families were left struggling for money to carry on the fight to get to the truth. The whole system in this country stinks," she said.

There was anger too at the toll the disaster was taking on her family. "I haven't been able to celebrate anything. When James was 18 his birthday was the same week as his dad's and he told him 'when I'm 21 you're going to be 50. We'll have a big double celebration.'"

At the time of James's death her four other children were aged six, seven, nine and 15. She dreaded each one's 18th birthday. "I had to get them past 18. I was terrified of them dying. That's another thing they've taken away. Not just my son but the good times I should have had with the rest of the family."

But what drove her on through those two years in Warrington was getting the right verdict, something she called her "ultimate gift" to James. The one thing she could give him when they meet again.

"After the first inquests the coroner asked us to pay £3 for a death certificate. As soon as I got home I wrote to him. 'Don't you ever send me my son's death certificate and have the cheek to ask me for £3 for a verdict that is so untrue. If you put the right words on his certificate I'll willingly give you £50. Don't you ever insult the memory of my son.'"

She never picked up that death certificate.

BIRCHWOOD PARK, WARRINGTON — *April 2016*

I'd always thought the phrases "coming out in a cold sweat" and "you could cut the tension with a knife" were lazy clichés.

But as I sat in that packed, pine-panelled room with the families, awaiting the verdict, I looked down at a hand shaking nervously, felt my armpits going wet and my head get so tight I thought my ears would pop.

In the 20 days that the jury had been out considering whether the 96 had been unlawfully killed, I'd spoken to Margaret many times on the phone. She was, like all family members and survivors, a nervous wreck.

Her main concern was that the judge had asked jurors to consider if fans' behaviour played any part in the deaths, after barristers for South Yorkshire Police had repeatedly alluded to drunkenness and unruliness. Were the jury to agree, then everyone who had swallowed *The Sun's* narrative that Liverpudlians killed their own would have been vindicated. That outcome haunted her, and most of us, more than not achieving an unlawful killing verdict.

So many families had descended on Birchwood not all could fit into the courtroom, so some watched the verdicts via screens in two annexes. Those who did, sat clutching others' hands, some holding framed photos of their lost loved one on their lap, fear etched on their drawn faces.

When the jury foreman stood up to give the verdicts anxiety hung so heavy in the low-roofed room you could feel it pushing down on your skull.

As he announced that the jury found David Duckenfield,

"responsible for manslaughter by gross negligence" there was an almighty communal gasp. Some shrieked or yelled "yes!" Others clenched their fists, closed their eyes and stared ahead. As the judge asked them to contain their emotions while the verdicts were announced, most of the women began to sob. Some of the men heaved their taut chests, let the shoulders drop and rubbed wet eyes. Finally, the lie about their loved ones dying in an accident had been wiped out. Their death certificates could now read 'Unlawfully Killed'.

When the foreman unanimously cleared the fans of all blame their tears turned to cheers, as relief cut through the tension. Finally the abysmal slur, the prime defence of the police, that drunken fans had killed the 96, had been banished for good.

Someone shouted, "God bless the jury" and the jurors were given a round of applause as they left. Outside the building family members from the annexe hugged those who poured out of the court, before spontaneously bursting into Liverpool's anthem You'll Never Walk Alone in front of the global media.

The joy on those tear-stained faces, laced with anger that it had taken so long for the truth to come out, was one of the most poignant scenes I've ever witnessed.

Now we officially knew that those 96 football fans who never came home from the 1989 FA Cup semi-final, 38 of whom were teenagers or younger, were crushed inside those Leppings Lane cages due to catastrophic policing, then allowed to die while officers and other emergency services looked on.

Up until that moment there had been a big lie about them dying in an accident daubed on their graves. Now the truth was written large. They died because those entrusted with their safety were criminally negligent.

People who'd been to hell and back were in a place they wanted to be. But they were also in emotional pieces. The anger was simmering below the surface about how long it had taken to get proper inquest verdicts.

The average age of the 96 victims was 24. Which meant the struggle to put the correct words on those death certificates had taken, on average, three years longer than the time they spent on earth. It said everything about the inhumanity of South Yorkshire Police, who refused to admit responsibility and end the pain suffered by these battered people.

Theirs was a shameless, unnecessary performance, funded lavishly by the taxpayer. It proved how impossible it is for the Establishment to hold its hands up, and how justified and magnificent the families and their supporters had been in refusing to let their lies prevail.

As I drove away from Warrington I felt so relieved for so many friends who'd endured 27 years of sleepless nights.

Now, I thought, it's time for the enemies to have theirs.

CUNARD BUILDING, LIVERPOOL — *November 2019*

If the families thought it was tough enduring two years without commenting on the slurs being spoken at the inquests, an even harder legal silence was coming down the line.

It took 14 months from the unlawful killing verdicts being returned for the Crown Prosecution Service to call the families to Warrington's Parr Hall and announce they were charging six men with offences relating to the 96 deaths.

But this time there was no triumphalism, no hugs of joy, no

tearful renditions of You'll Never Walk Alone. Just mixed feelings. On hearing that former South Yorkshire Police officers Donald Denton and Alan Foster as well as force solicitor Peter Metcalf were charged with carrying out acts with intent to pervert the course of justice, and former Sheffield Wednesday secretary Graham Mackrell faced three health and safety offences, there was a murmur of quiet satisfaction.

When they heard that David Duckenfield would face 95 charges of manslaughter by gross negligence and former Chief Constable Norman Bettison four charges of misconduct in public office, applause broke out from every family member in the room.

They had wanted more, many more than six men to take the rap, and there was disgust that The FA and the ambulance service were off the hook. But tempered with that was the charging of former Merseyside Chief Constable Bettison for his alleged role in the cover-up.

And of course, Duckenfield. The realisation he would be back in the dock 17 years after a judge ruled he was innocent and would never face a retrial, took Margaret's mind back to that bleak day in Leeds: "We left there on our knees telling each other it was all over. On the coach home nobody spoke. We were so devastated. We told each other we would never get that ruling overturned.

"The message this sends is 'never give up. Carry on fighting'. This should never happen again. No-one should go through this to get to the truth. That's the legacy us Hillsborough families will leave whatever happens now," she said.

The news of the charges came two weeks after the Grenfell Tower disaster which saw 72 people killed in a blaze at their neglected West London flats. The message many of the Hillsborough families wanted to get out to the bereaved and survivors of that tragedy was to follow their example and refuse to be beaten by the system no matter how hard the blows. And the Hillsborough families knew in their hearts that there were many more blows heading their way. A hammer one came the following summer when the CPS announced it was dropping all charges against Norman Bettison, after two witnesses changed their statements and a third died.

Their inability to air their feelings about that decision due to the impending trials of the other five defendants only added to their sense of betrayal and impotence. Still they maintained hope that in January 2019 when Duckenfield went on trial, that justice would be done.

If only. After a three-month trial at Preston Crown Court the jury found Graham Mackrell guilty of health and safety breaches but jurors could not reach a verdict on Duckenfield.

I sat with 70 of the families and survivors in Liverpool Cunard Building watching the trial via video-link, and they met the verdict with little emotion.

There were no angry screams, just exhausted faces turning to each other and asking, "When will it end?" It was ten days before the 30th anniversary of those trips to Sheffield to identify their dead children, and after half a lifetime of pain they were still being put through the wringer.

When they were told the CPS was pushing for a retrial they looked strained to breaking point, wondering how much more they could take. Some said they couldn't face it and felt it was time to walk away. But most realised, having come this far, they had no option but to go for a re-trial.

So by the November of 2019, Duckenfield was back in the dock in Preston and we were back in a room in the Cunard

Building, at the end of a six-week re-trial, waiting for the fresh jury to decide if the man who had admitted at the inquests that he was culpable for the deaths, was guilty of manslaughter.

For a week they waited patiently in a side room, drinking tea, eating biscuits and trying to lift each other's spirits by laughing about the funnier moments they had shared over the years and playing bingo.

They weren't confident of a result. They felt the CPS barrister representing them was weak. They also despaired at Judge Peter Openshaw's one-sided summing up and his sympathetic treatment of Duckenfield which extended to him being allowed to not give evidence because "the poor chap" as he called him, was suffering post-traumatic stress disorder. How that cut deeply those who had never stopped suffering.

By the time the judge said he would accept a majority verdict of 9-1 from the ten jurors, most believed a repeat of the first trial was on the cards and they would fail to reach a decision. But an hour after that ruling we were told a verdict had been reached, and optimism spread through the 60-strong gathering.

However, when the jury foreman announced they had found David Duckenfield "not guilty" of 95 charges of gross negligence manslaughter, the words felt like a cold dagger to their grieving hearts.

Up in Preston, Duckenfield, now 75, bowed his head and held his hands together. In the Cunard Building people just shrank into their own shell, lips quivering, heads shaking, the sense of betrayal and disbelief leaving them dazed.

When they spoke, the words were mostly the same. "The inquests said they were unlawfully killed so if Duckenfield didn't kill my son/brother/father, then who did?"

As we walked away from the Cunard Building struggling for words to say to each other I asked Margaret if she'd wanted Duckenfield to go to jail had a guilty verdict been delivered. She shook her head.

"If you'd asked me 30 years ago I'd probably have said I wanted him hung, drawn and quartered but I've moved on. I didn't want him to go to jail. If they'd put him away for 50 years it wouldn't have brought back one of the 96.

"I just wanted the word 'guilty' after his name and his pension taken off him. That would have done for me. That would have given me peace. But I haven't got it, have I? Still, you have to get on with what's left of your life, don't you?"

It would be another 18 months before the families could begin to get on with their lives. The trial of Donald Denton, Alan Foster and Peter Metcalf, for perverting the course of justice by changing statements from officers on duty at Hillsborough, was twice postponed.

When it finally came to court the week after the 32nd anniversary of the disaster in 2021 it soon became clear from the mood music that there was little chance of convictions. Sure enough, once the defence case had finished, the judge Mr Justice William Davis, called the trial off on the grounds that the statements that had been amended were presented to the Taylor Inquiry which was not a court of law. Therefore even if they had been changed to shift blame away from the South Yorkshire Police they could not have affected "the course of justice." So he closed the trial down on a technicality.

It meant that although 96 men, women and children were ruled to have been Unlawfully Killed at Hillsborough nobody in authority would be held accountable.

Despite the Hillsborough Independent Report concluding that 164 police statements were "significantly amended" in the aftermath of the disaster not one officer would be convicted of a cover-up. After 32 years of reports, inquiries, inquests, trials and former Prime Minister David Cameron apologising to the bereaved families as he told the Commons, "it was wrong that the police changed the records of what happened and tried to blame the fans", no-one in blue had lost a day's liberty or pay.

Only Sheffield Wednesday's former secretary, Graham Mackrell, was found guilty of any offence, that of failing to ensure there were enough turnstiles open on the day. He was fined £6,500. Which valued each of the 96 lives in the eyes of our law at £67.70. Where was the justice there?

No wonder the watching families could not contain their anger and disbelief over this final kick in the teeth.

Christine Burke, who lost her father Henry in the fatal crush, yelled at the judge in the court in Salford that his ruling had left the families heartbroken. And Margaret Aspinall screamed at the screen in Liverpool's St George's Hall which was showing the trial via videolink, "This is a kangaroo court. It's a cover-up of a cover-up."

As I left the scene of the final trial, Steve Kelly, who lost his brother Mike in the disaster, summed up what their remarkable fight had been all about: "Everyone should keep Hillsborough high in their thinking whenever they are feeling lied to, cheated or manipulated from above. We may not have the answers we fought so hard for but we have the decency."

As always, I was lost in admiration for the family members who had made it to court to see the final battle being lost. But the truth is that ultimately they won the war. They gave the accused decades of sleepless nights and they proved to everyone on the wrong end of an Establishment cover-up that you can get the truth out if you keep fighting.

More importantly, throughout those 30-plus years, these ordinary working-class men and women proved themselves to be the best of humanity.

I've always felt in awe of their strength and immensely privileged to have known them. Back in 1989 they were simply voiceless people who would spend the next three decades fighting for someone in authority to be accountable for their child, their partner, their sibling or their parent not coming home from a football match.

As someone who suffered at Hillsborough, as a Scouser, as a father and as a football fan, I thank them. For seeking truth in the face of vicious lies and prejudice. For fighting for people whose only crime was being naive enough to turn up at what was supposedly one of the country's finest sporting stadiums in the belief that their safety was paramount in the eyes of those charged with their care. I thank them.

For keeping the eternal flame burning. For letting the world know in the face of terrible slurs, criminal indifference and the power of the state, that the 96 who died that day were more than names engraved in cold stone.

For refusing to give in to the incessant calls to "let it go" from people who failed to understand the reason they couldn't. Because they were consumed by the most invincible of emotions: Love.

Love is the most powerful weapon in the human arsenal. Because, when it truly drives us on, it gives us something as precious as life itself: Hope.

And hope never left their hearts.

4

THE
LIBERATOR

MUHAMMAD
ALI

LOUISVILLE, KENTUCKY — *June 2016*

BY the time his burial casket reached 3302 Grand Avenue so many flowers had been tossed on to the limousine windscreen its driver was struggling to see.

But he'd slowed down by then anyway, so that the ten-deep crowds outside the small, pink-wooded, two-bedroomed house, could get a final sense of their hero's aura.

There were those who had been in the neighbourhood all their lives and remembered a gangly, cheeky teenager called Cassius Clay, who wept. Others bowed their heads or stood looking on, lost in admiration. Some kissed the window of the hearse and yelled at God to bless him. Most cheered and chanted his name, over and over again.

When the 18-strong motorcade pulled away from Muhammad Ali's childhood home to continue its 23-mile trip around Louisville some of the boys ran after the hearse, shadow boxing and trying to outpace it just as teenage Cassius had done with buses along the same stretch of tarmac back in the 1950s. They whooped and hollered and filled the hot summer air with a chant of "Ali bom ay-e … Ali bom ay-e."

It transported the mind back to footage of dozens of small Zairean kids chasing after his truck as it drove through the streets of Kinshasa in 1974, shouting that very phrase at him en route to his Rumble In The Jungle with George Foreman. And Ali stood proudly on the back of the truck, conducting his devoted orchestra.

So powerful was his charisma, so seductive his charm that he'd cajoled an entire nation into chanting that phrase "Ali bom ay-e." Ali kill him. Which, metaphorically, he did.

And now it was he who was dead. And while the wider world was mourning the loss of a sporting giant, black Louisville was mourning the loss of one of their own.

The cocky kid from Grand Avenue who put them on the global map, who lifted them, made them believe in themselves and their race, who told them it was possible to fight bigotry, beat life's odds and be proud of who they were, where they came from and how they looked.

As Louisville came to a standstill to applaud its greatest son, it felt like watching a lap of honour for a life we were honoured to have been blessed with. What other sportsman would get this send-off? What other human?

Everything about Ali left those touched by his magic awestruck. His face, his body, his wit, his strength, his athleticism, his will, his poetry, his personality.

Everything he achieved left us feeling somehow smaller by comparison.

In 1999 when the majority of respected polls made him Sportsman of the Century, the gap between him and the rest of the field was a chasm.

But he wasn't simply the author of the greatest sporting story ever told. He was a genuinely heroic figure whose beliefs made him defy the American government and give a voice to his country's black people.

More than a few of those same 1999 polls also made him Man of the Century, singling out his quote, when he refused to be drafted into the Vietnam War, as one of the most powerful of all time: "I ain't got no quarrel with the Viet Cong. No Viet Cong ever called me a nigger."

That wasn't just the greatest-ever pacifist slogan. It was the greatest anti-racist one, summing up as it did the futility of a colonial war and the centuries-old oppression of an entire race.

At the Muhammad Ali Center in downtown Louisville, a huge shrine had been growing all week bearing flowers, signed boxing gloves, butterflies, framed photos, balloons and messages of love from around the world.

One stood out: 'Farewell to the Last Great American Hero.'

On the lawn outside the house four doors down from Ali's childhood home, I asked 67-year-old James Patterson, a retired teacher who had lived in the neighbourhood all of his life, why he was wiping away a tear. "I'm so sad. I knew I would be but I didn't think it would get to me so bad." I told him the world was sad. It was why I'd come all the way from Britain and there were media from every corner of the earth in town for the funeral.

"Ah, but, with respect, he didn't give your life meaning, did he? You don't come from here. You don't know what it was like growing up and being black where you weren't just thinking you were a second class citizen, the signs on the restaurants and the buses told you that.

"And he beat it all. He showed the white people who ran everything that a black man could be better than them. And could look better as he was doing it. Ali gave us hope. Gave every black kid in every black part of every town in America, meaning. He told us we weren't no second class citizen just 'cos we was black. He freed us from the prison of our own inferiority."

Everyone I spoke to hailed Ali as a visionary and a prophet. Jerry Hines, 76, a retired electrician, who was forced, like Ali, to attend a blacks-only school said, "He showed all of us black people in the 60s, who back then were living segregated lives, that you didn't have to take that inhumanity. He was our beacon of light and hope."

I got the same response from black British friends of a certain age when I told them I was interviewing Ali in 2001. They told me how, when Ali was conquering the world, it gave them, growing up in an overwhelmingly white culture, an unimaginable lift.

One mate told me how he would walk to school the morning after Ali had won a fight feeling taller, more emboldened, prouder of who he was. He felt that, unlike the white boys, he could be Ali, but they never could.

Playwright and screenwriter Maurice Bessman, who suffered racial abuse growing up in the 60s in the virtually all-white town of Kirkby, on the outskirts of Liverpool, saw Ali as an empowering figure at a time of real fear in Britain following Enoch Powell's infamous Rivers of Blood speech.

From viewing racism as a personal battle he and his siblings had to fight, Powell made Bessman realise it was a national problem, and Ali, as he struggled against the white American hierarchy, that it was global.

"Some of the voices that surrounded me tried to mask their true feelings about Ali, hoping he'd lose every fight, and particularly if it were against a white opponent. But their masks were transparent to me. His skin colour was the problem, in the same way my skin colour and that of my family's was a problem to many," Bessman told me.

"But because of Ali and what he said and very importantly, how he said it, I realised the struggle against racism, or colour prejudice as it was then known, was an international problem. Knowing that Ali was going through similar struggles and speaking out against it, gave me a feeling of confidence to be stronger. That was one of the reasons I chose to take up boxing. He helped me psychologically when I needed it all those years ago, and in the longer term he helped shape me in a political sense. He showed us how to speak truth to power.

"When black people do well, there is often pressure to bestow on them an honorary white status. But he went against that. He said, 'I'm black and I don't need to be anything else. You can't bestow on me your whiteness because I'm happy in my own skin.' In doing so, he helped make us all feel comfortable in our own skin."

Imagine how it felt to be Ali, carrying that weight of expectation on your shoulders for all those years?

Before that fight in Zaire, he was asked by the Press whether he would retire if he won, as he would have earned so much from the bout he'd never have to step in the ring again. He replied, "You give me a hundred million today, I'll be broke tomorrow. We got a hospital we're working on, a black hospital in Chicago, costs fifty million dollars. My money goes into causes. If I win, I'll be travelling everywhere. If I win, I'm going to be the Black Kissinger. It's full of glory but it's tiresome. Every time I visit a place I have to go by the schools, by the old folks' home. I'm not just a fighter, I'm a world figure to these people."

Norman Mailer opened his classic book The Fight about that extraordinary sporting event in Kinshasa, with a description of what it felt like to meet Ali in the flesh. "Women draw an audible breath. Men look down. They are reminded again of their lack of worth. If Ali never opened his mouth to quiver the jellies of public opinion, he would still inspire love and hate. For he is the Prince of Heaven – so says the silence around his body when he is luminous."

When I got the chance to spend a day with him at his Michigan ranch I too looked down when I saw him get out of his car to meet me. A strange sensation took over my body. I tensed up at the sight of him. My lips felt parched, my legs weak.

Maybe that's how religious people feel when they meet the earthly leader of their faith. When Ali shook my hand, he did seem luminous. And throughout the six hours I spent in his company, the silence around his body was very real as the Prince of Heaven had been struck by the terrible disease of Parkinson's.

Personally, it was a remarkable encounter. One which left me feeling totally humbled. It must have come across that way when I submitted it as the editor chose to run it across the first five pages of *The Mirror*, under the headline The Greatest Interview. This was it …

BERRIEN SPRINGS, MICHIGAN — March 2001

The right hand shook violently as it was slowly willed towards the punch bag.

When it arrived he held it for a minute, concentrating like a brain surgeon as he tried to bring the wild muscle tremors under control.

He moved the left alongside it and kept them together for what seemed like an eternity. Sweat trickled down his unscarred brow, his eyes screwed tight, he bit his lip, inhaled deeply, got up on his toes, pulled back his fist and … bam, bam, bam, bam.

Three solid blows from the left followed by a right hook. He bounced back off the bag unsteadily, regained his balance, lifted his chin up, puffed out his chest and sneered at his opponent.

As the bag swayed back towards him, he called it on to his

trembling body as though asking it to tell him his name. Then the feet, which had moved him into the gym like a drunk heading for the pavement, attempted a shuffle.

Bam, bam, bam. Three more blows were unleashed. He stumbled sideways, hauled himself back up, stared at his prey, jabbed it and with eyes blazing yelled, "Ah'm dancin', ah'm dancin', ah'm dancin' again."

And the chills down my spine tell my brain what the eyes are refusing to believe. That I'm staring at the most potent sporting image of all time – The Greatest in action.

Dancing and jabbing. Smiling and hollering. Making the heavy bag sing. Just like he did a lifetime ago when he was king of the world.

And I'm close enough to see the one tiny scar on the right eyebrow that 21 years of boxing left on his face. Close enough to see the cluster of grey neck-hairs his razor missed that morning. Close enough to smell his sweat. I look into the gym wall mirror and the light plays tricks.

The bloated 59-year-old mountain of a man imprisoned by Parkinson's Disease fleetingly turns into the beautiful fighting machine who throughout the 60s and 70s made the world's top athletes look like clumsy, punch-drunk punks.

On the walls behind his reflection lie framed black-and-white reminders of all those glories. But I can't take my eyes off the man. He flies into the bag again and hits it with a flurry of lefts. Each thud brought back a familiar name. Bam. Bam.

Bam. Sonny Liston. Joe Frazier. George Foreman. Bam. Bam. Leon Spinks. Floyd Patterson.

Then, tiring, the jabs slow down to pat-a-cake speed. Bam. Jerry Quarry. Bam. Ken Norton. Bam. Ernie Terrell.

He stumbles forward like a felled tree and I move to catch him. Then he sways back and wobbles, eyes closed, like a stunned bear.

He gets up on the toes of his black Hush Puppies and staggers with an agonising palsy, his body at 45 degrees to the steps on the side of the ring, lowering himself down slowly, hanging on to the ropes.

His hand and head start to wobble but they won't stop his moment of triumph. He looks up, features drenched in sweat and forces his paralysed facial muscles into a huge smile.

"Didn't I tell you I still got it?" he says in a slow, slurred whisper. "What you saw was a miracle. People with Parkinson's Disease can't do that. Didn't I tell you I was the greatest of all time? Didn't I tell you I'm getting back in shape for my comeback at 60? Didn't I?"

He closes his eyes for a few seconds then opens them and mutters, "But first I need some ice cream."

He offers me his shaking arm. I grab a bicep so huge my hand won't fit halfway around it and realise if my jaw had met one of those punches he would have left me sipping hospital soup.

"You see I got special powers," he mumbles. "I can even levitate, watch." He turns his back and composes himself for a minute. Then his left foot leaves the floor and he's positioned me at such an angle that I can't see where his right foot is, creating the illusion that he's walking on air. I ask him how he does it and he says "it's spiritual" before giving me a big wink.

I turn away laughing and he flicks his fingers behind my ear making the whirring sound of a cricket then looks away whistling like a naughty kid in the playground.

It's one of the many tricks he has perfected to make the world believe he still has super-human gifts. To take our mind off the horrible disease that shackles him.

When he levitates he wants us to believe he can still "float like a butterfly, sting like a bee, your hands can't hit what your eyes can't see."

I am in the gym at his 81-acre ranch in Michigan which doubles as the HQ of his firm GOAT (Greatest Of All Time).

In the nearby office his 44-year-old wife Lonnie looks after his business affairs, helped by a team of workers.

The worldwide demands for Ali's presence are phenomenal and the money they raise go towards keeping his nine children, religious causes, charities like UNICEF, Sisters of The Poor and Best Buddies and projects like building an Ali Memorial Center in his home town of Louisville, Kentucky.

Outside, geese flutter in the winter sun and his two Doberman pinschers, Champ and Sasha, chase each other down to the river. Back in the Roaring Twenties, Al Capone had the place. Now, like its current owner, most of the time it's covered in a blanket of stillness.

But today Ali is on form. Today people have come all the way from London, the town he calls his "second home" and the great entertainer won't disappoint his guests.

He guides me into his office where he works on the days he's not travelling. On his desk is the Koran, two copies of the Bible, letters skimmed from the top of four full baskets in his mailroom and two piles of photographs which he signs and sells through a dealer for $100 each. But mostly just gives away.

His day revolves around religion. He prays five times and devotes most of his mental energy to highlighting contradictions in the Bible, spending endless hours poring over it, searching for inconsistencies. It's as though he wants us to know his brain is still so sharp he can outsmart the fount of Western wisdom.

He says, "I can prove there are 30,000 contradictions in the Bible but not one in the Koran. Not one. People in England don't know that. You gotta tell 'em.

"And look at this," he says, pointing out the word 'piss' in the Old Testament. "Bet you never knew they said 'piss' in the Bible." And he gives me his famous "scared by a ghost" look and says, "ma-a-an."

As I laugh he asks a question he posed four times that day. Was I getting enough information from him? Was he doing ok? When I say yes he draws me closer and whispers, "Good. Because what I'm telling you will be passed on to millions of people and it would take me 20 years to go round and tell them all myself. I predict this article will astonish everyone in Britain when they read that Ali is as great as ever.

"When it does I'll come over and shake the whole place up again like I used to when I fought Henry Cooper.

"I'll go and speak to them at Wembley Stadium and I'll tell them the truth about God and they'll go wild and I'll turn to you and say, 'didn't I tell you I was the greatest? Didn't I?'"

Parkinson's Disease is a non-life threatening disorder of the nervous system that stiffens his muscles, freezes his face, gives him the shakes and leaves him very fragile. Ali was diagnosed in the mid-80s.

Balancing is difficult, speaking hard, swallowing a trial. It takes him minutes to take a small sip of water and as he fumbles to co-ordinate glass and mouth, it spills. When he eats a chicken sandwich it is an even more pitiful sight.

Talking is even harder. He pieces his words together with a painful difficulty and his sentences are often inaudible. The result is Ali spends most of his time like a phantom. Not moving. Not speaking.

Millions of people have blamed boxing for his condition, particularly the punishment he soaked up in the seven years he fought on after regaining his world title from George Foreman in 1974. But Ali is not among them.

The man who proudly declares that in many parts of the world he is still more popular than The Beatles says, "Parkinson's is just something that happened to me. One day I was on top of the world – the fastest, prettiest, the best boxer of all time. The next day I was shaking, shaking.

"Like it happened to the two million other sufferers out there. Some are worse than others. Some shake very, very badly. But I don't think about it because it's not important. I'm not bitter or angry. Why I caught it I don't know. Nobody knows for sure.

"It wasn't boxing. Were the two million sufferers boxers? No. Now think of all the boxers who have ever been then tell me how many of them got Parkinson's.

"It is simply a message from God. All I know is He had a plan. This is the way He wants me to do His work.

"He put me on the top of the world and now He's testing me. It's made me stronger. It's made my religious beliefs stronger. It makes me pray more. It's just a trial from God."

Many people mourn the sight of a man who was once so fearsome being reduced to such frailty. They see high tragedy in the fact that someone who shook the world with such a rare charisma should be silenced. But if there is one thing you learn on meeting Ali it's that he neither seeks, nor needs, pity.

I had expected all the vitality to be drained but the opposite was true. He was funnier, sharper, more passionate than I had expected. And when, after a few hours of listening I cracked his speech patterns, I understood nearly all he said.

Ali is far from incapacitated. He dresses, shaves, writes and laces his shoes. As if anyone else could.

He understands everything you say. At times his head will slump to his chest, his eyes shut and you imagine he has gone to sleep. You strike up a conversation with someone else and minutes later he cuts in with a correction or a quip.

Sometimes you catch him staring into the distance in a world of his own, but then you realise he is serene, content, a man at peace with himself and sure of his destiny.

"Oh, man, I'm really happy. I know the purpose of my life. It's to spread the word of Allah. People never really knew the name Ali until I changed it from my slave name Clay. But now it's known in so many countries. There are 1,000 million Muslims on earth and they all know me. That's why I'm the most recognisable person in the world. Not because I was a good boxer but because I'm a good Muslim."

Lonnie, the woman Ali calls "The Boss" and his nurse, manager and soulmate rolled into one, had already told me that in 15 years of marriage she had never seen him get irate about his condition. But I asked him if it ever gets him angry, anyway.

"Why should I be angry?" he says. "Everything that happened to me was for a purpose and made me more popular.

"God made me the most popular man on earth even if I got criticised for changing my name and not going to war. But in the end I was proved right. God was right to make me do those things, so how can I get angry with Him for the way I am now? It is His will.

"People ask if I regret being a boxer. No. If I hadn't been a boxer I wouldn't have gotten famous. If I hadn't gotten famous I wouldn't be able to help my people and spread the word of God."

Religion is Ali's saviour. He says without hesitation his conversion to Islam was his proudest moment. It gives his life purpose and meaning in the face of his illness. It draws on his most enduring quality: Courage.

It was courage that led the poor boy from Kentucky to Olympic Gold in 1960 and to become the first boxer to win the world heavyweight title three times.

It was courage, not fear, that kept him from the war in Vietnam in 1967. He was denounced in Congress, stripped of his world title for three-and-a-half years, demonized by White America as a coward and a subversive, made a bankrupt and a criminal and deprived of his profession, but Ali's stature only grew.

How many of today's high profile black Americans would say what he said in the late 60s: "I can't take part in nothing where I'd help the shooting of dark Asiatic people, who haven't lynched me, deprived me of my freedom, justice and equality or assassinated my leaders."

How many would put everything on the line for their people or their principles? Any? When I raise this with him he denies he was striking a blow for black Americans. He says, "My refusal to go to Vietnam did not just help the black people it helped more white people. More whites rebelled against 'Nam.

"It made me a hero to many white people as well as black people because I had the nerve to challenge the system and all the people who hate injustice backed me for that."

It is the courage Ali is showing in the face of Parkinson's today which makes him grow even taller.

Which of the 3.5 billion people who watched his shaking hand light the Olympic flame in Atlanta in 1996 did so without being in awe of his heroism?

Something which bothers me though is his appearance at company functions. I hate seeing him being hauled before cameras like some corporate trophy. I ask if he feels exploited by it.

"Exploited? What? Who else earns $100,000 a day just for turning up? Man, I can turn up. I tell you I love turning up. I love what I do. I love meeting my fans. I even love doing commercials."

His slow, slurred voice is interrupted by one such fan. An electrician in his early 20s who was working on his house had asked to meet him. There is a long silence as Ali weighs him up.

"I know you" he mumbles. "No sir, I don't think so," comes the nervous reply. "Yeah, ain't you the boy who called me a nigger?" he asks, and the white man, believing him to be serious, almost faints as he splutters his denials.

Ali tells him he's only joking, then asks him his name and he tells him it's Jim. "Ok, Jim, your chances are slim," he says before signing a picture and motioning that he also wants the names of his friends. He signs half-a-dozen before the man runs out of mates, and leaves Ali shouting after him "hundred dollars each." Which is the price he is supposed to be selling them for.

"Most famous people never give autographs," he says. "I always do. I never ignore one. You won't get another celebrity to do what I do. People don't do nothing for me just because they are famous. I'll give a downtrodden man on the street more time as he needs it more.

"One day we're all going to die. The angels are recording all our actions. One day we'll wake up and it will be Judgement Day and you'll be judged on how you treated people. Forget about hatred and pray hard."

Apart from Islam, death is the subject that occupies him most. He is obsessed with it.

"I sleep a lot. Sleep is the brother of death," he slowly mutters. "Life ain't nothing. You can have a girl but it don't last that long. Take a drink, it don't last that long. Nothing lasts that long. Tell them people in England to look at all those castles they got. Where are the people who built them? Dead. The kings and princes who lived in them? Long dead. What did their castles mean when the Judgement Day came? Nothing.

"Al Capone once owned this place. Dead. He had holes that ran underground to get him out when the cops came. I have been down them holes. Full of skeletons. Do something decent with your life. Impress the angels. Make them record something good about you."

He stops to catch his breath, to regain energy and concentration, then slowly mumbles a series of his own philosophical soundbites.

"Service for others is the rent we pay on earth. Love is the net where hearts are caught like fish. A man's wealth is his knowledge."

His use of language and imagery is still as potent as ever. It sounds even more stirring when delivered in a voice like a dying Marlon Brando in The Godfather.

I tell him he could have been a great rapper. "I am a great

rapper. I invented rap. Those young guys just copied off me." He says, "Give me five" and holds out his hand to be slapped. I slap it and he moves it away. "I'd give you 30 but your face is too dirty." He likes getting a laugh so delivers some jokes.

"There's a Mexican, a black man and a Puerto Rican in a car. Who's driving?" I shrug. "The police," he answers.

"What did Abraham Lincoln say when he woke up after being drunk for two days?" Another shrug: "I freed WHO?"

He appears to nod off. Then he opens his eyes and asks if I've got enough to write about. When I tell him he's doing brilliantly he pulls a mock Uncle Tom look and says: "Still a nigger though."

It reminds me of the way he used to taunt Joe Frazier, labelling him a white man's stooge, which still pains Frazier 30 years after they first fought. I ask him why he hurt his famous rival so.

"I got nothing against Joe. Without Joe I wouldn't be who I am. How could I hate Joe for making me all that money?" he asks with a grin.

Does money matter, I ask? "It matters if you get it honestly. Some people get it immorally and that offends God. They have to compromise their faith. But if you get it and still worship God then that's fine." What about his boxer daughter Laila who is set to face Frazier's daughter Jackie in the ring?

"I wish she wasn't doing it but I can't stop her so I support her. They're paying her thousands but I don't like it. I want her to stay beautiful."

He stops for a while then asks, "You all heard of her in London?" When I nod he shakes his head. "Wow, who'd have thought that? Who'd have thought that one day Muhammad Ali's daughter is more famous than him?"

I ask if he misses boxing. "No. Boxing misses me. I was the

resurrection of the fight game. I got people to watch it. When I was fighting more people watched than ever. Not today. They don't watch it like they did back then.

"People used to wake up and ask: 'How did the Ali fight go last night?' Now they just say: 'Was there some fight last night?'" The statement is unerringly true.

Surprisingly he says his proudest boxing moment was not winning any of his world titles against Liston (1964) Foreman (1974) and Spinks (1978) but winning Olympic Gold for the U.S. in 1960. "Meant more to me than any title fight," he says.

It is a strange admission from a man who on returning to his home in Kentucky in triumph, was refused service in a whites-only restaurant and threw his medal in the Ohio River in disgust.

Was he ever scared in the ring? "Only scared because I thought the other man wouldn't get up."

I remind him that we British were once scared he would not get up after Henry Cooper floored him in 1963. He remembers, "Cooper hit me with a left hook so hard it jarred my kinfolks in Africa. But he didn't floor me. I tripped."

For a man supposedly struck dumb he has an answer for everything. While there is still a tongue in his head no-one will be quicker.

During the six hours I spend with Ali he occasionally turns, out-of-the-blue, and asks unconnected questions:

ALI: *What colour are your socks?*
ME: *Black.*
ALI: *Let me see. (I show him). Good, I like black.*
ME: *Why?*

ALI: Cos I'm black. You keep 'em black. Am I still pretty?
ME: Yes, you've still got all your hair. And it's your favourite colour, black.
ALI: No it ain't. It's dyed. You should try it. You need to. Then you may look as pretty as me. Did you always know you'd be a writer?
ME: Not really.
ALI: Shame. You should have done. Great people always know their destiny. How old are you?
ME: 43.
ALI: How old were you in 1964?
ME: When you fought Liston? (He nods). Six years and three months.
ALI: You even remember the month. You ain't as dumb as you look.

He shows me the framed photos that hang on the walls around the ring of his gym. Iconic images that capture some of the greatest moments in 20th century popular culture. When we get to the one where he looks like he's knocking The Beatles down he asks if I recognise them. When I tell him that we come from the same city, he replies, quick as a flash, "Then you ain't no fool, if you from Liverpool."

He says he loved The Beatles before starting to sing: "It's been a hard day's night and I been sleepin' like a dog." He stops for a few seconds. "That's me now, always sleepin' like a dog." He pretends to sleep, snores, then wakes up and goes "boo."

He reminisces about how crazy the world went over The Beatles before asking where they are now. I tell him the three who are alive made a billion dollars last year by releasing their old records. "A billion dollars? Still that popular?" he asks, and I tell him they are probably as popular as him. He doesn't like that, thinks for 10 seconds then plays his trump card.

"One place I guarantee they ain't more popular than me is Mecca. And Pakistan and Saudi Arabia ... before listing all the Muslim states where he is known and The Beatles are not. He may be vain but he is also right.

Ali's religion is his saviour in every argument. He was brought up a Baptist but two days after winning the world title in 1964 dropped the name Cassius Clay and joined the Nation of Islam, viewed by Middle America at the time as a radical race hate sect.

Ali was their greatest capture, publicity coup and source of funds. It is estimated that between 1966 and 1978 he gave them $16 million, a third of all his fight earnings. Most of the rest went to the taxman, his former wives, family and charities. He gradually became disillusioned with the Nation of Islam and in 1983 embraced a more orthodox form of the religion.

I ask if he has any regrets about joining them and he becomes more passionate than at any time during the day. "No. Islam taught me who I was. Made me challenge white America, made me change my name, change the way I am and who I am. Their teachings helped me to be a better person. Taught me not to eat pork, which is full of worms and maggots.

"They were the reason I kept telling everyone I was the greatest and I was pretty. I wanted the world to know that black is beautiful, to let my people take pride in being black.

"Because it's hard in a culture like ours. They tell the kids that Jesus was white, the Last Supper was for whites only and the angels are all white. They even made Tarzan white.

"What was a white man doing in the middle of the African jungle doing all that "ahh-ahh-ahh" stuff? King of the Jungle! White! Ahhh-ahhh! Maaaa-an!

"Where does the president live? The White House. Good people? They're whiter than white. Now think about all the bad black words – blackmail, blackleg, blackball, black cat means bad luck. Maaaa-an. Yet all colours come from black. All people come from one single black man. We are all brothers, white and black. All equal before God.

"So I was proud to tell the world that I was the prettiest, I was the greatest. That's why I did it all the time. I was saying 'look at me black people and realise you don't be ashamed of your colour, you have to be proud. A black man is the greatest so you can be great too.'

"And I wanted black men to be proud of our women. Some black stars like Chubby Checker and Sammy Davies Jnr. took white women. Not me. All my wives were black. I wanted to show black people they could be proud of what they had, that you could be a new kind of black man."

Ali starts to get tired. His head slumps, his eyes close more often, his breathing gets harder and it takes him longer to answer questions. He takes another drink of water. The hand shakes, water spills, he cradles the glass on his chest.

I have the urge to help him but know I shouldn't. He struggles to get the glass to his lips then slurps like a baby and puts it down slowly. The whole process of getting a mouthful of water takes three minutes. It embarrasses him so he tries to entertain again.

"Don't forget to tell Britain that I'm going to make a comeback on my 60th birthday. They'll call it a real miracle when I beat the champ and the number one contender. I'll shake up the whole world."

I ask him how he would like to be remembered? He struggles with an answer, gets it right the third time and says, "That I took a few cups of love, one teaspoon of patience, one pint of kindness, stirred it up and gave it to every deserving person I met."

He tells me he just made that up and I tell him he's lying because I know he's said it before: "Ok, I get asked that question a lot," is the quick reply.

Never stumped, never beaten. Still the Louisville Lip. Still The Greatest. Is that how he sees himself? "No, Allah's the Greatest. I'm just a man."

Indeed, he had his share of human flaws. He could be cruel beyond the call of duty as Joe Frazier found out with his shameful Uncle Tom slurs. He was a serial womaniser and some of the propaganda he spouted when he was being fleeced by the white-hating Nation of Islam was embarrassing.

But despite all of that, Muhammad Ali holds a unique place in our hearts. He transcended sport like no-one else has ever done, disputing all our beliefs about how an athlete should behave and what he could achieve. And he was entirely his own creation.

I help him up and we walk at a snail's pace to the door, past a picture of his greatest-ever night: The Rumble In The Jungle when Ali chewed up George Foreman in Zaire, spat him out, regained his crown against all the odds and put down a marker few sportsmen could hope to match.

I ask if he remembers a poem he made up at a press conference leading up to that fight. A poem whose stunning imagery eclipsed anything they ever taught me at school.

As I start to recite it he doesn't hear me, or pretends not to. But as we stand on his step saying our goodbyes the poem floods into my head: "I done wrestled with an alligator, I done tussled with a whale. I done handcuffed lightning, and thrown thunder in jail. I can run through a hurricane and not get wet. Only last week I murdered a rock, injured a stone, hospitalized a brick. I'm so mean, I make medicine sick."

His shaking hand takes mine, he puts his mouth to my ear and I hear that slurred mumble for a final time: "Don't be a fool. Just be cool."

It feels like he wants me to know he heard my question and although his memory is not what it was, he is still a poet. Parkinson's may have changed the way he looks, talks and moves, but mentally he is still running through hurricanes and wrestling with alligators.

As photographer Roger Allen and I drive down the long chipped-stone pathway from his ranch, he waves and blows us a kiss. It takes us 30 seconds to say anything to each other.

When we do, our words are almost identical. We have never met a more extraordinary man. And doubt we ever will. Twenty years on, I still haven't.

5

THE
UNBREAKABLE

DONNA MARIE
McGILLION

EDINBURGH — *September 2010*

I'D headed up to Scotland hoping to witness one of the ugliest holy scraps since the Crusades. Or at least the funniest one since Father Ted kicked Bishop Brennan up the arse: God's Catholic Rottweiler versus God's Protestant Pitbull.

Pope Benedict was on a tour of Britain, with many viewing the arrival of this right wing Pontiff and former Hitler Youth member as the most unwelcome visit by a German since Herman Goring sent his pilots over.

But as his bullet-proof Popemobile drove down Princes Street on a fresh autumn day, past tens of thousands of flag-waving Catholics, some weeping tears of joy at the sight of a Bay City Rollers-type tartan scarf planted on his holy garments, the love for Benedict was clear.

Yet outside Holyrood Palace knots of protesters, some clutching banners saying: 'Stop Protecting Paedophile Priests' and 'Condoms Save Lives' made their objections known. And in a quiet side street in Edinburgh Old Town his nemesis lay in wait, warming himself up before his supporters by caricaturing the Pope as a glorified snake-charmer.

The Reverend Ian Paisley had been drawn to the Papal visit like a vulture to a rotting carcase. And there he proudly stood, aged 84, at the head of a group of Free Presbyterian ministers leading a protest march against an office he once called the Anti-Christ.

Paisley was now known as Lord Bannside, an elder statesman viewed widely as a man of peace. But the mischievous twinkle in his eye hinted that his appetite for spewing bile in the direction of Rome was not yet satiated.

I'd seen him on the streets of Liverpool during the previous Papal UK visit in 1982, when he jeered loudly as John Paul II went past, and a photographer took a picture which appeared to show the Pope blessing his red, volcanic features.

"Are you hoping for another Papal blessing today?" I asked outside the headquarters of the Scottish Reformation Society in Cowgate, reminding him of that previous humiliation.

His face blazed fire and brimstone as he replied, "I was not blessed then and I do not want his blessing today. In fact, I will be keeping as far away as I can from him. This whole thing is a load of hokey-cokey nonsense."

"Why do you call it hokey-cokey nonsense?" I asked, which made him turn to his crowd of supporters and strike the kind of pose favoured by stand-ups at the nearby Underbelly comedy venue, and answer, "Well, I've just read on the Vatican website that if I pay £25 and go to today's Mass, it will get me out of Purgatory quicker. Ha, ha. Can you believe such utter nonsense?" And his merry band of dissenters laughed along with him.

"So what are you doing here, then?" I asked.

"I'm a member of the House of Lords and I'm entitled to travel anywhere in the United Kingdom, my friend. Now out of my way, I have God's work to do."

But I didn't move out of his way, instead asking what he was trying to achieve in Scotland, a country he wasn't from, as it courteously welcomed the head of a religion many of its citizens followed.

He pointed at me and other members of the media who had been drawn away from the Papal route in the hope of witnessing trouble, grinned and yelled, "Getting YOU all here, for a start."

The journalists laughed along with the Reverend's groupies.

And he strolled away gingerly, grinning from ear to ear, eyes glinting, leading his tribe once more unto the sectarian breach.

A strange thing happens when certain men who have either engaged in, or advocated, violence reach an age when their anger appears to have mellowed. We embrace their new-found pacifism, seek out their good points, applaud their self-effacing humour. I'd observed this interviewing retired gangster Mad Frankie Fraser, who after years of indulging in murder and torture, wowed a younger generation as a raconteur.

Halfway through telling me another gruesome anecdote about ripping "'orrible fuckers" teeth out, a couple came up to our table in a North London pub and asked Frankie for his autograph. He obliged. And they swooned at a figure popular culture was clamouring to give National Treasure status to.

I told him I had to phone my son who was making his first Holy Communion the following day and he gave a big "ah, nice." Then added, "I'm a Catholic too. It never leaves you, does it?" Unlike the teeth and organs of his many victims.

Paisley was the same. He was already adored by Ulster's Loyalist masses. To them he was the greatest of heroes for denouncing Sinn Féin, the IRA and any attempts by the British government to placate them.

He earned the nickname of Doctor No for steadfastly refusing for decades to hand any concessions to the Nationalist minorities in Northern Ireland, or deal with Dublin.

In the late 60s, Paisley led Loyalist opposition to the Catholic civil rights movement in Derry and Belfast, a major factor in Northern Ireland being plunged into the dark period known as The Troubles, which would lead to 30 years of bloodshed, claiming at least 3,532 lives and injuring 47,500 people.

As MP for North Antrim, then an MEP, and leader of the Democratic Unionist Party he was the face of Protestant resistance to power-sharing with Irish nationalists, bringing down the 1973 Sunningdale Agreement, vilifying the Anglo-Irish Agreement of 1985 and vehemently opposing the Good Friday Agreement of 1998.

Paisley was also a pivotal figure in creating a paramilitary movement called Ulster Resistance which smuggled in a huge arsenal of weapons to the province that would eventually be used in the murder, or attempted murder of 70, mostly Catholic, citizens.

As a new century dawned and the people of Northern Ireland enjoyed the relative peace brought about by the Good Friday Agreement and the disbanding of many key terrorist groups, it was clear they weren't prepared to return to the days of the terror.

So, after the 2007 St Andrews Agreement, Paisley's DUP finally agreed to share power with Sinn Féin. He and Martin McGuinness, who for decades had been sworn enemies, embraced each other so warmly they were referred to as The Chuckle Brothers.

It was a remarkable, barely-believable transformation which would lead to Paisley being ennobled as a life peer. From being derided as a warmonger to being hailed as a peace-maker. From Doctor No to Lord Yes in an instant.

When he died in 2014 glowing obituaries referenced a giant of a man, a hero to his people who brought peace to his country, but other voices were unafraid to speak their truth.

Former Alliance Party leader John Cushnahan said he was astonished at the "rewriting" of Ian Paisley's political life. "While I welcome the fact that he ultimately embraced power-sharing, it was too little, too late, and should not be used to excuse the pain and suffering that he inflicted on the people of Northern Ireland for the majority of his political life. A life that was punctuated with nakedly sectarian acts and deeds."

When the other Chuckle Brother, Martin McGuinness, died just over two years later, amid all the gushing tributes to a genuine all-Irish hero, once again dissident voices questioned whether he deserved such status.

THE CREGGAN, DERRY — March 2017

The former IRA commander of Derry had heaved many a fallen comrade's coffin on to his shoulder before walking proudly through the streets of Bogside.

But watching Martin McGuinness's final journey through those streets was to see how much the backdrop had irrevocably changed. With The Troubles long over, there were no IRA insignia, berets or balaclavas on display, no gun salutes or British Army helicopters drowning out the lament of the lone piper at the head of the mourners.

Many of the old signs like 'Brits Out' were still nailed to lamp-posts or written on house walls. There were still plaques to the fallen, and those huge murals commemorating IRA heroes like hunger striker Bobby Sands and those who fell on Bloody Sunday, that darkest of Republican days in 1972, when 14 innocents were killed and 15 injured by British paras in the streets of Derry as they peacefully protested internment without trial. The day when the man who was now inside the Tricolour-draped coffin roamed Bogside with a sub-machine gun in his hand, with the British alleging he was looking to pick off their soldiers.

As McGuinness's vast funeral cortege moved down the steep hill from his family home towards Free Derry corner, every inch of Westland Street was filled with mourners, many of them men of McGuinness's generation: faces set hard and uncompromising against the bitter cold, their eyes full of knowledge of the tortuous past. Young mothers and schoolkids hung from house windows, taking photos of the final journey of the man many in that part of the world believed to be the finest of Irish martyrs.

It gave a much-needed reminder that not that long ago decimated limbs were strewn across other UK streets thanks to gunmen and bombers killing in the name of their cause.

Men like the one whose funeral had brought Derry to a standstill. A man who stopped believing that violence in the name of tribalism solved ancient conflicts and turned his mind to overcoming injustices through peace and inclusion.

And it took Bill Clinton, in a powerful eulogy inside St Columba's Church, to crystallise how far Northern Ireland had come. He pointed at the DUP leader, Arlene Foster, who was seated near the altar, and thanked her for taking the difficult decision to attend. As he did, the 1,500-strong, overwhelmingly Catholic, congregation burst into applause.

It was a powerful moment and, after years of reporting on The Troubles, a privilege to be present at. Never in my lifetime could I have imagined that a Protestant political leader like Foster, who as a teenager saw her school bus blown up by the IRA, would attend the Catholic Requiem Mass at the funeral of a former IRA commander.

Clinton, that most charismatic of communicators, stole the show with a typically articulate appreciation of Northern

Ireland's former Deputy First Minister who had died aged 66. Speaking for 10 minutes when he was asked for three, Clinton said, "He persevered and prevailed. He risked the wrath of his comrades and the rejection of his adversaries.

"He made honourable compromises and was strong enough to keep them and came to be trusted because his word was good.

"And he never stopped being who he was – a good husband, a good father, a follower of the faith of his father and mother and a passionate believer in a free, secure, self-governing Ireland.

"The only thing that happened was that he shrank the definition of 'us' and expanded the definition of 'them.'"

Gerry Adams said of his old and dear friend, "There was not a bad Martin McGuinness or a good Martin McGuinness, there was simply a man, like every other decent man or woman, doing his best."

Words which, when reported to the wider world, drew anger from those who believed a virtual state funeral being granted to a man who had sanctioned killings was an insult to his victims.

More than 100 people died in political violence in Derry between 1971 and 1973, and McGuinness later justified his role in it by saying "a little boy from the Catholic Bogside was no more culpable than a little black boy from Soweto".

The disgust wasn't contained to parts of Derry or Belfast. Lord Norman Tebbit said, on hearing of McGuinness's death, that he was a "coward" who only posed as a man of peace once he knew the IRA was beaten.

"The world is a sweeter and cleaner place now. I hope that his Roman Catholic beliefs turn out to be true and he'll be parked in a particularly hot and unpleasant corner of hell for the rest of eternity," said the Tory grandee whose wife was paralysed after the

IRA's bombing in Brighton. However, Jo Berry, whose father Sir Anthony Berry died in the same atrocity, rebuked Tebbit, calling McGuinness "an inspiring example of peace and reconciliation."

The truth, as with the conflicting judgements after the death of Ian Paisley, lay somewhere in between.

The journey McGuinness took from reputed IRA butcher to Northern Ireland's Deputy First Minister, who denounced dissident republicans as "traitors to the island of Ireland" and shook hands with the Queen, was simply astonishing.

I'd briefly met him in a break during the 1998 Good Friday Agreement talks, when he was Sinn Féin's chief negotiator, and it was hard to believe I was in the presence of a man who had reputedly sanctioned terror. He was warm and generous with his time, especially as I was a British journalist, and appeared sincere when I asked if he genuinely believed he'd see peace in Northern Ireland in his lifetime.

"Absolutely," he told me. "There is simply no other way forward for our people. The past has to stay in the past. If we fail to give a peaceful future to younger generations then our struggles, our fights on their behalf, have been a sham."

The most honest assessment of both Paisley and McGuinness was that they were tribal hawks who eventually became inclusive doves. Men who began as militants and encouraged their followers to indulge in the worst aspects of sectarianism only to end up as peacemakers.

But trying to convince their enemies to embrace or forgive the other side of their complex characters is a very tough ask. In that sense, they perfectly sum up the land and the struggle they were born into.

Heroes to their own people, undoubtedly. But to the whole of

Northern Ireland, never. Because you can't escape from the fact that in their name many innocent people from working-class communities were tortured, murdered and horrendously maimed.

One of them is possibly the bravest woman I've ever met. A survivor of the bloodiest atrocity of The Troubles, at Omagh. Her resilience in the face of the bombers, her refusal to be cowed or have an ounce of self-pity as she faced them down, did more to ultimately bring peace to her country than any politician like Paisley or McGuinness.

A woman who refused to buy into either of their visions, whose courage and determination not to give into the bullet or the bomb showed why both sides would eventually have no option but to go with the will of the majority of ordinary, peace-seeking citizens and compromise.

OMAGH — August 1998

The morning after the car bomb ripped through this quiet market town, the main shopping street resembled a post-apocalyptic landscape.

Helicopters pounded high above the waterlogged rubble, alarms raged and the only people on the blood-stained pavements were white-suited forensic teams picking through glass in shop windows which the day before housed the mutilated limbs of men, women and children.

Outside a newsagents, bundles of Sunday newspapers lay soaked and untouched, still in their string, the 'OUTRAGE, SAVAGERY, BARBARISM' that screamed from their front pages seeming utterly inadequate. How could a single word fairly describe the callous murder of 29 people, nine of them children and 14 of them women, one of whom was pregnant with twins, and the injuring of 220 others?

This wasn't just the worst day's killing in three decades of The Troubles as those newspapers reported, it was the worst death count since the 1920s when the British Army and Republicans were engaged in all-out war. But back then most of the casualties were soldiers and volunteers who knew what to expect, and were willing to die for their causes.

In Omagh's Market Street, on one of the busiest of shopping days, the Saturday before the kids went back to school, all we saw was innocents who were going about their normal lives unknowingly herded to the slaughter.

There had only been one bomb previously in this neat, middle-class County Tyrone town which the 30-year reign of terror had largely by-passed. In 1995, a small blast outside the courthouse left a security guard needing treatment for shock.

This time all of its 20,000 citizens needed that treatment, especially the hundreds who had narrowly escaped but who would remain physically and mentally scarred for the rest of their lives.

One of them was 22-year-old Donna Marie McGillion who was out shopping with her fiancé Gary, his sister Tracy and her 21-month-old daughter Breda on that Saturday afternoon when the blood-lusting cowards detonated their bomb without warning.

They were buying shoes for Breda who was to be a flower girl at the couple's wedding the following Saturday and their mood was as sunny as the August sky. At 3.10pm as Donna Marie pushed the toddler's buggy five yards from a maroon Vauxhall car, a 500lb bomb exploded. Breda was instantly killed.

Donna Marie suffered lung damage and severe lacerations and was so badly burned across two-thirds of her body that her family could no longer recognise her. She was read the last rites and given only a 20 per cent chance of living.

As her immune system weakened she suffered lung infections, pneumonia and septicaemia. According to doctors in Belfast's Royal Victoria Hospital only her willpower saw her through.

For six weeks she lay in a coma unaware that Garry was in the same hospital being treated for severe burns down his right side and that her family had closed ranks around her to ensure she regained consciousness.

Her gently-spoken father Malachy later told me how a communal tranquility saw her beat the horrendous odds stacked against her: "We told every member of the family not to get angry. Donna Marie has two brothers who were 17 and 25 and we knew that anger would lead to revenge which would destroy us.

"We decided to let God deal with these people. No one was allowed to cry at her bedside. I think she sensed this calmness from us all and it helped to pull her through."

The last thing she can remember from the day was buying Breda's shoes. Then nothing. When she came around, she assumed she'd been in a car accident. When she was told the truth, and saw how she had been left, her first instinct was not to drown in self-pity but to fight back by setting herself goals. The unacceptable alternative was to let the Omagh bombers claim another victim.

Three months after the blast she achieved her first goal by leaving hospital. Then she drew on all the courage her battered body and mind could muster and revisited the plans for her wedding.

Amazingly, in March 1999, she made it down the aisle of Sacred Heart Church on a day drenched in raw emotion. It felt like most of the town had turned out to applaud a couple who would go on to symbolise Omagh's defiance in the face of the bombers.

On the first anniversary of the atrocity Donna Marie let me into her home to tell me her feelings. And as soon as I set eyes on her, she shamed me.

I saw the horrific scars all over the exposed parts of her face and body. The small black spots on her neck where shrapnel was still trying to escape. I felt intense pity for her as she placed a mask on her face to stop her cheek from sagging and ached with her as she climbed painfully from a chair.

But when she spoke with a warm smile, the ugliness the terrorists had created disappeared and all I noticed was the power of her spirit. A power that kept her alive when lesser humans would have given up and shamed the politicians who, in 1999, were dragging the fragile peace process to the brink of collapse. Her words were the most powerful I had heard from anyone about the Northern Irish situation in my time covering The Troubles.

"I love this country and I love being close to my family but if there is ever another Omagh I would seriously consider leaving. I want my children to have the best possible future in a place where people aren't fighting on the streets but fighting for better education and investment."

It was a voice that spoke for a new generation which was tired and sickened by the centuries-old squabbling and just wanted to grasp a normal future.

"I want my children to live in a place which has all of this, not one that sucks them into a sectarian divide. I could never cope with that now. Whenever bombs went off in Ireland before I'd go, 'oh that's awful' and then get on with my life. I never realised how the physical and mental pain drags on years down the line. But now I know, and it's so pointless."

She took me through the thought process that led to her holding a wedding seven months after the terrorists had left her at death's door.

"At first I thought it might be best to go for a quiet wedding but then I thought that would be giving in," she said.

"So we decided not to change anything. I was a bit worried beforehand, mainly about my wedding dress and the problems with my dressings but from the moment I woke up until I went to bed, I enjoyed every minute of it.

"Seeing Garry at the altar after all we had been through was amazing. And then seeing the crowd outside was unbelievable. I didn't get to bed until 3.30am and it was the only day since the bomb that I haven't felt any pain."

Four months down the line she said married life was everything she hoped it would be. "We're no different from any other couple but I think what has happened has brought us even closer together. He understands what I'm going through and I know what he's going through.

"We realise that we came so close to death that to survive makes us very lucky people.

"And it has made us realise that life is too short to worry. Before the bomb we would save for things, now if we want something we just go and get it. We realise now that we took so much for granted. It makes you realise how precious the present is."

I realised the main weapon in Donna Marie's armoury was a

refusal to let the terrorists believe they had spoiled her life or changed her in any way.

"I get out of the house whenever I can. I figure if I sit in here moping they will have taken a 30th victim and I refuse to let them win. I don't have control of my past but I certainly have control of my future," she said.

Although she was in pain every day, the hardest part of her life was being tied down to a schedule where she had to have dressings changed and attend regular therapy and physio sessions.

She had recently been back in hospital so more skin could be grafted on to her upper body and arm. Only 95 per cent of the grafting took, which meant she still had ten more raw areas yet to heal. She wore a mask because the ligaments and cartilages in her face snapped, making her skin sag. She was told she would still be having surgery in four years' time. Only after that could she think about cosmetic surgery.

Garry, then 25, was also in need of constant hospital treatment as the muscles on the right arm of this former boxer were wasting away. But cosmetic surgery was way down the list of Donna Marie's goals a year after the bombing. Her next one was returning to her job as a sales assistant in frozen food store Iceland.

She wanted to go back in the autumn to do the odd hour but thought it more likely to be Christmas. As she talked, I was left in awe of her cool demeanour and inability to feel anger. I asked her why she didn't fly into a rage about the callous butchers who had done so much damage to her and destroyed so many lives in Omagh the year before.

"If I get angry it stops me getting better and means I have given in. They want me to get angry but I refuse to give in to intimidation. I can't say I was never angry. I probably was early on for five minutes and then I looked around and thought, 'I'm alive. And I have my sight, my hearing and my limbs.'"

Did she ever try to get inside the heads of the bombers?

"No, I try to steer away from it because I could go on forever saying 'why me?' and no-one will have the answers. I have no pity for them and I will never forgive them but I can't help feeling sorrow that all they had to do with their lives was leave a bomb in Omagh while families were going about their Saturday shopping."

Did she feel upset when people stared at her in the town?

"Kids are funny. They stare at you and ask what happened. How do you explain it to a child? I just say I fell and hurt myself.

"If someone takes a second look it doesn't bother me but the odd time someone constantly stares I think, 'God I'm not that bad am I?'

"I wouldn't come home and cry but I would certainly notice. But it's all about how you feel about yourself inside, not how others think of you that counts."

I asked how Omagh was feeling as the first anniversary approached.

"People are a bit scared about how they'll be on the day but overall they've been very strong. They refuse to let this beat them and they refuse to be divided. If anything, the bomb has driven us all ten times closer together. I will feel a sense of relief when the anniversary is over but I know it will be an emotional rollercoaster.

"The main thing is the bombers didn't destroy this town. They just made us stronger and more determined to get on with our lives."

During her stay in hospital she wrote to Gerry Adams and David Trimble pleading with them to achieve peace. Both vowed to do their best but their words left her unimpressed:

"It's so very sad that they can't get together and sort it out. It just leaves you thinking, 'how many more Omaghs need to happen before they do?'"

OMAGH — May 2013

Fifteen years after the bombers did their worst the contrast in the mood on Market Street could not be more stark.

On a beautiful early summer's morning, watching happy, carefree shoppers pop into boutiques and chat outside chic coffee shops on a tree-lined street, I could have been staring at a prosperous stop-off town on a European tour.

The only reminder that that bloodiest of days in 1998 had happened here was the tall glass pillar, which bears no words, just a crystal heart, on the spot where the car bomb exploded on that August Saturday afternoon.

The changed picture mirrored a bigger shift in Northern Ireland's fortunes to the point where the following weekend, 35 miles away, world leaders such as Barack Obama and Vladimir Putin were set to gather for a G8 summit.

Which was an astonishing symbol of progress that left locals, who not long ago had the army in their faces if they strayed into the wrong area, disbelieving but proud.

I had returned to talk to Donna Marie, now a 37-year-old mother of two beautiful children, to see how she and Omagh were doing.

Not only had she given birth to Cara, who was then 11, and Cormac, six, she had gained herself a degree in event management.

She was still suffering from acute physical and mental pain and the memories of what the bombers did to her and her town still haunted her, mainly because not one of them had been brought to justice. I was still gobsmacked at the absence of anger in her words and her calm expression and told her that I didn't know how she did it.

"Containing my anger can be hard. Like the time one of them was in court and charged with 29 counts of murder but he wasn't charged with what he did to me.

"But I still remind myself that I'm a survivor not a victim, and I won't let them win by seeing myself as a victim. They didn't take my life. They just distorted it."

The deepest pain, what she calls "the heartache" of knowing she survived and others didn't, is the most difficult to cope with. Others such as little Breda, who would have been a flower girl at their wedding the week after the bomb went off.

She told me that her lowest point came during her 12-year fight for compensation: "It was awful. I remember walking out of the High Court in Belfast crying. I felt so low, as though I was back there again. The system made me feel like I was begging for something.

"They would ask to check my scars and stuff, and I was thinking, 'can't you see them?' Justice is not something I'll get in this life. Even if they do get them and put them away, they'll do a short period of time. But I don't think they'll get them now anyway. Too much time has passed. It's a struggle but we have to move on. Maybe not move on. Move away."

I told her Omagh looked like it had moved on, at least economically, and she nodded. "I always say to outsiders when you think of Omagh don't just think of what happened, think of the people who came out of that and how strong we were.

"A lot of survivors were fantastic, inspirational people who showed real willpower and spirit to get back on their feet. If you're an employer, think if you had those people in your workforce how good your business would be?"

By 2013 they were teaching kids about the bomb in local schools although it didn't stop one of Cara's friends staring at Donna Marie's face and asking what had happened.

"Cara said, 'It was the bomb' and her friend went, 'What bomb?'" That amused Donna Marie almost as much as seeing her kids recoil in horror on a trip to London when they spotted a soldier carrying a gun.

"I was just killing myself laughing at their shock. How times change. In many ways. I mean, never in a million years did I think world leaders would gather for a summit a taxi drive away from Omagh.

"Northern Ireland has changed so much that I couldn't bring my children up here if it went back to how it was. Cara's going from a Catholic primary into an integrated senior school and, to me, that's the way forward."

Disgracefully, no-one has been found guilty in a criminal court for those 29 deaths despite numerous attempts and overwhelming evidence. Not one conviction, despite the then Royal Ulster Constabulary Chief Constable Sir Ronnie Flanagan vowing in 1998 "no stone would be left unturned until we bring these people to justice".

But Omagh did achieve something. It shamed all of those on

either side of the Loyalist/Nationalist divide who did not believe the slaughter had to end.

The unique thing about the Omagh bombing was the nature of the victims. They ranged from unborn children to a 66-year-old gran. They were Catholics and Protestants, they were brothers, sisters, mothers, sons and daughters, even a 12- year-old Spanish student on an exchange visit. They posed no threat to anyone.

And because the atrocity was so abhorrent, a decision had to be made. Northern Ireland could carry on in this senseless cycle of butchery or it could fundamentally change. And everyone with any sense of morality chose change.

On the 20th anniversary of the bombing, the Omagh Community Youth Choir performed a concert to mark the occasion. One of the singers was a 17-year-old called Cara McGillion who composed her own song, called Empty Promises because she "wanted to write about something close to my heart."

Her mother was beside herself with pride. What an achievement to take the full blast of a 500lb bomb from five yards away, to be read the last rites, but to rise above it all. And two decades later have your daughter sing a song about the failure of the men who almost killed you, to break the human spirit.

A glimpse of Donna Marie McGillion's face as she speaks with such composed defiance makes you realise it wasn't Martin McGuinness or Ian Paisley, Tony Blair or Bill Clinton, Sinn Féin or the DUP, Dublin or Westminster, who finally ensured the worst of The Troubles would end. It was invincible working-class people like her who were the real game-changers.

RIP those who weren't alive to enjoy the peace that their courage insisted upon.

THE
PRINCIPLED

6

THE
LIVERPOOL —·—
DOCKERS

HISTORY seeps from Hope Street's every Grade II Listed pore. Towering over its south end, like some brooding Gothic beast, is the longest cathedral in the world, Giles Gilbert Scott's sandstone Anglican masterpiece in whose shadow lay the bones of such fabled figures as statesman William Huskisson, the first human to be killed by a train when he was hit by Stephenson's Rocket.

At the north end, built on the site of Britain's biggest-ever poorhouse, stands the futuristic Metropolitan Cathedral, intended by Sir Edwin Lutyens to be the second-largest church in the world until spiralling costs forced on it the more modest title of England's largest Catholic cathedral, or locally: Paddy's Wigwam.

Opposite you'll see the distinctive curved facade of the Medical Institution, one of the city's 2,500-plus listed buildings, where poet and slavery abolitionist William Roscoe was born.

Next to that is a theatre which in the early 60s was Hope Hall, a Bohemian hang-out for radical artists like sculptor Arthur Dooley, and poets Roger McGough and Adrian Henri, which gave birth to the counter-cultural Liverpool Scene, and Britain's first hippy Happening.

After they'd turned on, tuned in and dropped out, it became The Everyman Theatre which spawned an explosion of talent in the 70s, led by writers Willy Russell and Alan Bleasdale and actors Julie Walters, Bernard Hill, Jonathan Pryce, Pete Postlethwaite, Antony Sher and Bill Nighy.

Its junction with Hardman Street is dominated by the art deco Philharmonic Hall, where some of the finest composers and musicians have played, and where sits a plaque to the members of its orchestra who were part of the band that played

Outside Jack Jones House in Liverpool city centre, spring 2021. Jack provided the inspiration for the book. I wanted to write about working-class 'diamonds' who should be celebrated

At the 25th Hillsborough Memorial Service at Anfield and beside Tom Murphy's monument. The relentless campaigning of women like Anne Williams helped destroy the wall of lies

'We were our children's eyes, their ears. We were their voices. And we were never going to be silenced'. With the inspirational Hillsborough mum Margaret Aspinall

'A black man is the greatest so you can be great too.' Me and photographer Roger Allen with the one and only Muhammad Ali. We had never met a more extraordinary man

In Louisville, Kentucky, June 2016, beside the limousine carrying Muhammad Ali's burial casket. Thousands gathered to chant his name over and over again

'Are you hoping for another Papal blessing today?' With Ian Paisley in Edinburgh, 2010. Despite a life 'punctuated by nakedly sectarian acts', Paisley was ennobled as a life peer

In Derry for the funeral of former Sinn Féin leader Martin McGuinness in 2017. But it was invincible working-class people like Donna Marie McGillion who were the real game-changers

With Tony Nelson at The Casa – the centre became a legacy of the Liverpool dockers dispute. They put a brass plaque on their Supporters Wall in honour of my mum Sheila

Interviewing Tony Benn in his London home. He was a left-wing giant but Dennis Skinner's wit and his torpedo-like ability to score direct hits on Tories resonated more deeply with me

'You must be the ace reporter then, son?' At Liverpool's old training ground, Melwood, in July 1975, interviewing Bill Shankly for the school magazine

On the Kop in 1994 on the last day there was standing. Bill Shankly and Bob Paisley don't need letters adding to their names to remind fans of their deep and lasting impact

Eltham, 1999. I struggled to find the memorial in south east London, marking the spot where Stephen Lawrence was killed. It had recently been attacked by racist vandals

Fading graffiti sprayed 30 years previously on the walls of the old railway bridges around the Brook Estate in Eltham. A twisted philosophy passed on to a new generation

'This isn't charity. It's solidarity.' At Goodison Park, helping collections for the Fans Supporting Foodbanks initiative set up by Ian Byrne and Dave Kelly

'Power to the People': Few Britons of his or any generation did more than Jack Jones to turn that slogan into a reality. I'm pictured here with the great man on his 90th birthday in The Casa

on while the Liverpool-registered Titanic sank. Diagonally across the traffic lights is the iconic Philharmonic pub, which gives working-class gentlemen the unique opportunity to piss against ornate marble, while getting pissed in two spectacular Art Nouveau drinking lounges, aptly named Brahms and Liszt.

Further down Hope Street towards Toxteth is the Institute of Performing Arts, originally the Mechanics Institute where Charles Dickens, Anthony Trollope and Ralph Waldo Emerson lectured. It became The Institute School for Boys where Paul McCartney met George Harrison, next to the art school where John Lennon met Stuart Sutcliffe.

Round the corner is the 19th century pub, Ye Cracke, with its famous War Room, to which every drinker in the mid-1850s who bored on about the Boer War was sent. It was also where Lennon hung out with a group of artists and musicians called The Dissenters.

According to Hitler's sister-in-law, Bridget, 23-year-old Adolf would often walk down Hope Street towards their nearby flat in 102 Upper Stanhope Street, during the five months he spent with his half-brother Alois in 1913 after escaping the Austrian Army draft (giving rise to the wonderful image of the moustachioed one sitting in Ye Cracke's War Room waving his arms manically, and telling those boring on about the imminent Great War that he had an even greater one planned for 1939).

But the building which truly encapsulates the radical, ground-breaking spirit of this extraordinary street, is a three-storied one that sits halfway between the Everyman and the Philharmonic called The Casa. If you're looking for a truly heroic Scouse yarn plus an education in modern social history, pull up a bar stool.

In 1999, the semi-derelict shell, which had last opened as a late-night drinking den called The Casablanca, was bought by Liverpool dockers who had been sacked after one of the longest disputes in British employment history. Sacked because of something that resides deep in the Liverpudlian psyche: a refusal to cross a picket line. Sacked because, to them, a principle is a principle worth fighting for to the death.

Liverpool has a long history of trade union resistance. In 1911, the General Transport Strike brought the city to a halt and so frightened the Establishment that then Home Secretary Winston Churchill sent a gunship to the River Mersey to put down the insurrection. *The Times* sent a reporter up from London too. And he called it "as near to a revolution as anything I have seen in England." Unsurprisingly, when it was over, the dockers were the last workers to go back.

At the core of the 90s dispute was a fear among dockers of the management's plan to bring back casualisation. A return to the pre-war days when men would wait in pens each morning to be picked out for work that day. I knew from personal experience how much that scheme was detested as both of my grandfathers had been Liverpool dockers.

My mother's dad, Vic, would rise at dawn and walk, in every type of weather, five miles to the docks in the hope of gaining a very long day's work. And five miles home when he often didn't get any.

He would tell about tallies being tossed into the crowd by bowler-hatted foremen, who would then watch as men scrambled and fought like stray dogs for the privilege of offering their labour. He would describe how some were so desperate for money they would sleep on the docks to be first on the stand the next day.

And of the humiliation it brought on men, not to mention the poverty on their families, if you weren't among the minority favoured by the foreman. Favoured for anything from nepotism, your religion, what pub you drank in and whether you bought the foreman a drink there.

In 1947, the National Dock Labour Scheme was set up by Clement Attlee's post-war Labour government to dismantle casualisation and give workers job security, daily work, or fallback pay, and proper training. More than 78,000 dockers in 86 ports became "regulated" employees with the bosses' unchallenged right to hire-and-fire replaced by joint union-management labour boards.

However, when Margaret Thatcher came to power in 1979 she declared war on the unions, as she believed they were the prime cause of Britain's poor economic performance.

Her plan was to break the power of the workers by allowing unemployment to surge and introduce repressive laws which would smash the solidarity between different unions and allow her to face them down one-by-one.

Throughout the 80s the Tories secured a series of victories against unions, most notably against the miners, who were effectively starved back to work by pre-emptive stockpiling, cheap imports, the recruitment of non-union haulage firms, scab workers, the sequestration of union funds and the deployment of the riot police as a paramilitary arm of government.

In the docks, the crisis came in 1989, with the abolition of the Dock Labour Scheme, which was abolished with little resistance from the dockers' union, the TGWU. Detested casualisation was a reality once again.

The union leadership was too slow in approving membership

calls for a national strike and by the time the dockers walked out, the employers had been granted legal backing to use non-registered dockers and slash thousands of well-paid jobs. With private enterprise salivating at the prospect of booming profits, and their ever helpful police enforcers, the strike collapsed. Once again, the Liverpool dockers were the last to go back.

At virtually every port, workplace organisation was destroyed, union representatives de-recognised, mass redundancies forced through and the National Port Shop Stewards Committee effectively dissolved. Only in Liverpool was there a temporary compromise.

The Mersey Docks and Harbour Company (MDHC) agreed to carry on recognising the union but jobs were slashed from 1,100 to 500. That was a move to buy them time. In the longer term the employers would be satisfied with nothing less than the destruction of trade union organisation on the Liverpool docks.

They began a demoralising and provocative process aimed at breaking the morale of the men and undermining the power of their shop stewards. Despite dockers handling the highest cargo levels ever recorded in the Port of Liverpool they saw their wages and their numbers fall, with any new men recruited from sub-contracted firms offering inferior pay and conditions.

They were told to be available for work at any time and be on call even on their days off. If the bosses couldn't contact them by phone they'd send them hand-delivered messages ordering them to return to work. This was zero-hours culture-plus, decades before it became a despised notion.

In 1994 MDHC decided to "de-recognise" elected TGWU shop stewards. When the dockers opposed the move they placed adverts in the *Liverpool Echo* inviting applicants to replace the entire workforce. Thousands applied but nobody was hired. It was a cynical ploy to force dockers to sign inferior contracts, involving big cuts in pay, under which "all existing jobs including your own are to be eliminated with new jobs being created which fit into the new working system."

As Jimmy Nolan, chairman of the shop stewards, said at the time, "I fought 30 years ago to end ten-hour shifts and now we were being told that it's twelve hours or the sack."

The sense of intimidation allied to the disruption of their lifestyles, plus a decline in health and safety, saw resentment and anger surge.

"Our husbands were on 12-hour shifts, and would then find themselves called back for another 12, just five hours after getting home," said Cathy Dwyer, whose husband Andy had worked on the docks for 33 years. Other women spoke of their husbands being disciplined for not being by the phone on their day off and messages being left with young children asking them to find their dads and tell him to get back to work.

Shipping industry journal *Lloyd's List*, which had described Liverpool's dockers as 'the most productive workforce in Europe' commented, 'One does not have to be left-wing to have sympathy for the sacked dockers of Liverpool, who now find themselves effectively victims of a markedly macho management.'

A powder keg had been created which needed only a match to set the anger alight.

The 850-day dispute started on September 25, 1995, when Bootle-based docks sub-contractor firm Torside reneged on an overtime agreement and dismissed five employees.

The sacked men formed a picket line which fellow Torside

dockers refused to cross, allowing the company to dismiss its entire workforce of 80.

Many of the sacked workers were sons and relatives of dockers whose families had worked on the Mersey for generations and knew only one thing to do. They formed a picket line at Seaforth container terminal, handing out leaflets and displaying a defiant banner saying, 'Save The 80: Say No To Casuals.' Immediately, 329 workers employed by the MDHC refused to cross their picket line. The match had been lit.

The workforce, referred to so recently as the most productive in Europe, was sacked in its entirety three days later with management saying, "The striking men are in breach of their contracts and we have therefore terminated them." They advertised for replacement labour within 24 hours, at lower rates of pay and inferior conditions.

It sent shockwaves through the thousands of family members reliant on the docks to put food on the table and pay the bills. A typical response came from Pat Dooley, whose husband had been a docker for 28 years: "It felt like someone in our house had died," she said.

Canon Nicholas Frayling, the Rector of Liverpool, who tried to mediate in the dispute but was cold-shouldered by management said, "The working man in Liverpool has always worked in a culture of fear but since Thatcher that has become a culture of terror. However, some would rather be unemployed than exploited. For them, it is better to die in the fight than admit defeat."

The men knew they had walked into a trap. Even though the dispute was not theirs, their refusal to cross Torside's picket line made it illegal under Thatcher's anti-trade union laws. MDHC, who had been very clever, claimed Torside was an "entirely independent" company.

But those who knew the score, knew that Torside was a Trojan horse sent in to kill off the established dockers' livelihoods and bring in cheaper, more compliant, less well-trained labour. Their workers were even recruited at interviews held on MDHC premises.

Local politicians met with management to try to find a solution but to no avail. Management had got what they wanted and the Tories' anti-union laws backed them to the hilt. The 1980 Employment Act made it illegal to take part in secondary action except in limited circumstances. A later Act, in 1990, outlawed those limited circumstances and unions could be taken to court if they organised secondary actions.

In October, Eddie Loyden, Labour MP for Liverpool Garston told the Commons, "It is 1995, and we are returning to the dark days of threatened casualisation. I believe that that is a serious threat. I believe that people are entitled to work with dignity under conditions that are human, and to be part of the process of developing the industry."

The TGWU took the Establishment line that, because the dockers' action was technically illegal, they could not make the dispute official. Yet had its leadership shown more guts it could have immediately launched a national campaign championing the dockers on a cause of principle, highlighting the exploitation and intimidation they were facing, and probably achieved a swift victory. Thatcher was gone, John Major's days were numbered as Prime Minister, and it was the perfect time to pick a fight when right was on the workers' side.

Five months after the sackings, TGWU General Secretary Bill

Morris came to Liverpool and made an emotional speech to the dockers and their families. "I am proud to be with you. Your struggle is so important that our grandchildren will ask, 'where were you at the great moment?' And you will either stand up with pride and say, 'I was there,' or you'll hang your head in shame, without an answer. There can be no turning back and no backsliding until victory is won."

Morris, although refusing to make the dispute official, vowed that his union would "keep going until we get this company to understand that a negotiated settlement which gives people their jobs back is the only way." Before telling them, "God is on our side."

But he was either being knowingly duplicitous or foolishly over-blowing expectations, because he would later summon the dockers' committee to London to tell them MDHC wasn't playing ball, the unions' hands were tied and they would have to swallow their pride and take the redundancy money. So much for the power of God.

In theory, the dockers were on their own. Even the Labour Party, which came to power during the dispute, refused to support them or overturn Thatcher's anti-union laws for fear of alienating the Middle England voters they had so recently wooed.

But in practice they never walked alone. With a largely unsympathetic and thus virtually silent media in Britain they looked further afield, calculating that support for their cause among foreign workers would impact on Mersey Docks' profits and raise their profile back home. The solidarity offered by comrades around the world for their demands to be reinstated was astonishing.

In December 1995, three months after the start of the dispute, longshoremen in Newark, New Jersey, refused to cross a 6am picket line set up by three Liverpool dockers which almost cost MDHC the business of huge American shipping company Atlantic Containers (ACL).

They kept the picket line going for a week, and as ACL began to lose serious money it brought pressure on Mersey Docks, eventually suspending its Liverpool operations for a month.

In Los Angeles, a picket was set up at the port and among those who refused to cross it was a convoy of low-paid, un-unionised Mexican truck drivers. In Montreal, four Liverpool dockers walked in on a morning shift, climbed a gantry and unfurled a banner announcing that the Canadian Pacific-owned container firm Cast was employing scab labour in Liverpool. When police tried to arrest them, a ring of Canadian dockers protected them until the management agreed to meet.

In January 1997, almost a year before the dispute would end, the dockers called an International Week of Action and workers in 105 ports across the world rallied to the cause. Backed by the International Transport Federation, the action directly hit shipping in at least 13 countries in the week beginning January 20.

On the west coast of America, all Oregon ports were shut for 24 hours with Los Angeles, Long Beach, San Francisco, Oakland, Tacoma, Seattle and Dutch Harbour, Alaska closing for eight hours.

In Los Angeles alone, more than 100 cranes were stopped, with 32 ships in harbour and another 16 due that day. In Japan action hit 50 ports, with meetings held under the slogan 'Stand Against Deregulation: Strengthen International Solidarity' and the union contributed one million yen (£8,000) to the cause. America longshoremen donated nearly £80,000. There were

24-hour stoppages in Canada, Sweden and Denmark. Germany, France, Greece, Holland, New Zealand and all major Australian ports disrupted trade.

Even workers in countries with no ports offered their support. In Switzerland they occupied the Rhine Shipping Company in Basel and glued door locks at the British Consulate in Zurich. Messages of support and reports of solidarity action came in from as far afield as Kaliningrad, Mombasa, Mexico City and Mauritania.

Back in Liverpool they were overwhelmed at the scale and the depth of the solidarity. Jimmy Nolan, Port Shop Stewards Secretary, sent out this heartfelt thank-you message: "The Week of Action was a magnificent achievement for the international dockworkers' movement and for workers worldwide. We thank you all. We would ask that the supportive actions are maintained right up to the moment when the Liverpool dock workers march proudly back to their jobs within the Port of Liverpool. That day now looks within reach. Make no mistake, the dockers are winning this one."

In September 1997, 30 ports worldwide stopped work for 24 hours, bringing the US east coast to a standstill. Ports in Japan and South Africa came to a halt with workers in the latter withdrawing their labour "in solidarity with the Liverpool dockers who stood by us during apartheid." On one day, September 8, 50,000 dockers worldwide in 16 countries acted in solidarity.

Maritime Union of Australia's Jim Donovan told journalist John Pilger at the time, "In a lifetime as a union official, I have never seen anything like the Liverpool campaign. It's a phenomenon. They've gone to every corner of the earth to seek support, to places they've never been before, and they've done it on their own, with no backing from their union.

"They've held two international conferences in Liverpool – I've been to both – and they've had 18 countries represented. I took over 60,000 Australian dollars for them last time. We've blacked a major Liverpool customer, the ABC Line, and the pressure added so much to its financial difficulties it's gone out of business. There is a fundamental human right at issue here: the right of ordinary people to secure work at decent rates and conditions."

The International Week Of Action drew huge coverage in foreign media. CNN's cameras followed the action, showing footage of the picket at Seaforth, and other TV stations and newspapers across the world reported on it.

The Los Angeles Times wrote this, 'Pacific Rim trade sputtered to a halt and dozens of mammoth cargo ships sat idle in their ports as union dockworkers from Los Angeles to Seattle stayed off the job in a one-day show of support for striking longshoremen in Liverpool, England.

'At the Los Angeles-Long Beach harbour complex, the nation's busiest, 33 ships were either stranded in berths with no-one to handle their cargo or were anchored in the San Pedro Bay with nowhere to go.' *The Tribune Business News* quoted Karsten Lemke, chairman of the Steamship Association of Southern California, saying, "The industry is again a mess." And Wilmington trucking executive Mike Johnson, President of the Port Intermodal Operators Association, said, "This is going to cost us millions of dollars in delays. Half a billion dollars in commerce is shot down the drain."

But back home the dockers were struggling to get any support in the local media or so much as a word or an image printed nationally.

One of the first meaningful references to the dispute in the national press came more than two months after they had been sacked. In a letter to several newspapers from four Scottish writers, including the Booker Prize-winner James Kelman, they alleged "a conspiracy of silence" and a "gentleman's agreement" between John Major and Tony Blair. It was, they suggested, less the dispute Britain forgot than one that Parliament and the media did not want us to hear about.

Kevin Bocquet, the BBC's Merseyside correspondent said he had done only four pieces for television and four for radio in the 14 months since the dispute began. His pitch to the newsdesks would be that this is a stirring human story with poignant images of men and their wives standing defiantly outside the dock gates in the early morning light. Only for his editors to ask him, "who is suffering and how does it affect the economy?" When he argued that the creeping spread of poorly-paid casual work was a critical issue facing millions of people he was told, "They're casualising at the BBC, mate. That's life."

At the *Daily Mirror*, despite it being a staunchly Labour-supporting newspaper that speaks up for the working-class, I hit a brick wall when I pitched features about the dockers. The feedback I was given was that the paper was backing Blair's New Labour and its moderate Third Way philosophy, and the readers would rather hear about that and how it could see off the Tories than tub-thumping rhetoric about striking unions which harked back to a bygone age.

It was only when their dispute received global recognition from workers, and support at home from celebrities, that the

Mirror finally allowed me to spend a day with the dockers and do a piece on their struggle. They ran it on the eve of a second anniversary demonstration in Liverpool under the headline: 'Heroes or fools. It depends on whether we still place value on dignity and collective support.'

SEAFORTH DOCK GATES — September 1997

D*awn at Liverpool docks. Through the mist, a trail of juggernauts and cars snaking back as far as the eye can see stands paralysed before a human wall.*

Ninety men in yellow dockers' jackets and women in calf- length coats block the dock gates, glaring at their enemy with a mixture of contempt and pride.

Two van-loads of police in riot gear descend on the crowd mouthing threats of arrests, and the shop stewards order the pickets to disperse. Within seconds, they have regrouped either side of the road, yelling, "Scabs, scabs, scabs", as the snake slowly glides into the docks.

An Escort door opens. A shaven-headed youth, crossing the picket line to go into work, screams, "Get a job. Get a life", and laughter explodes from the steamy car windows and cuts the morning mist with a deafening cruelty.

Two years ago, the men outside the cars had jobs and lives but then the dock gate was blocked by a picket line they refused to cross. Thus began one of the world's longest-running strikes and an astonishing tale of human resilience in the face of awesome odds.

The striking dockers have been out on a limb, without union support, political support or state benefits. They have been offered redundancy payments but refuse to accept. They will settle for nothing less than their jobs back. Not for them, they say, but for past and future generations. Welcome to Old Labour's Last Stand.

"It's all about the definition of a job. What is it? Is it a fair and honest agreement between a man and his employer, or is it simply an animal being put to work?" said John Deaves, 55, who has been on the docks 37 years, like his father and grandfather before him. "Most of us are in our mid-50s and would be better off taking the money tomorrow, but we won't without winning our jobs back. We want whoever goes back in there to have real jobs with pension rights and holidays and decent conditions."

The dockers believe they have been forced into a corner by a macho management desperate to implement total casual- isation of the workforce. "This firm was hell-bent on destroying everything past generations of dockers had fought for," said 52-year-old John Turner, 25 years a docker.

"We can't throw away all that and sell out future generations. It goes against everything we have been taught since we were knee-high. It's a question of 'to thine own self be true'."

For the last 24 months that sentiment has been stretched beyond the pale. Marriages have crumbled and homes have been repossessed, as adults and children have struggled on handouts. But they've got by with a little help from their friends.

On Merseyside, extended families have taken over the bills, strangers pay for them at supermarket checkouts, pensioners and students throw pound coins into their collecting buckets.

Abroad, there has been financial and moral support on an extraordinary scale. Earlier this month, an International Day Of Action crippled 30 ports worldwide. But it is the solidarity much closer to home that has stunned the men and seen them through. Their wives, sisters, mothers and girlfriends have turned themselves into a life-support machine called Women Of The Waterfront.

Chairwoman Doreen McNally says, "We were just housewives catapulted from the washing line to the picket line. We are there to cope with the reality of the dispute: To clothe everyone, put food on the table, tell kids why they have to go without, lift the men up from the floor, support each other when it all gets too harrowing to go on."

Doreen has taken the dockers' message around the world and recently went to Libya to pick up a human rights award. The women have held candlelit vigils outside the homes of the MDHC bosses. On the day that American east coast dockers refused to handle ships from Liverpool the women toured the directors' houses, singing, "New York, New York, it's a wonderful town." They took a birthday cake along to chairman Trevor Furlong, just after he awarded himself an £87,000 pay rise which took his wages up to £316,000 plus share options. Furlong's response was to phone the police.

The MDHC admits that the dispute cost it £600,000 last year but with profits up 60 per cent to £22 million in the six months to June, the action is having no real effect.

Port operations director Peter Jones says, "We have made the men a generous final offer and we are waiting for them to put it to a secret ballot. We have the greatest sympathy with some of those who have been dismissed, but at the time they were dismissed we had to protect our business."

It is doubtful if this strike could have happened anywhere else. Earlier this century, Liverpool was the second-busiest port in the world, but the labour was casual and the dockers' lives were ruled by prejudice and fear.

That is the nightmare that haunts every one of today's strikers. A nightmare their heritage will not allow them to repeat. It is why they refuse to listen to the offer made by the MDHC eight months ago: 40 of the 329 jobs back, and £28,000 redundancy apiece for the rest of the men.

The MDHC wants the shop stewards to put the offer to a secret ballot. The men refuse. They held a previous secret ballot on a redundancy offer and it was rejected by 85 per cent. Every Friday, they hold a mass meeting and put the offer to the men on a show of hands. It is always unanimously thrown out.

"We know what the result of the ballot would be, so why give them the benefit of saying we have officially turned down their 'final offer'," says Billy Lomas, 57, a docker for 37 years.

"Where would it leave us? The point is, it is a ballot about the size of our redundancy cheque, and we've already told them redundancy is not an issue."

Speaking to the men gives you the sense that they are fighting for something bigger than themselves. That they are fighting for all working people, to prevent the degradation dockers had once suffered being revisited on future generations.

Some who were nearing retirement would have been better off taking the redundancy cheque and an enhanced pension that was on offer but could not dream of doing so because they believe there is more to a human being than ownership of money. To their minds they would be selling a job passed down by their grandfather and father, which should be available for their son if he wants it. To sell it would be to never hold their heads up again or look themselves in the mirror.

So how can these obstinate men win? "How can we lose?" says shop stewards' chairman Jimmy Nolan. "We'll be outside those gates for as long as it takes to get our jobs back, because we have done nothing wrong.

"The only crime we have committed is refusing to cross a picket line. We know we are right. And the pain no longer hurts."

Is he proud of the second anniversary? He shakes his head vigorously. "No. Outsiders may say it is the greatest strike that ever existed. We think it's gone on too long. We just want to get back to work."

What should we make of these men? Bolshie dinosaurs from a bygone age? Or brave individuals embracing the new, caring ideals of decency and fairness espoused by New Labour? Are they heroes or fools? It depends how we look at life.

Whether we still place value on qualities such as dignity and collective support. Whether this country still believes it has room for men you would give a limb for to have standing next to you in a trench.

What struck me that day was the courage of the men, the stoicism of the women and the generosity of passers-by, many of whom honked their horn in support with some stopping to hand out fivers and tenners to the strikers.

They were being sent postal orders or money in envelopes, sometimes anonymously, as well as having groceries delivered to their doorstep. An 84-year-old former miner's wife turned up at the picket line in late 1997, offering savings left to her by her late husband to help towards the hardship fund.

It was a support that spread way beyond Liverpool and trade unions' traditional allies, typified by the anti-globalist movement Reclaim The Streets joining in the struggle. Before the dispute, Tony Nelson was a senior shop steward on the docks. Knowing that Reclaim The Streets were no fans of trade unions but warmed to people committed to environmental issues, he asked to meet them, along with Billy Jenkins, with a view to gaining their support.

Nelson told them the story of how, in 1998 he, and fellow shop steward Mike Carden, got wind of a shipment of uranium hexafluoride heading to Liverpool. When the cargo arrived, with country of origin documents stating Sweden, they barred it from being shipped onwards to Canada, arguing correctly that there was no uranium to be found in Sweden. It had come from South Africa.

Despite intense pressure from the MDHC, Special Branch and the South African government, they refused to touch the cargo on the grounds that Liverpool dockers do not collude with apartheid governments.

Reclaim The Streets were won over and it wasn't long before their supporters travelled up from London to occupy the Mersey Docks and Harbour Company offices in support.

Then there was anarcho-punk band Chumbawamba, who, at the 1998 Brit Awards changed the words of their hit Tubthumping to 'New Labour sold out the dockers, just like they'll sell out the rest of us.' Singer Danbert Nobacon famously poured a bucket of icy water over Deputy PM John Prescott, saying, "This is for the Liverpool dockers." Prescott, who was seated with his wife Pauline, was incandescent, and his office later released a statement saying, 'Mr Prescott thinks it is utterly contemptible that his wife and other womenfolk should have been subjected to such terrifying behaviour.'

Chumbawamba hit back with their own statement: "If John Prescott as a representative of the government has the nerve to turn up at events such as the Brit Awards in a vain attempt to make Labour seem cool and trendy then he deserves all we can throw at him."

Comics Jo Brand, Mark Steel, Julian Clary, Jeremy Hardy and Lee Hurst, and musicians such as Noel Gallagher did fundraisers. A few of them like Mark Steel and Jeremy Hardy stayed in touch with the dockers after the dispute ended, and would give tickets to them when playing concerts in the city, accepting invites to be plied with large quantities of drink in The Casa, a bar and social justice centre that became a legacy of the dispute.

Jeremy Hardy once said he was nominating The Casa for a Guinness World Record as the pub where the phrase "those Tory cunts" was spat out most by drinkers in any given minute. When he died in 2019, pints were raised and stories swapped by dockers and comrades who never forgot the support he and other comedians gave them when few politicians wanted to know.

Sacked docker Micky Tighe, who became good friends with Steel and Hardy, explained how the bond came about: "The most successful benefit was one organised by the comedians in the London Palladium. We were asked to a meeting with Mark Steel and a group of comedians and they decided that something had to be done.

"One day, Mark took us to London's Comedy Store and told us, 'I don't know how this is going to turn out, you've got to remember that most of the people here work nights.'

"There were over thirty people in the room: Jo Brand, Sean

Hughes, Harry Hill, Linda Thomas, all the famous faces off the television. Lee Hurst was chairing the meeting.

"They came to a decision to put a show on at the London Palladium. You can imagine how it felt. I remember when I was a kid and shows came on the telly from the Palladium, we had to have quiet in the house." The Palladium sold out and raised more than £30,000. They also put on gigs at Greenwich comedy club Up the Creek, where Arthur Smith compered and Jools Holland and Squeeze played the music.

The dockers tried to repay this solidarity whenever they could. A year after the dispute ended a group travelled down from Liverpool to picket outside *The Guardian* in protest at the newspaper terminating Mark Steel's weekly column for failing to toe their New Labour line. Steel had ruffled the feathers of too many Blairite figures with friends in the *Guardian* boardroom and he had to go.

One of them was the TGWU general secretary Bill Morris who objected to a column about his shabby treatment of the Liverpool dockers. Steel wrote that Morris's version of trade unionism was little more use than Yellow Pages, as they both seem to be able to help you get insurance and credit cards.

He quoted a complaint from Morris that John Pilger had given the dockers "false hope" by claiming they could win, and accused him of defeatism: "If Bill Morris had been at Agincourt his stirring speech would have been: 'I wouldn't bother going into the breach, boys. Have you seen the size of some of them French? Anyway, it's illegal to flare your nostrils.'"

A year into the dispute the dockers stumbled on an idea that would create positive global coverage.

"I saw someone wearing a Calvin Klein T-shirt, and thought

we could fit the word dockers around it," said Tony Melia, a sacked docks shop steward. A red T-shirt was produced which incorporated the Calvin Klein "CK" into the word "doCKer" with the words "500 Liverpool dockers sacked since September 1995."

"Basically we wanted to attract the attention of young people and the T-shirts had the desired effect because you had to take a second look before you realised what it said," he added.

They received massive attention when two Liverpool footballers, Steve McManaman and Robbie Fowler, both Scousers with links to the docks, decided to sport the shirts as a show of solidarity. The pair wore them under their Liverpool tops for a European Cup Winners' Cup game with SK Brann at Anfield in March 1997.

They agreed not to display the shirts until exchanging their Liverpool tops after the final whistle, believing the gesture would have the same impact but they would escape censure from football authorities.

But when Fowler scored his second goal of the night, giving Liverpool a comfortable 3-0 lead, he forgot about the agreement, lifted his jersey, and the 'Support the 500 sacked Liverpool doCKers' was captured by the cameras and shown to the world. Maybe this was what Bill Morris meant when he said that God, Fowler's nickname, was on their side.

A week later, UEFA fined Fowler £900 but effectively apologised for their disciplinary action: "It may seem strange and even unfair but by lifting his shirt and displaying the message, Fowler violated UEFA regulations. Although we may sympathise with such support, it is a strict rule that a football ground is not the right stage for political demonstrations," said a spokesman.

Fowler later explained why he did it. "The dockers were getting a lot of stick for what they were doing and what they believed in and we believed in what they were trying to do. I was fined but there were collections going round Anfield which proved how much that support meant to them."

The gesture only made Toxteth lad Fowler a bigger idol among Liverpool fans and his shirt-raising moment was voted one of the top 100 Days Which Shook The Kop on the club's official website.

On the other side of Stanley Park, Everton's Duncan Ferguson publicly stated his support for the dockers and Liverpool's Norwegian international Stig Inge Bjornebye turned up at Seaforth docks one afternoon, following training, and tagged himself on to the picket line to show solidarity.

The T-shirts took on a life of their own, gaining cult status among some of the biggest acts. The dockers were invited to sell them at concerts by groups such as Oasis, Cast, Space, Dodgy, Chumbawamba and Primal Scream. It was claimed they sold almost 50,000, at £5 each, which went into the hardship fund.

Benefit gigs raised thousands for the cause and after the dispute ended huge names like Oasis, Paul Weller, The Chemical Brothers, Ocean Colour Scene and Billy Bragg donated a track to an album called Rock The Dock, which raised cash for families who were still struggling. Bragg's 'Never Cross A Picket Line' was especially poignant. In a message to launch the album, Gallagher said, "It's a disgrace their cause has been largely ignored for so long. People need to support them. Buy the CD, or next time it could be you."

Despite all the moral and financial support, the dockers' resolve was draining away as they headed into their third winter enduring real hardship. By the end of 1997, families faced unmanageable financial circumstances, with the weekly £12 union payments impossible to live on and more than 90 homes under repossession orders.

In January 1998, after 28 months out of work, the dockers reluctantly agreed to settle. The Port Shop Stewards agonised over the decision, but after several heated and emotional meetings they agreed to accept the £28,000-per-man redundancy offer and share the payouts with the 80 Torside workers who had been offered nothing.

Shop stewards leader Jimmy Nolan sent them all a letter explaining that with the heaviest of hearts, rather than see "good men and women lose everything" the committee had decided to settle on the best terms achievable.

He cited the lack of political support at national level, the deaths of two more picket line stalwarts and the extreme suffering the families were facing as the key factors in bringing their "heroic struggle" to a conclusion.

And he concluded by saying, "We have to build upon our internationalism, upon the experiences of all our struggles, and let the words of the great trade unionist and former Liverpool docker James Larkin capture our thoughts: 'Who is it speaks of defeat? I tell you a cause like ours is greater than defeat can know. It is the power of powers.'"

The dockers had been broken mainly due to the apathy of their own union leadership and a Labour government having no stomach for the fight. But the dangerous new world that those two supposed bastions of working-class rights had ushered in, was exposed in all its brutality three months later, by the fate of a young man called Simon Jones.

Jones, an unemployed 24-year-old, had been sent by his local

JobCentre to work as a casual labourer at Shoreham harbour in Sussex. It was an offer he had to take or his Jobseeker's Allowance would be lost.

He arrived for his first day's work at 8am, and was told to assist in the unloading of bags of stones and loose aggregate from the hold of the Cambrook, a Polish cargo ship that had docked that morning. Two hours later he was dead.

Jones had been given no training by anyone in a position of responsibility and was issued with no safety equipment. His job was to attach the bags of stones to chains hanging from the underside of a clam-shaped grab, which was open.

When the lever operating the jaws of the grab got caught in the crane operator's clothing, the jaws closed above him and his head was severed. Within seconds, the young man who had recently been a promising student at Sussex University, died of massive fractures to the skull.

Shipping company Euromin, and Richard Martell, general manager at Shoreham, were eventually taken to court on manslaughter charges, where it was revealed that operating instructions posted inside the cab of the excavator crane had been blatantly ignored. To no-one's surprise, Euromin was fined a mere £50,000 for breaching safety regulations and Martell was acquitted of manslaughter.

In a painful twist to this tragic tale it transpired that Simon Jones had been a member of the Brighton-based direct-action group Justice? which had offered support to the Liverpool dockers during the dispute. Ironically, one of the dockers' main objectives was establishing proper apprenticeships, better safety at work and no untrained casual labour anywhere near dangerous dockside workplaces.

In September 1998, on what would have been Simon's 25th birthday, protesters invaded Euromin's Shoreham base and unfurled banners from two 80-foot towers reading, 'Simon Jones RIP' and 'Casualisation kills'.

Same as it ever was.

Losing the dispute, after such a long fight, was a shattering blow to the men and their families. As Cathy Dwyer later said, "It was sheer devastation at the end. It still eats away at us. It always comes back, on anniversaries, when you read about the docks, when you drive past them. It still haunts us."

The dockers may have lost the battle but they decided they weren't going to wallow in self-pity. They weren't going to view the past through a bitter lens. They were going to move on and build a lasting testament to their 28-month struggle and the remarkable community spirit it had unleashed. They wanted to give something back.

An opportunity arose out of retraining workshops which the Workers' Educational Association (WEA) had started in 1996 for sacked dockers and their partners. An idea grew for a writing class to develop their story-telling skills and document their own struggle.

Liverpool screenwriter Jimmy McGovern was invited by the WEA to become a part-time tutor at the class, which he agreed to, as did Trainspotting author Irvine Welsh. McGovern is one of British television's greatest-ever dramatists, not just because of his brilliant scripts but the subjects he chooses. He gives voice to working-class people, especially those battling injustice, he takes on established thinking and asks tough moral questions.

The knowledge he was picking up about the dispute inspired him to write an article in *The Observer* newspaper declaring his support for the sacked men while strongly attacking the MDHC and the General Secretary of the TGWU. It was read by Channel 4 producer Gub Neal who urged McGovern to turn their story into a docu-drama, as he had done with the Hillsborough Disaster.

Eventually McGovern agreed, on two conditions. First, dockers from the WEA class had to write the screenplay which he would nurture and edit, and secondly, they would receive all the proceeds.

When I heard he was attempting to tell this epic story I interviewed him for the *Mirror* on the set of the Cammell Laird shipyard in Birkenhead, where 200 of the sacked men were employed as extras and technicians, and asked him why he had chosen to effectively let the dockers and their partners tell their own tale. "I didn't want to be a vulture. To pick the brains and explore the hearts of people who have been through hell then walk away and pick up BAFTAs which I did with Hillsborough. This time I said I would tell their story with them. And only if it worked," he said.

For the first few workshops Jimmy listened to the sacked dockers talk and said nothing. Then he asked them to stop talking and start writing. Marty Size, who had worked for 22 years on the docks, told me, "I was expecting some glamorous star, but this fella with a grey beard and a ciggie dangling from his mouth came in, and I thought he was the caretaker.

"And all he could say was 'go away and do it yourselves.' Anyway, I had a crack. It felt great. Just like going to work again. And I was really proud of what I'd written. Then I showed it to Jimmy and he went, 'That's shite, Marty.' But he was letting us make our own mistakes, which is the only way to learn."

The plot centred on a fictional family, the Waltons, loosely based on the Mitchells, with sacked docker Colin Mitchell and his wife, Sue, writing some of the scenes. McGovern floored them when he announced that one of the main characters had to be a scab, and even worse, a loveable one.

"They were gutted. I thought some of them would walk out and not come back. These people had watched scabs take away their livelihoods and here was I telling them to love them. They just didn't get it," he said.

In the end McGovern wrote the scene himself about the courage it takes to cross a picket line and how ultimately a man's principles boil down to what's best for his wife and children.

"When I finished there was total silence with few of them holding back tears of anger and grief," he said. But it worked.

"The following week one of the dockers, Tony Weedon, brought in a piece written from their perspective and it was one of the most powerful scenes I have ever read," said McGovern.

The dramatist had got his way and he topped off that triumph by persuading Ricky Tomlinson to play the scab. Which was a bit like asking Ian Paisley to play The Pope as Tomlinson was one of the Shrewsbury 24, jailed for two years in a 1972 building workers' strike for conspiracy to intimidate on a picket line. Tomlinson told me it was the hardest role he'd ever played.

"In a scene where I crossed the picket line, I had to go into the locker room and cry. And they were real tears because it was an awful feeling sitting there. I felt so lonely and desolate. And the tears were genuine."

He wasn't the only one to shed tears. At the end of the first rough-cut showing of the film, McGovern walked out of the London studio and sobbed his heart out.

"When we were writing it we had our battles and quite a few sessions ended in tears as they relived the events. But mostly we were laughing so much that I forgot how abominably these people had been treated. And then it hit me at the screening. Every aspect of how these people were betrayed. And it all just left me emotionally drained."

I asked Jimmy what he had learnt from it all. "Expressions, mainly. I was born within a stone's throw of the docks but I'd never heard phrases like 'he couldn't pull a cat off a well-polished table.' I realised how all across the world dockers have their own language and culture.

"And someone explained it to me. Whether you are in New York, Sydney or Liverpool, you all work in the same factory. Container ships are just floating factories and men from all over the world leave their identities there."

What did he hope the film might achieve?

"It just might remind people what has been lost. Not lost because it was crushed by Margaret Thatcher but by the leaders of their own union and their own movement, led by a man called Tony Blair who went to public school. And what a loss it was. These people who have been thrown on the scrapheap simply for refusing to cross a picket line are some of the finest people I have ever met in my life."

After 14 months of blood, sweat and tears, Dockers made it to the screen starring Ken Stott, Crissy Rock, Katy Lamont, Christine Tremarco and Tomlinson. It was critically acclaimed and went on to earn a BAFTA nomination for Best Single Drama. But its true legacy was far more significant.

The writers gave their £90,000 fee, plus the 40 per cent of its production fee Channel 4 donated to them, to the Initiative

Factory, a workers' co-operative set up by dockers to re-train and give out advice. With that £127,000 (£230,000 in 2021 prices) they bought and restored a run-down, three-storey building in Liverpool's Hope Street, turning it into a community hub run on not-for-profit, socialist ideals promoting "fairness and justice for all."

The Casa opened on Christmas Eve 2000 and became known across the world as a lasting testament to the spirit of collectivism. A monument to defiance, enterprise and solidarity. The living embodiment of a principled defeat turned on its head.

The bar and function room serve as meeting places for locals, a welcoming point for trade unionists who visit Liverpool, a venue for radical thought, plays, meetings, parties, charity fundraisers, recitals or rallies to promote progressive political causes. In short, an open house for anyone who needs it, run by a formidable manager, Jacqui Richardson, whose professionalism, humour and dedication have been crucial in keeping The Casa afloat.

Her partner Tony Nelson, who runs the business side with fellow sacked docker Terry Teague, said, "The Casa has been used by the Burjesta Theatre group, South Liverpool Against Poverty, Cuban Solidarity, Friends of Palestine, all the trade unions, the Shrewsbury pickets, Spanish Civil War veterans, the Voice campaign against gun crime in Croxteth, members of the Liverpool 47 (former rebel councillors), Liverpool and Everton supporters' groups, Merseyside Asylum Seeker Health and many, many others.

"A member of staff once rang me to say a group meeting in the back room had gone over time and the group waiting in the front were getting angry. It was the pagans in the back and the Christians in the front! But that's us. We don't turn anyone away."

This liberal policy of believing everyone is genuine until proven otherwise has caused the occasional problem. Like the time a group of university professors booked the function room for a fancy dress party.

What they didn't tell The Casa was it was a World War II fancy dress party. Halfway through the night one of the dockers who was drinking in the front bar, Frank Lanigan, went to the toilet and found himself standing next to Adolf Hitler.

After a swift double-take, and self-questioning about how much he'd drunk, he asked, "What the fuck are you doing in The Casa? We detest fascists, you twat," then knocked him out.

Another Hitler appeared to confront him. "Jesus Christ," said Frank, "we only had to fight one Hitler in the war, now there's two in the fucking Casa." The lecturers' wife, dressed as Eva Braun, called the police. And when one of the party, dressed as Benito Mussolini went to give his statement, the police had had enough and sided with The Casa.

Profits from the bar and function room are ploughed into what happens upstairs. Initially, the first-floor became an IT training and enterprise centre, which helped people gain computer skills and find work. The floor above became the home of the Community Advice Services Association, offering free, expert help from professionals about benefits, debt, employment, asylum, health, homelessness and tribunal support.

On The Casa's 99-year lease, agreed with the city council, it was stated that the building's primary function would be to relieve "poverty, sickness and hardship, and advance education in Merseyside." And that is what they have done, winning tens of millions of pounds worth of benefits for people in desperate need, through the care and expertise of volunteers like Tony

Thompson, who sadly passed away, and Terry Craven, a former council welfare officer who received Liverpool City Council's award for Services to Elderly People.

They are there for asylum-seekers who have fallen through the gaps in the system and need to be told how to get back into it. They are there for the homeless, holding open days for those living on the street, giving out hot drinks, food, clothing and a haircut. They are there for people who simply want advice on how to fill out a form to get benefits they are due, then guided in the right direction to claim them. They are there for anyone who doesn't know where to turn and are on the verge of giving up on life.

Tony Nelson believes it has survived because of the honesty, generosity and experience of the people who work there and their supporters: "Us dockers were accused of living in the past but the reason The Casa exists is so we can move forward and try to do something in the community. We had the choice of crying into our beer or re-inventing ourselves as an organisation and still being relevant.

"We are working men and women and it survives because there is no-one in here who gets above themselves. Everyone is on the same wage and we listen to each other. Everyone who comes in here and who works in here is treated with respect and dignity.

"We have saved people's lives in this place. Many people who come to us are desperate for money or advice or just some hope. And we've given them that hope. It doesn't matter who you are, you are going to get help. And we didn't want it to be like a solicitor's office so there are no suits here."

A typical example of their work would be the elderly couple they helped claim an extra £300-a-week benefits due to both being terminally ill and the mother with an autistic child who gained a £200-a-week increase in benefit and £8,800 in arrears. On average, The Casa assists at least four clients a week to claim disability benefits and represents people at appeal tribunals.

These are life-changing interventions for thousands of people at a time when welfare advice centres are being closed as part of an austerity drive that batters the poorest and most vulnerable.

Nothing better summed up their vital work than the case of Stephen Smith, a 64-year-old who was so ill with a series of complex conditions, including chronic obstructive pulmonary disease and osteoarthritis, his weight fell to six stone and he could not walk ten metres without getting out of breath.

Despite his obvious health issues the Department of Work and Pensions (DWP) declared him fit for work and he was told to sign on for a £67-a-week Jobseeker's Allowance and visit the Jobcentre every week.

He was put in touch with The Casa and Terry Craven took up his case, sending two doctors' opinions stating he had difficulty walking even short distances. But the DWP rejected that appeal despite the overwhelming medical evidence. Terry did not give up and battled for a year to be granted a tribunal hearing.

Stephen had by then contracted pneumonia and was taken to hospital. During that stay in Christmas 2018 he was forced to get a pass to allow him to attend the tribunal, which he won. When the story hit the national media the DWP apologised, reassessed his case and gave him all the benefits he was entitled to. He was paid back £4,000 for the Employment and Support Allowance payments he should have received over several years and received more cash when Terry argued successfully that he had been entitled to a Severe Disability Premium.

At the time, Stephen told the *Liverpool Echo's* Liam Thorp that he would have died were it not for Tony Nelson and Terry Craven. "I had nowhere to turn, they saved my life," he said. However, his pneumonia worsened and a few months after the tribunal victory he died.

When Terry heard of Stephen's death he said of him, "He was simply a nice man who had fallen on hard times and when he asked the government to help him, he was humiliated. That he never got the chance to spend the money The Casa won back for him, which is now being used to pay for his funeral, is the ultimate kick in the teeth."

John Pilger wrote during his time doing pieces on the dockers' dispute that, 'As a keeper of the secrets of the blood, sweat and tears of ordinary people, Liverpool has few equals. That is why it excites such prejudice, even hatred, and why the unfashionable resistance of its people endures.'

That unfashionable resistance was amplified by Liverpool's most famous Anglican bishop, David Sheppard, who argued that no people care more for "the community of the left behind" than Liverpudlians. And few people sum that up better than the sacked dockers and those who work today in The Casa honouring their legacy.

I've been a regular visitor since it opened and can be found there most Fridays, arguing and laughing over pints with like-minded friends who I've known since school and others I've met along the way. I celebrated my wedding and my 60th birthday there. My eldest daughter Christie held her 21st party in the back room and they gave my son Phil a job behind the bar in his student days.

When my mum died in 2002 the organising committee held a

meeting to decide how to mark her passing, even though they'd never met her. They just wanted to show their solidarity with me for supporting them during their dispute.

They decided to place a brass plaque in her honour on their Supporters Wall, which read: *Sheila Reade. Lifelong Socialist. One of Us.*

That's the kind of people they are.

The type who would do anything for you. Ones who don't just talk about socialism but put it into practice every day. Which was why, in 2015, when council funding dried up and a long-term tenant moved out, I organised a fund-raising concert for them at Liverpool's Philharmonic Hall featuring John Bishop, The Farm, John Power, and comedians Mark Steel, Ricky Tomlinson, Neil Fitzmaurice and Chris Cairns. Every ticket went within a fortnight, proving how much love was out there for a building so vital to the city's radical identity.

And that's why every penny I make from this book will go to The Casa. To help them sustain their noble fight against poverty and injustice.

When I'm in the bar, I sometimes imagine what my docker grandads would have made of the willingness of a future generation to lose everything to protect the jobs they once had. What they would make of this monument to that valiant struggle built in a street called Hope. I know they would both be immensely proud.

Because this remarkable story says that no matter what you throw at working-class people, when they stick together and fight relentlessly for what they believe in, they won't be beaten.

They will find a way to survive and come back even stronger.

THE PIONEER

7

BARBARA CASTLE

DIAMONDS IN THE MUD

THE SCILLY ISLES — June 1995

THEY packed the small grey-stone church in a far-flung corner of the British Isles to honour the man who won more general elections than any other 21st century leader.

Under blue skies, on the tiny Scilly Isle of St Mary's, the great and the good of the Labour Party paid their last respects to Harold Wilson, who, as Lord Tonypandy said in his eulogy, "burnt himself out for Britain".

My old MP, whom I'd watched merrily puffing on his pipe as 1970s election nights were celebrated like Cup Final wins in Huyton Civic Centre, went out as he lived – simply, without fanfare, pomp, circumstance or fuss, surrounded by the people who cared for him in the tranquil place he loved.

What a contrast with the later passing of Margaret Thatcher, who won one general election fewer than his four, yet was afforded a state funeral in Westminster Abbey. Harold would have loved that. He'd have taken pride in being treated as just another citizen, not some fetishised re-incarnation of Boadicea.

Although, had the Queen and her hubby been allowed into this celebration of his life, his wicked sense of humour would have enjoyed watching them attempt a lusty rendition of the socialist hymn Fight The Good Fight that rocked this little island church.

Centre-stage were the two main women in his life: Mary, his wife of 55 years, and former secretary and gatekeeper Lady Falkender, both dressed in black suits with white blouses and gloves. But there was another woman central to Wilson's political life whose style and aura drew everyone's eyes. The flame-haired dynamo fondly nicknamed The Red Queen, whom Wilson admired so much he pencilled her into all of his cabinets and described her as "perhaps my best minister." Barbara Castle.

When Lord Tonypandy said the following about the man who had died weeks earlier from Alzheimer's, aged 79: "He fiercely believed that the ordinary working people were entitled to live in a just and compassionate society," the Red Queen shook her head and clenched her fist in solidarity.

When he added, "There were no important people in Harold's world. He looked at people and saw them in terms of their possibilities, if only they were given a chance in life," the woman who Wilson made the most influential in Labour's history looked around the church as if to say "and here's your living proof."

Barbara, like me, loved the brilliant man with the pipe and Gannex coat, who smashed the established British rule that you had to be an ex-public schoolboy to enter Number Ten. And when Harold Wilson got there, despite his many difficulties with the economy, he left the country a more educated, open, equal and caring one. And saved many young lives through ignoring pleas from Washington to send our troops into Vietnam, unlike some of the ego-driven glory-hunters who succeeded him.

It was why, after we had followed the six lifeboatmen carrying his coffin out of St Mary The Virgin church towards a beachside graveyard, I sidled over to Barbara and asked if I could have a word.

"What paper are you from?" she fired back. "*The Daily Mirror,*" I replied.

"Well, of course you can have a word with me dear, I used

to work there, didn't I?" she said, referring to her brief time as housing correspondent on the *Mirror* during World War II.

"I thought you were from one of those nasty, Tory rags and were going to ask about my affair with Harold."

My face froze and my mouth had no words to release. Had I stumbled on a world exclusive? Had she decided to finally confirm the rumours now that Harold was gone to the first journalist she spoke to? I had a vision of the first five pages of the next day's *Mirror* covering her bombshell admission and right-wing papers following up with headlines that screamed variations of 'Reds Under The Bedsheets.'

She saw the shock on my face, laughed, and grabbed my arm. "I had you there, didn't I? Of course that's what your colleagues on other papers would have liked to have asked. For years their pages were full of innuendo about us being lovers. It was the same with his secretary, Marcia. All rubbish of course. Just more smears. Oh, how they smeared Harold. And all out of fear."

My face unfroze but my mouth could still release no noise, mainly because I couldn't get a word in.

"And oh, how they hated me for being a powerful woman when such a thing was unheard of," she continued. "I don't know if the editors despised me more for making them get breathalysed after a few drinks in their clubs or giving their women workers equal pay.

"What they could never get their heads around was that Harold trusted women and loved to be in their company. He kept promoting me because he believed in me. He believed in women. He was the first feminist Prime Minister."

Throughout our chat there were constant interruptions from people wanting to give her a hug or kiss her cheek. There was a wave of genuine love towards the closest thing Labour had to royalty. Even though she hadn't been in a Cabinet for two decades.

I asked what she made of the man sat next to her throughout the service, Tony Blair, who was a year into the job as party leader. She thought for a few seconds, then said it was early days, and even though she had backed John Prescott to be leader, she had grown fond of Blair.

"He's shrewd, his heart's in the right place, he has total self-belief, and he could just be the man to evict this awful Tory government that is doing so much harm," she said.

When she asked whether I agreed, I said she was probably right, but she sensed I wasn't 100 per cent with the New Labour project. And inquired why.

I told her that I'd seen something on the coach as we travelled to the church that jarred with me. When we passed Harold's small, grey bungalow, Lowenva, which had been his Scilly Isles holiday home for nearly 40 years, some of the Bright Young Things in sharp suits pointed at it and guffawed.

One of them said in a hushed tone, "why would you spend your holiday in a little council house?" as those around him muffled their laughter. I don't know what angered me most. The disrespect, the disgusting air of superiority or their ignorance of the fact that Harold had been elected to power by people from Huyton, most of whom lived in council houses. Whatever it was, I briefly felt like I was in the wrong political tribe.

The oldest of Old Labour women narrowed her eyes, shook her head and asked, "Really? If that's the future of the Labour Party, then God help us."

I thanked her for the chat and told her I'd like to have a longer one with her at some point so I could do a piece on her which would grace the pages of her old newspaper. "Give me a ring then. I've plenty of time on my hands these days," she said.

So three months later, when we were both attending the Labour Party Conference, I did.

BRIGHTON — September 1995

She gave me two alternatives, but no choice.

"You can see me for a rushed half hour in the morning, darling, or you can take me for a nice, long lunch. By the way I love fish."

The Thinking Man's Lucille Ball, a couple of weeks shy of her 85th birthday, was doing what she'd been doing with such style and nous all of her life: Wrapping men around her finely-manicured fingers.

I met her in the lobby of her Brighton hotel and as I walked her down the steps, her major worry was that the wind rushing in off the Channel would blow her sweep of honey-blonde hair out of place and ruin that morning's work in the hairdressers.

Just as outside that Scilly Isles church she was the focal point of attention. Heads turned and passers-by stopped to thrust their hands at her frail five-foot frame. She was hugged, kissed and feted.

When we reached the restaurant and I guided her to our window table, veteran journalists Jeremy Paxman, John Humphrys and Anthony Howard rose from their seats to greet and pay homage to her.

As she perused the menu it was clear her eyesight was fading, but when I asked her questions she articulated her thoughts with a majesty of language and certainty of mind that shamed politicians half her age.

"Dogs and politics keep me young," she said, dressed in a chic leather jacket with trendy gold chains around her neck, knocking back a large glass of Chardonnay. "Dogs make you walk, politics makes you think. Only boredom makes you old.

"I know I'm losing my eyesight, but it has its advantages. I bump into handsome young men who help me across the road," she said, telling me it's important for a woman to stay a flirt for as long as she can.

"Keep your sex, I once advised my niece Rachel. Use it for power but never give it away," said the woman who was the political role model for every female who wanted to succeed in politics years before Thatcher came along.

"They say opportunity maketh the man, but it's even more so for women. Women always sell themselves short. They're too submissive, too self-denigrating. I never had any problems like that. Although I was never an aggressive feminist, never a man-hater. I love men."

Barbara Betts was born into a staunchly left-wing family in Chesterfield in 1910 and grew up in Bradford. She was the youngest of three children born to Annie, a William Morris socialist, and Frank, a tax collector, and devourer of literature, who wrote socialist poetry and edited the radical left-wing newspaper the *Bradford Pioneer*.

Although the family had a relatively comfortable lifestyle due to Frank's job she came from solid working-class stock. Her maternal grandmother left school at 12 to walk several miles a day to a pen-filling factory in Coventry and had an intense hatred of snobbery. Her daughter, Barbara's mother Annie, who left school at 14 to become an apprentice milliner, was brought up with those same qualities: Hard-working, independent-minded and empathetic to the people she came from.

It was from her gran that she got her doggedness of character. From her father she got her intellect, her love of learning and her politics.

"My father believed in the freedom of ideas. When he married my mother he taught her to smoke because it was unladylike. He hated conventions that held people back. He taught me to believe in myself and never to care what others think," she told me.

Frank also taught her to "despise the money-manipulators in the temple of life" and to align herself "with the oppressed against the rich and powerful." Growing up in Bradford in the 1920s, she saw plenty of oppressed people around her.

He also taught her to despise the phoney patriotism that was being churned out as propaganda during the First World War, a conflict he described as a scrap between competing imperial powers using the working man as cannon fodder. He taught her to never sing Land of Hope and Glory, saying, "love of one's country should broaden one's vision, not narrow it." And he railed against the Treaty of Versailles, calling it vindictive and counter-productive as it would come back to haunt the victors.

"He loved beauty. That's what made him a socialist. I hate ugliness and the fact that people are condemned to live in it. That's why I am a socialist and why my beliefs strengthen as I get older," she told me.

Barbara and her siblings were encouraged to put on plays with socialist themes and the house was always filled with people eager for political discussion.

When the miners were locked out in 1921 her mother, who went on to become a Labour councillor, set up a soup kitchen in the backyard and dished out food to struggling families on a weekly basis.

Her Old Labour credentials were untouchable, but in the 1990s New Labour world, I asked, was she still proud to call herself a socialist?

"Of course I am. It's a beautiful but misinterpreted word. It's not about communism or dictatorship. Socialism simply means sharing things in the national interest. And God knows we need that today.

"You can physically touch the anger, repulsion and hatred people feel towards the fat cat bosses and all this Tory sleaze," she said banging the table, with blazing eyes, making me realise I'd have hated to be on the wrong side of an argument with her in Cabinet.

The bright schoolgirl went to Oxford in 1929 where she became treasurer of the Labour Club, the highest position a woman student could hold at the time. She became a Labour councillor in London's St Pancras in 1937 and a reporter on the left-wing paper *The Tribune* where she fell under the spell of Michael Foot and had a passionate love affair with married journalist William Mellor.

"William taught me a lifelong maxim that's kept me young. 'Think. Think. Think,' he said. 'It will hurt like hell at first but you'll get used to it.'" After Mellor died during the war, Barbara married her night editor at the *Daily Mirror*, Ted Castle.

Despite their inability to have children they enjoyed a blissful married life at their home in the Chilterns until Ted died in 1979. "He was the most generous of men. He would have loved to have entered politics himself but sadly he had to live vicariously through me. That was very hard.

"He envied me but he was never jealous. That is the ideal relationship between a man and a woman. I adored him."

Barbara was elected MP for Blackburn in 1945, and when Labour won power in 1964 she became only the fourth woman ever to hold a Cabinet seat. Michael Foot called her "the best socialist minister I ever saw in action". Her achievements, in her time as Minister for Overseas Development, Minister for Transport, and Secretary of State for Employment and Health and Social Services, were many and varied.

She introduced the statutory right to belong to a trade union, seat-belts, permanent speed limits and breathalysers. She initiated the idea of compensation for unfair dismissal and she replaced the family allowance with enhanced child benefit, ensuring the money was paid to the mothers, not the fathers, against bitter male opposition in the Labour movement. She moulded the first Ministry for Overseas Development and phased out pay beds from the NHS.

When she introduced State Earnings Related Pension Schemes (SERPS) which ensured women would have equal pension rights with men, she was told that was unfair because women retire earlier. Her reply? "Okay, for a change we'll have a bit of sex discrimination against men for a few years shall we?"

She famously intervened to resolve the Ford sewing machinists strike against wage discrimination in 1968 bringing the women up to 92 per cent pay parity with men. More importantly she used that victory to convince the almost completely male government of the need for equal pay and got it on the statute books, making it illegal to hire a woman to do the same job as a man for less money.

Many years later the Ford strike became the subject of the film Made In Dagenham, where Castle was played by Miranda Richardson. In one scene, Richardson delivers this speech to the doddery male civil servants in the Ministry of Labour who told her that her argument had no credence. You can feel Castle's spirit in every word.

"I am what is known as a fiery redhead. Now, I hate to make this a matter of appearance and go all womanly on you, but there you have it. And me standing up like this is in fact just that red-headed fieriness leaping to the fore. Credence? I will give credence to their cause. My God, their cause already has credence! It is equal pay. Equal pay is common justice and if you two weren't such a pair of egotistical, chauvinistic, bigoted dunderheads you would realise that."

Like most politicians who go out on a limb for their beliefs and relish the art of combat, Castle wasn't universally loved, even amongst her own. Transport and General Workers Union leader Jack Jones, who fell out with her over her doomed In Place Of Strife paper which sought to limit the power of the unions by outlawing wildcat strikes, called her "The Queer One." Gerald Kaufman, citing her undoubted vanity, referred to her as "the Norma Desmond of politics always ready for her close-up." And when Harold Wilson retired in 1976 on health grounds his successor, and her nemesis, James Callaghan, chucked her out of the Cabinet.

He asked her to resign, under the excuse that he wanted to lower the average age of the cabinet. She refused, saying he'd have to sack her. So he did. Later she would say that one of her biggest regrets was not saying back to Callaghan, who was a mere 18 months younger than her, "If you want to bring the average age down by sacking older people why don't you start with yourself."

The Guardian's then political editor Ian Aitken came up with four reasons why he believed she was overlooked to be party leader in favour of Callaghan, whom she was a far superior performer to: "Because she was a woman, because she was too left-wing, because she didn't go out of her way to make friends and because she didn't try to build herself support." Roy Hattersley put it more succinctly: "She had an infinite capacity for annoying people." Castle herself knew it was her attempt to take on and reign in the trade unions when they were at the peak of their power that did for her.

After 34 years as Blackburn's MP she became an MEP in the North West, where she was once accused at an election rally of being "too old and past it" by Liberal MP Cyril Smith.

Quick as a flash she came back with, "Well, you're too fat and never made it."

In 1990 she was made a life peer. I told her I was surprised such a passionate socialist as her accepted the offer to join the House of Lords and she told me she did so reluctantly and after much thought.

"Ted was made a peer in 1974 which meant I was technically Lady Castle but I refused to use the title or be addressed by it because I hadn't earned it. It was patronising and wrong. But when the Labour Party offered me a peerage in my own right I thought maybe I should join the hated cosy club, and because Labour had pledged to abolish it, I could be there to help close the place down. Besides, I love its library."

As she finished her meal I asked what she thought were the greatest qualities a politician could have. "Be true to yourself, aim high and stay unflinching in your refusal to let down the people you represent.

"If you see an injustice, always attack the perpetrator. I've attacked all my life. You've got to dare to be yourself. To come out of your corner fighting for what you believe in. And never apologise."

As the waiter took her plate she touched up her hair, and asked him for a sprig of parsley telling me she couldn't risk the meal leaving a smell of garlic on her breath because "you never know who you're going to meet."

The next time I met her was four years later at a Labour conference when she showed exactly what she meant by fighting for what you believe in regardless of who you upset.

Her first conference speech in 1943 had been a fierce attack on the wartime national government's proposals to delay implementation of the Beveridge Report which recommended setting up the welfare state. In 1999 at Bournemouth, 56 years later, she took to the stage to tear into her own government over its refusal to restore the link between wage rises and pensions, a policy she had introduced.

She was a year short of her 90th birthday but attacked them with such vehemence and style, and drew such raucous approval from the audience, it went down as one of the great moments in Labour conference history. And forced Tony Blair and Gordon Brown into an embarrassing u-turn.

She was helped on to the stage by conference managers who were always happy to let her have a socialist rant as they felt it helped make New Labour look like a broad church. But the business of modern conferences had become so controlled they knew her radical demands would never be put to a vote. So it was really a sop to a bygone era with little risk to the party's ratings among Middle England focus groups. Well, in theory at least.

The fiery orator who began her political career in the 1930s by touring the country talking publicly on street corners and packed halls was in her element that day. She was as skilled at old-fashioned rabble-rousing as the best of them. Plus, she had immense stage presence and a natural star quality. Which she knew. And milked.

She looked her usual immaculate self as she made it to the podium, wearing a gold top that matched her earrings and a red waistcoat that matched her soul. Her eyesight was so bad by now she couldn't read her words with any confidence, so she consigned her 12-minute speech to memory, delivering what felt like a spontaneous tour de force. The more she looked like a cuddly old granny the more she bared her teeth and showed what a ruthless operator she was. By linking pension to inflation not earnings, she told them, it meant just a 1.1 per cent rise for the backbone of the nation. "This means a pension increase of 72p – a fair price for a bag of peanuts."

When her time overran, and conference chairman Vernon Hince ordered her to finish her speech and get off the podium, the delegates who were lapping up her every word booed and jeered him. She finished off with a stark warning: "Just bear in mind comrades what you are doing here this afternoon." And was serenaded off-stage with a thunderous ovation.

Back in the press room the New Labour PR spin doctors were briefing against her, spreading patronising poison about an old dear who was well past her sell-by date. I became involved in a row with Gordon Brown's press officer, telling him Barbara had more Labour DNA in a single fingertip than half the Burton Dummies in the Cabinet. When he tried to win the argument by bringing in a prominent *Daily Mail* columnist to back him up by denigrating Castle, I told him he'd proved my point.

The Red Queen had certainly proved hers. That afternoon she took her one-woman pensions campaign on to national radio accusing Blair of delivering a "mishmash of moralising" and said, "I get so cross at this suggestion that people who have contributed all their lives to the basic pension are trying to scrounge off the taxpayer.

"What worries me is that the government keeps on saying that the basic pension is to be the foundation of security for everybody. But that is shrivelling in value in relation to the national income by the government's refusal to restore the link with the movement of earnings, which I introduced as a minister in 1974."

That day's performance shamed Gordon Brown into properly addressing pensions and Tony Blair to admit it was his most serious mistake in office. Mind you, that was before Iraq.

As I headed back to my hotel room, I saw her holding court in the lobby and waited my turn to tell her she'd been magnificent in the conference hall. She could barely recognise anyone due to her failing eyesight so I reminded her that I'd taken her for lunch in Brighton four years ago and she said she remembered. I also told her we'd spoken after Harold Wilson's funeral, which she couldn't recall, so I reminded her of my misgivings over some of the characters in the New Labour project. But, ever-loyal to her party, she refused to put the leadership down.

"Oh, undoubtedly some of them are charlatans and opportunists. But there's good people at the top of our party too. And at least we're in power now. So it's up to us to keep our ministers on their toes by fighting the good fight. I might not have long left but I'll keep fighting until my last breath," she said, before being mobbed by a new group of admirers, some of whom were young enough to be her great-grandchildren.

Barbara died in 2002, aged 91, of pneumonia and chronic lung disease in her small house in rural Buckinghamshire. The tributes, from across the political spectrum, hailed her as one of the pivotal female figures in British political history.

Despite being attacked by her in her final years, Blair called her "courageous, determined, tireless and principled, never afraid to speak her mind or stand up for her beliefs. She was loved throughout the Labour movement and recognised as an outstanding minister."

Labour's Minister for Women, Patricia Hewitt, said, "Barbara was a hero to millions of British women. She inspired a new generation of women to become active in Labour politics. Unlike Margaret Thatcher, who never appointed another woman to her cabinet, Barbara was a feminist who staunchly advanced the cause of women."

I wrote a tribute to her in *The Mirror* saying that British politics had produced no woman better than her and few men her equal. That she was, at national level, Labour Party's one true, genuine heroine. Indeed, to a generation on the Left, she had been the only female political icon to aspire to.

In truth, she reminded me a lot of my mum who died four months before her. Sheila, like Barbara, had the same hatred of privilege and desire for equality that fired my political spirit from an early age. My mum, like her mother and her sisters, loved Barbara Castle because she took no shit from men and gave their generation hope that real change could be brought about for working women.

Growing up, some of my happiest memories were in the Wavertree Labour Club and Huyton Civic Centre, where I would go with my mum in the 60s and 70s on General Election nights in the hope of cheering home a Labour victory.

I can still smell the beer and the smoke and hear the raucous cheers on the nights that Harold Wilson won. I can see his broad smile above the trademark pipe in Huyton waving at us all before going back to the Adelphi Hotel to pencil in his new cabinet of heavyweights containing the likes of Barbara Castle, Michael Foot, Denis Healey and Tony Benn.

Those precious memories ensured whatever happened in my life I could never put an 'x' in a box for someone standing against a Labour candidate. There have been times when I found myself unable to vote for a Labour man or woman but never, ever for another party. It's what you are. Where you come from. What I was brought up to be loyal to. The side I was born on.

The Red Queen had died three weeks after Britain came to a standstill for the funeral of The Queen Mother. The contrast in the way each passing was treated by the nation was stark.

One had the TV schedules wiped out, 40-page newspaper supplements published in her honour, a week of official mourning and a state funeral with no fanfare spared. The other received a one-page tribute in the paper she used to work for, *The Daily Mirror*, and less in most of the others.

I know which one I regarded as the national treasure. Not the one with her own standard, a crown with the Koh-i-Noor diamond on top, and a host of palaces where she spent a pampered century living off the State. But the one who devoted her life to ensuring the State worked for its people.

The one who did more for her own generation in that one conference analogy about a bag of peanuts than the other did in her entire 101 years.

Not the Windsor but the Castle.

THE JOY
BRINGERS

8

BILL
SHANKLY

BOB
PAISLEY

ANFIELD — *July 2020*

EVERYTHING about the occasion seemed surreal.
The sun was still out on a muggy July evening, the pubs around the ground that should have been so rammed half their customers were carousing on pavements had their doors locked and the stadium was silent except for the eerie echoes of warm-up instructions being barked at the players.

That night the sign above the entrance to the pitch should have read This Isn't Anfield.

The fastest-ever winners of the English league title, in terms of games, had endured the longest-ever wait to pick up their trophy. And when they did, their home was virtually deserted.

But this was 2020. When Covid struck and football stopped at a point when Jürgen Klopp's relentless team was almost able to reach out and put polish on the silverware that had most eluded them. They were 25 points clear with nine games to go when their fans plunged into purgatory as calls were made to scrap the season and void all results, just as England had done in 1939 when war was declared on Hitler.

And this after the most painful of waits for an English league title that felt like it had stretched as far back as that war. Thirty years in which a regular habit had become a serial curse. When there had been so many near-misses, so many anti-climaxes, so many rival fans telling Kopites their sense of entitlement was embarrassing. Because no big club goes three decades without a league title, especially when minnows like Blackburn Rovers and Leicester City have etched their name on the trophy.

But in some ways July 22, 2020, was the most familiar of nights. Anfield Road was lined with crowds festooned in red-

and-white, flags were out, anthems were roared and there were even cheers when news spread that the enemy, Manchester United, were losing at home to West Ham.

And then the bus came into sight bearing a Liverpool squad who had just obliterated all domestic opposition to regain a status that used to be bestowed on them with unprecedented regularity. The 21st century version of rattles – plumes of red smoke rising from flares – lit up the L4 sky as the bus cut through a crimson summer mist to enter the bowels of the old citadel, Anfield.

Inside, it was business as usual for a Liverpool title coronation. Five goals were put past a London side (Chelsea) in a crushing exhibition of superiority, just as in 1964 when Arsenal were thrashed to end the previous longest title drought of 17 years.

And the celebrations may have belonged to a more modern, pyrotechnically-choreographed age, but there was no doubting the sense of ecstasy that connected the players and manager to supporters who gathered outside the ground or huddled around TV screens in every corner of the world.

The eloquent Jürgen Klopp had issued a carpe diem call to his players. A decree to seize the day, embrace the fruits of their hard work, and imagine that the stadium was packed to the rafters. He and the squad took to a makeshift stage on the Kop looking like a shower of matchday tourists who had wandered in from the museum: Scarfs around wrists, reverse baseball hats and flashing phones, their faces beaming as they looked down at the green brilliance of the Anfield pitch under floodlights.

The man chosen to hand over the medals and the trophy was Kenny Dalglish. Chosen because he was the club's most celebrated player and the manager who was last in charge when Liverpool were crowned English champions in 1990. An umbilical link to a glorious past.

Outside Anfield, as the delirious crowds thickened against police advice, fireworks soared and the vast repertoire of songs was plundered. One in particular: "We've conquered all of Europe, we're never gonna stop. From Paris down to Turkey, we've won the fuckin' lot. Bob Paisley and Bill Shankly, the fields of Anfield Road, we are loyal supporters and we come from Liverpool … allez, allez, allez."

Those wise old sages, Paisley and Shankly, who built, then expanded, Liverpool until it became a dynasty that conquered the bloody world were looking on in bronze.

As fans clambered on to the statues of the two simple, working-class men who made it all possible, you couldn't help but think how chuffed they would have been had they lived to see this day.

Paisley's statue evokes an image of the ultimate servant of 44 years, carrying an injured player, Emlyn Hughes, off the pitch, with these words of his etched on to the plinth: "This club has been my life. I'd go out and sweep the street and be proud to do it for Liverpool FC if they asked me to."

Shankly's statue captures him celebrating the 1973 title win in front of the Kop: A fan's scarf around his neck, arms outstretched, chin jutting, clenched fists pumping the air and the simple but profound words on his plinth saying, 'He made the people happy.'

Both encapsulated the spirit of this globally-respected sporting institution, mainly because they forged it. A spirit based on collectivism and solidarity which the manager inside the stadium that night, Jürgen Klopp, claimed as the bedrock of his own political philosophy and cited as a big reason he was drawn to Liverpool and the gargantuan task of returning them to the pinnacle of world football. Which he succeeded in doing by following in the tradition of Shankly. By turning Anfield into a bastion of invincibility that made even the best players in Europe cower at its full-throated force.

As cameras relayed images of that long-awaited title celebration around the globe, Liverpool in its newly-rebuilt stadium, with its squad of expensive players, its vast fan base, rich American owners and stable of blue-chip sponsors, looked wealthy. It was. With an estimated value exceeding £2 billion, only a handful of clubs were more affluent.

But that wealth was largely sustained through those three long decades when Liverpool could not win their own domestic title by the legacy of those two titans, Shankly and Paisley. The club remained one of the world's biggest because the foundations that supported it were so strong that its allure only grew.

It was why, when civil war broke out in European football in April 2021 as a dozen of the biggest clubs announced they were breaking away to form a closed-shop Super League, Liverpool's American owners took the biggest kicking. Not least from their own fans who expressed their disgust by hanging flags outside the ground that read 'SHAME ON YOU RIP LFC 1892-2021' and demanding their banners be removed from the Kop.

There were even calls to take down the Shankly statue from people who rightly pointed out that this shameless wealth-grab went against everything he stood for.

Liverpool's principal owner John Henry relented after two days of ferocious personal attacks and issued a grovelling apology. But the damage had been done and it felt like he would struggle to ever be welcomed into Anfield again.

The morning after the European Super League story broke I was sat on the steps of Liverpool's St George's Hall, waiting to go inside to watch a video-link to the trial in Salford of three men accused of perverting the course of justice following the Hillsborough Disaster.

Despairing at the unjustifiable act of greed that Liverpool's owners had signed up to, I doubted I'd be able to renew my Kop season ticket if the breakaway went ahead.

As the reality of that dawned, an image came to me of my 13-year-old self, almost 50 years earlier to the week, gazing at the same steps amid a vast crowd that had descended on Lime Street to hear Bill Shankly speak.

And I wondered how football had allowed itself to lose sight of its one and only point: Making the people happy.

LIME STREET, LIVERPOOL — May 1971

I t was the first time I had felt the power of oratory raise my neck hairs.

Less than 24 hours earlier I had been inconsolable, left devastated by the sight of Arsenal's Charlie George lying on the Wembley turf with arms outstretched while, behind him, Liverpool goalkeeper Ray Clemence was on his knees gripping the post, with the net still rustling.

I'd seen the Reds lose an FA Cup final for the first time in my life and it hurt badly. On the Sunday I awoke feeling empty and in need of reassurance that this new Liverpool team we were witnessing would come back stronger next year.

That the five-year trophy drought would soon be over and I'd watch the birth of Bill Shankly's second great team. I sought strength in a solo pilgrimage to welcome home the beaten team in Liverpool city centre not knowing what to expect.

When I arrived early into Lime Street, unable to get within 50 yards of St George's Hall, it was clear that almost a quarter-of-a-million people had sought similar solace.

Up there on the steps of the vast neo-classical building the defeated team stood stony-faced in their Wembley suits. Then Shankly took the mic, spread his arms out and standing under those huge columns like Caesar on a triumphant return to Rome, told us, "Chairman Mao could never have seen such a show of red strength."

The appreciative yells made the cement below me shake. And then a reverential silence descended as the great man addressed us…

"Yesterday we lost the Cup. But you, the people, have won everything. Since I came here to Liverpool, to Anfield, I've drummed it into my players, time and again, that they are privileged to be playing for you. If they didn't believe it, they will now."

His speech was punctuated with wild applause and chants of "Shankly, Shankly" which only ceased with the raising of his hand. He promised us that this team was going places. He vowed that he would take them back to Wembley and win it for us. And we believed him because he had drawn us under his spell. His mesmeric performance had left us putty in his hands.

I walked away from St George's Hall feeling as though I'd just had an audience with a messiah who was part Robin Hood,

Martin Luther King and Jesus Christ. It certainly felt like a religious event, one where the preacher helped us to exorcise the demons of defeat by convincing us we would soon be feasting on the milk and honey of the Promised Land.

Shankly cultivated this divine connection, claiming that supporting Liverpool "is more than fanaticism, it's a religion. To the many thousands who come here to worship, Anfield isn't a football ground, it's a sort of shrine."

Three years later, when the Scot kept his word by leading Liverpool back to the FA Cup final in which they thrashed Newcastle 3-0, photographers caught an image any religious leader would have been pleased with. Two grown men, on their knees, bowing down and kissing his shoes.

It is easy for a football manager, any leader really, to tell their followers how much they mean to them, but with Shankly it never appeared remotely fake. Not least because he backed his words up with actions.

He brought the fans with him on the journey to the top, making them central to his vision. His greatest fear was that anyone might think he'd cheated them. He loathed selling others short.

It's why virtually every person who ever wrote to him had a personal reply, hammered out on his old typewriter, in the parlour of his small semi-detached house in West Derby. Why every kid who knocked on his door was given what they wanted: A chat, a joke, an autograph or a "yes" to a request to have a kick-about on the nearby playing fields that now bear his name.

Few other managers or players were doing that at the time and hardly any today would recognise that level of devotion, let alone engage in it. It continued after he'd retired as Liverpool manager and stood with fans on the Kop for a match in 1975. Throughout the game the fans sang, "Shankly is our king."

He once wrote an article in the *Liverpool Echo*, saying that he would help any genuine supporters who were having difficulty in obtaining tickets. Many took him up on that offer, including me, with a heart-jerking begging letter rewarded with a ticket for the 1974 FA Cup final. It was reported that after John Lennon asked the club for tickets for the 1971 FA Cup final, Shankly replied, "I've never seen any of The Beatles standing on The Kop. Any ticket I have spare will be going to my mates on the Kop."

England goalkeeper Ray Clemence recalled coming home from an away game on the same train as the fans and when Shankly saw an inspector threatening to throw some of them off for not having a valid ticket, he paid their fares. Then thanked the fans for their loyalty in following his team and asked the players to do the same.

He would instil into every footballer he signed that the fans weren't the most important people at the club – they were the only people. And while they were paying your wages you never treated them with anything less than utmost respect.

Liverpool supporters have taken a lot of stick over the years for a perceived mawkishness and, especially in the 30 years the club couldn't win the English title, an unearned air of superiority. When the club's own marketing gurus cashed in on that perception by dreaming up a slogan 'This Means More', it was hard to shoot down the accusations.

Rightly or wrongly, Shankly made us feel that way. He instilled the idea that Liverpool fans were the most special part of the most special club in world sport. He believed that 90 per cent of success was in the mind. You must believe you are the best or you have no chance of succeeding. He imbued a sense of invincibility which shone through on those famous European nights when teams would cower when confronted with the primitive roar of Anfield and miracles would happen.

That started before a European Cup semi-final in 1965 when Shankly sent out two injured players, Gerry Byrne and Gordon Milne, to parade the FA Cup they had won days earlier, whipping the crowd into a frenzy which blew away Inter Milan.

The fans adored him for it. At other clubs it's the star striker or midfielder whose name is sung and whose image adorns flags, but Kopites elevated Shankly to idol status. It's a tradition respected to this day. Indeed, before every game, a huge banner passes over the Kop with images of the managers who have brought home the trophies. Shankly forged that unique communion between the dugout and the terraces and any manager who has failed to appreciate that has not lasted.

In 2008, when Liverpudlians realised that their new American owners were hedge-fund sharks who had bought the club with loans that would leave a crippling debt, a hardcore of fans formed a union whose aim was to evict them from Anfield. Its name was unanimously agreed on: Spirit of Shankly.

It was a badge of defiance. It said we have certain standards at this club which date back to the man who built the modern version of it. His principles of honesty, self-sacrifice and communal effort for the greater good are the ones we live by. Tom Hicks and George Gillett were told that their get-rich-quick ethos was the very antithesis of those principles, meaning they did not belong at Anfield. And they would eventually be evicted. Because Liverpool FC is guided by the Spirit of Shankly or it dies.

Shankly's granddaughter Karen Gill, a woman who has inherited many of her grandad's finest traits, sent this letter of support when the union was formed. It said it all.

'I would like to thank each and every one of you for honouring my grandfather's name by calling this union Spirit of Shankly. For me though, it's more than just honouring his name. In these times of corporate gluttony I am truly heartened to discover there are still so many people who embody my grandad's spirit. It's an Olympic spirit – passionate, pure and true. It's a dream of greatness and glory which comes from dedication, hard work and integrity. In this dream money is only a means to an end, not the end itself.

'My grandad had a dream for Liverpool Football Club and you are all helping to keep that dream alive. It's the people with dreams who achieve things in the end because they have a vision which drives them on.

'We know Bill Shankly 'made the people happy' but I know that you would have all made him happy were he alive to see this legendary support today. I speak on behalf of the Shankly family when I say that we are wholeheartedly behind the Spirit of Shankly.'

Bill Shankly was born in 1913 in the Ayrshire coal mining village of Glenbuck which had a population of fewer than 700 people. By the time he was leading Liverpool to glory in the 1960s it was bordering on a ghost town.

Shankly's parents, John and Barbara, had ten children; five boys and five girls, with Bill, or Willie as the family called him, the youngest boy. All five Shankly lads went on to play professional football with Shankly typically claiming that, at their peak, they'd have beaten any other five brothers alive.

Times were bleak during the First World War and the Great Depression of the 1920s and coal-mining communities were among the hardest hit. Abject poverty and genuine hunger was all around him.

When Bill left school, aged 14, after a very basic education, he worked as a miner for two years until the pit closed and he was thrown on the dole. But by now the football fanatic was playing for local sides, most notably Cronberry Eglinton, cycling the 24-mile round-trip from Glenbuck to get to games. It was there he was spotted by Carlisle United who, in 1932, offered him a contract. As someone who had always known that football was his destiny, he didn't hesitate to sign.

A year later he joined Preston North End, where he established himself as a hard, tough-tackling, exceptionally fit right-half and stayed at Deepdale 16 years, where there is now a stand named in his honour.

The crowning moment of his career was victory in the 1938 FA Cup final, although he played 12 times for Scotland and said that pulling on the dark blue shirt against England filled him with "unbelievable pride."

Shankly was 26 when the Second World War broke out and like so many professional footballers of his generation it claimed his best years. He joined the RAF and played as an amateur throughout the war but he also made a name for himself as a middleweight boxer, winning a trophy when he was stationed in Manchester. One wartime result he would never regret was meeting and marrying Nessie, who was in the Women's Auxiliary Air Force.

Shankly's knowledge of the game and the natural authority he exuded in the dressing room made it inevitable he would move into football management. But at first it was a struggle. He started at Carlisle, then had spells with Grimsby, Workington and Huddersfield. The highest position he would achieve during those years was 12th in the Second Division.

Yet his tactical nous was being noticed. He was one of the first managers to realise that while width was an essential, in modern football it was not enough for wingers to stand on the touchline waiting for the ball to reach them. They had to track back and cut inside.

And his knack for spotting and developing young talent, such as the precocious Denis Law, whom he gave his Huddersfield debut to when he was 16, brought him to the attention of bigger clubs.

As Shankly would tell me years later, "I can figure out if someone is a footballer by throwing a ball at them when they walk into a room. How they react, how their body approaches that ball and whether they succeed in controlling it can tell me if they have what it takes."

Liverpool were in no doubt that he had what it took when they approached him to be their manager in the winter of 1959. Chairman T.V. Williams asked him how he would like to manage the best club in England, and Shankly replied, "Why? Is Matt Busby packing it in?" But he took the Liverpool job, albeit with some preconditions: That he had total control of all aspects of the training and playing, and that he picked the team without any interference from above. Demands that were unprecedented in 1950s English football.

That decade had not been kind to Liverpool. They had been

relegated to Division Two in 1954 and, before Shankly's arrival, had finished four successive seasons in the top four without winning promotion. Cynics believed this suited the unambitious board who were happy to hang around the upper-half of the Second Division on healthy average gates of 35,000 with little need to spend or take financial risk.

The infrastructure was also in a state of dire neglect, especially at the Melwood training ground where they didn't even have running water. Shankly initiated a seismic shift in priorities, transforming the place through sheer force of his personality, demanding the money to refurbish Melwood and build a team around his two prime targets: fellow Scots Ron Yeats and Ian St John. He introduced modern training methods and treatment rooms. He gave the club a new professionalism and instilled the self-confidence and optimism that saw it fly.

In 1962 they won the Second Division title by eight points, and remarkably, the First Division title only two years later, followed by the FA Cup in 1965, for the first time in the club's history, and a second league title the following year.

There then followed a seven-year trophy drought, in which Liverpool were always near the top of the league, but never capable of regaining what Shankly referred to as "this club's bread and butter." It was widely-believed that he was too slow to break up that great team of the mid-60s because he almost looked on them as sons.

But when he did wield the axe his fine eye for young talent saw him rebuild a team in the early-70s around unknown lower league players like Kevin Keegan and Ray Clemence, who would become the finest in Europe in their positions.

Shankly won his third league title in 1973, along with the UEFA

Cup, making him the first manager of an English club to win a European trophy in the same year as becoming champions.

By now, Liverpool fans were utterly besotted with him and the feeling was mutual, his respect for them summed up during a lap of honour after Liverpool regained the title at Anfield in 1973.

A boy at the front of the Kop threw his scarf at Shankly's feet, and a policeman kicked it away, only for his wrath to descend. "Don't do that" said Shankly, picking up the scarf and tying it around his neck. "That scarf is this boy's life."

In 1974 Shankly's young side put on a masterful show at Wembley to demolish Newcastle 3-0 and bring home the FA Cup, but to everyone's surprise that would be Shankly's last competitive game in charge of the club. After 15 years he called it a day.

It wasn't the first summer he had told the board he had taken the club as far as he could. In 1967 he typed his resignation letter after missing out on the signing of Preston's Howard Kendall, who instead joined Everton. But in July 1974, at the age of 60, after writing this letter to the chairman, he stuck to his guns.

Dear Sir,
I would like to retire as Manager of Liverpool Football Club as soon as possible and would be grateful if you would take the necessary steps for my pensions to commence.
Yours faithfully,
W. Shankly.

A press conference was held on July 12, at which the chairman John Smith announced Shankly's desire to retire and the news hit Liverpudlians like a blow from a blunt instrument. Half the city was plunged into a state of deep shock, summed up by a banner headline on the front of the *Liverpool Echo*:

SOCCER BOMBSHELL – SHANKLY RETIRES

Nobody could figure out why he was going. There were many theories, from an irreconcilable fall-out with the board to a misguided belief that his insurance company which held his retirement fund was about to fold. His own explanation was that he felt burned out.

One of Shankly's most intelligent players, maths graduate Brian Hall, put it down to the heat of the job. "He put enormous pressure on himself because every time he stood up in front of people, whether it be the media boys, fans at a dinner or a school function, he had to produce a performance that was Shankly-like.

"It had to be dramatic, it had to be poignant, it had to hit nails on heads. I just have a sneaky feeling that the pressures of football management and the pressures of who he was and how he had to perform in front of people became too much in the end."

None of it made sense to me, a besotted 16-year-old whose idol had broken his heart, so a year later I tried to find out for myself, by writing to him and asking if I could interview him for the school magazine.

With characteristic generosity he wrote back on his battered typewriter:

Dear Brian, I am at Melwood most mornings between 10am and noon. If you can come down we can have a chat.

I could come down.

MELWOOD TRAINING GROUND, LIVERPOOL
— July 1975

I t may have been a baking hot summer's day but my blood was shivering.

He pulled up in a green Ford Capri and bounced out looking full of health, a smile cracking his craggy features. "You must be the ace reporter then, son?" he asked, reaching for my hand. "I hope you've got some good questions for me."

A year after he'd walked into the Anfield boardroom to announce his retirement, feeling, as he put it, like he was walking to the electric chair, he still saw Liverpool's training ground as his workplace, heading there, whenever he was allowed, to be close to the things that mattered to him most outside of his family – football, football pitches and football people.

That line about being at Melwood "most mornings" wasn't strictly true. He was there in the mornings when the first-team players were not. And this being pre-season when only the groundsmen and the odd apprentice were in, Shanks had the keys to his old palace.

Halfway through the 1974/75 season, chairman John Smith was forced into doing something which a few months earlier would have had him hung for treason: Barring Shankly from Melwood when the players were there.

The club justified it on the grounds that his successor, Bob Paisley, was finding it hard enough stepping into his shoes without having him around players who, throughout their careers, had called one 'Boss' and the other 'Bob'.

But it was hard for Shankly to take and didn't sit right with many Liverpool fans when news of his exile became public.

Especially after Shankly revealed in his autobiography that he had found sanctuary across the city's great divide. 'I have been received more warmly by Everton than I have been by Liverpool,' he wrote.

Indeed, he would often turn up at Everton's training ground, a stone's throw from his house, where he would train and help coach the junior teams. But there was no resentment visible at Melwood that hot July day in 1975, when he skipped up the steps to the changing rooms and beckoned me to join him. "Magnificent isn't it?" he purred, picking up a shirt and shorts from a big wicker hamper. "This is where we prepare for greatness, son."

He talked as he changed. About my school De La Salle, which he at first frowned at, fearing it was a rugby school. "I hate rugby son. Why would you want to change the perfect round shape of a football into one so ugly?" he asked, only half joking.

When I threw the kind of questions you would expect a smitten teenager to ask, about his favourite this and his best that, he barely needed to think before the reply was out.

Best game at Anfield? Inter Milan, 1965, when "we tore apart the finest side in Europe, only to go over there and be denied the chance to become the first English team to reach a European Cup final by a travesty of refereeing justice."

Best player? "Of all time, Tom Finney, without a doubt." Best one he'd had at Anfield? He name-checked a dozen before settling on an unlikely winner, full-back Gerry Byrne. "The best professional of the lot. Hard and skilful every game but above all honest. And that is the greatest quality of all."

I listened entranced, nodding in agreement. But I couldn't help thinking that the more I probed him about the great players and past glories, the spark in his eyes dulled. An air of sadness hung over him as he looked around the changing room pointing out to me which pegs the likes of Ian St John and Roger Hunt used to hang their slacks.

This had been his home for years, where the legends he had brought to the club like Kevin Keegan, Emlyn Hughes and Ray Clemence still thrived. But a home he no longer inhabited, simply because something had told him when he reached 60 that it was time to call it a day.

It felt like looking at a weekend dad who had seen his kids taken away, and despite his love for them being as strong as ever, was being denied all but the most fleeting of contact.

"You see here? You see Melwood," he rasped when I asked him what the club had been like when he arrived in 1959. "It was a wasteland. I built it up with these hands. Every blade of grass, Every single brick. Aye. All of it."

It was as though he were talking about a love he had rashly abandoned. As though he'd jilted a woman then realised she was the irreplaceable passion of his life and he would never have her back. His soulmate gone forever.

I could tell he was beating himself up, searching for something to fill the great void in his existence, and failing woefully. He had few other interests.

He would do a spot of gardening and clean the oven as self-punishment whenever Liverpool lost. He hated golf and travel, holidaying for one week every year in the same Blackpool hotel. He didn't have the patience for books, cinema or theatre and all he really wanted to watch on TV, apart from old Jimmy Cagney films, was football.

He couldn't even let alcohol blot out the sadness because

he didn't drink. Football was his drug and he had sentenced himself to a life of cold turkey.

The main reason I was there, apart from being able to share the same air as my all-time hero, was to find out why he'd walked out of our lives a year ago. I hoped for the answer he'd given no-one but got the one he gave everyone.

"Well, the time felt right. We'd won the league, the UEFA Cup and then the FA Cup, so I knew I'd given Liverpool a second great team that could really reach the heights again. It felt like I'd done my time and it was time for someone else."

I told him that it didn't make sense. He'd gone through those hard, lean years when we couldn't win a title and had to break up his first great team and now he had a second one, that could be even better. So why not lift the club to even greater heights?

"I felt tired, son, if I'm honest. It comes to us all. I wasn't getting any younger and the break had to come at some time. I couldn't go on forever. And I felt I owed it to my family, after 40 years in the game, to step back."

I argued that he, of all people, could have handled it, because he was mentally tough and was the fittest 60-something I'd ever seen. I expected him to laugh and put me straight but his expression intensified and he looked into the distance as though that very thought now haunted him.

"Maybe I could. Maybe I couldn't. But you have to understand what this job is like. My work followed me everywhere and it was there every waking moment. You don't have a spare second to think of anything outside it. It grinds you down. You need a break."

"So why didn't you take one and come back?" I asked.

"Oh no, son. That's not the right thing to do. The right decision for me and the club was to make a clean break and give someone else a chance. And Bobby Paisley is doing a fine job." I asked if he regretted it and he gave off a forced laugh.

"No, no, not at all," he barked, unconvincingly. "You can't afford to have regrets in life. It gets you nowhere. Besides, I'm having a great time. Never felt better. I've plenty to keep me happy with my family. And the phone never stops ringing with people asking for advice or offering me jobs. I give advice but I won't take the jobs. I'm enjoying retirement too much. Besides…"

He let that word drift off without finishing the sentence but it was clear he was thinking, 'where could I go after here? This was my life. To go anywhere else would be betrayal.'

The emptiness he was feeling and the act he was putting on to disguise it was tragic to behold.

Back then, like virtually everyone outside of family, I didn't know the inner-turmoil Shankly was putting himself through. How the knowledge he had gone too soon, plus the cold shoulder he was now being shown by the club, was eating away at him. How his belief that the Liverpool hierarchy were intentionally ostracising him had left him feeling deeply wounded.

I didn't find out why Shankly walked away, the main reason being I don't think he honestly knew. I guess it was a combination of things – he was feeling exhausted and thought the grass would be greener in his garden.

Maybe after the demolition of Newcastle in the 1974 FA Cup final, and the plaudits that followed, the student of boxing thought back to the greats who had punched on for too long and persuaded himself that the only way to go was at the top.

The seven years Liverpool had spent in the wilderness and the breaking up of that first great side had left mental scars. Maybe he decided he couldn't risk that painful wilderness again. But I think it had more to do with the principle he held closest to his heart: Loyalty.

When he joined Liverpool in 1959, the backroom staff of Bob Paisley, Joe Fagan and Reuben Bennett expected to be shown the door. But Shankly believed in giving people a chance. He told them their jobs would be safe so long as they gave him their 100 per cent allegiance.

Shanks had demanded and received loyalty throughout his life. Possibly he thought it was time to pay back some of the same to his long-suffering wife Nessie, and his two daughters. That by letting them have some of the hours in the day which had all been given to football he was doing the right thing.

Maybe he had decided that by sharing himself with his family he was staying true to his political beliefs. Shankly's politics were of the old school of Christian socialism, honed in that small, tight-knit Ayrshire mining community. His most famous quote on the subject is this one: "The socialism I believe in isn't really politics. It is a way of living. It is humanity. I believe the only way to live and to be truly successful is by collective effort, with everyone working for each other, everyone helping each other, and everyone having a share of the rewards at the end of the day. That might be asking a lot, but it's the way I see football and the way I see life."

When I asked him for an example of how he saw politics in a practical sense he came up with this gem:

"Liverpool is a great city but right now it's not a clean city. If I became a binman tomorrow, son, I'd be the greatest binman who ever lived and I'd have Liverpool the cleanest city on earth.

I'd take over the whole cleaning operation and make it work, properly, for the people.

"And I'd have everyone working with me, succeeding and sharing out the success. I'd make sure they were paid a decent wage with the best bonuses and that we all worked hard to achieve our goal of total cleanliness.

"Some people might say, ah, but they're only binmen why do we need to reward them so well for a job that anyone with two arms and legs can do? But I'd ask them why they believe they are more important than a binman? I'd ask them to think how proud they would be if this dirty city became the cleanest in the world?

"And who would have made them proud? Aye, the binmen."

Sod studying for A-Levels to get into university. I wanted to pick up a brush, join his army of cleaners, get out in the streets around Melwood and start straight away.

Here was the main reason that Shankly struck a chord with the majority of Scousers. His core philosophy chimed with theirs. Once, when chatting with former Labour Prime Minister Harold Wilson on local radio, Shankly told him proudly that his football teams were always "a form of socialism."

His idea of socialism wasn't mired in party politicking but came from somewhere deep inside. It was of his essence. It defined how he treated other humans: as his equal and with respect. It was about recognising the dignity of the working-class: "I'm a people's man. Only the people matter," he once said.

No other manager at that time had dared to talk about politics, least of all bang the drum about socialism. Probably because they feared being kicked on to the dole by the fine, upstanding Tory businessmen in the boardroom who kept their grounds like abattoirs, their players like slaves, but themselves in the lap of luxury.

Before Shankly, managers were mostly 'yes men' who just picked the team. But this man of vision who demanded full control over playing affairs when he was offered the Liverpool job wouldn't suffer interference from above. As he pointed out in a quote that must have left the more traditional board members raging: "There's a holy trinity at all football clubs. The players, the managers and the supporters. Directors are only there to sign the cheques."

God, I loved him for that. I loved the way he seemed to encapsulate everything I held close to my heart. A Liverpudlian, a football man and a socialist. And captured those concepts with such wit and fire. And when he died, like many thousands of others, I felt bereft.

In September 1981, he suffered a heart attack and was rushed to Liverpool's Broadgreen Hospital. Three days later he had a second one which was fatal. He didn't drink or smoke and took daily exercise. And he was only 68. "When I go, I'm going to be the fittest man ever to die," he would vow. Maybe he was.

The city of Liverpool, not just the red side, was stunned and saddened. The wider world mourned his loss, with the Labour Party Conference standing for a minute's silence in honour of the lifelong socialist.

There were those who said this fit man who had no signs of ill-health had, due to taking retirement too early and being snubbed by the great love of his life, died of a broken heart.

He certainly knew very quickly that retiring at 60 had been a terrible mistake. Football, specifically Liverpool Football Club, had become his everything, his reason to be alive. And he couldn't live without it. As his granddaughter Karen Gill said, "He lived and breathed football from morning to night. If he wasn't watching it, he'd be talking about it or playing. Even when he was having lunch, the whole table would turn into a massive football field and he'd be moving objects around. He couldn't get football out of his mind."

Like all men he wasn't a saint, and had his flaws. He could be cold and dictatorial, treating players who were injured like lepers. Anyone who gave less than their all was told he had "a heart the size of a caraway seed." Tony Hateley, who was one of the finest headers in the game, turned out not to be good enough with his feet for Shankly's liking. "Football's Douglas Bader," he called him before swiftly moving him on.

He distrusted most things foreign and reputedly refused to adjust his watch to local time when he travelled abroad. He could be vain and attention-seeking. He had an overpowering belief that his way was the right way. He expected journalists who worked the Merseyside patch to be as blindly loyal to him as the fans and would savage those who were critical of his work.

But for all that, he was special, inspirational and unique. This book is filled with descriptions of people who have moved me almost beyond words. But none could touch the effect Shankly had. No-one's philosophy has stayed with me through life more than his.

When he wanted to finish the interview he told me he had work to do and shook my hand with his iron grip, walked out of the changing room and broke into a jog, floating off into the distance past the famous sweat-boards he introduced to improve his players' touch, across the pitches he re-laid when he arrived at the dilapidated training ground. Pitches that became the drawing board for the most successful club in British football history, founded by a manager whose popularity has never been matched.

One of the most illuminating examples of the esteem Shankly was held in is a report from Granada journalist Tony Wilson who broke the news of his retirement to passers-by in Liverpool city centre. People of all ages were disbelieving and devastated. A boy of no more than 13 looked as though he was about to burst into tears, and famously said, "You're 'avin' me on, aren't ya?"

It's how you imagine the crowds outside Buckingham Palace will react when they hear the Queen is dead.

If the King of Anfield's abdication left Liverpool fans numb it had also left the board with a seemingly insoluble quandary. How do you replace the man who had become the club? His personality and methods were sunk so deep into the foundations he had laid 15 years earlier, how could Liverpool successfully move forward without him?

Should they go for an equally magnetic personality, and proven winner, like, say, Brian Clough? Do they attempt to repeat the trick they pulled off with Shankly by going for a promising young manager with potential and giving him the platform to fulfil it, like, say Jack Charlton?

They were the routes most observers expected Liverpool to go down. Very few, including the prime candidate, thought they would look much closer to home and promote Shankly's right-hand man Bob Paisley.

The strengths were there for all to see. His loyalty to the club, and his knowledge about it, were unparalleled. But had Liverpool fans become used to a leader who oozed charisma?

And was the club's profile rising to such an extent that to hand the baton down to the number two appeared a lazy move that threatened to take the club back to the unambitious pre-Shankly days of caution and insularity?

Partly inspired by Shankly himself, and the increased media attention of football, by the mid-70s the role of the manager had become box office. Brian Clough, Tommy Docherty and Malcolm Allison were witty, frank-talking, hip-shooting TV gold in natty suits and kipper ties. Paisley seemed as far removed from them as a eunuch from George Best. Neither did he possess the track record to project himself as a wise, vastly experienced, genial uncle figure like Matt Busby or Joe Mercer.

Paisley had been the ultimate man in the shadows. He was the quiet Geordie who never spoke about his Second World War heroics, when he spent four years fighting in North Africa and Italy, helping to liberate Rome. The tubby, Brylcreemed trainer who ran on to the pitch with a bucket or was spotted awkwardly grinning with the rest of the backroom staff behind the photogenic Shankly when cameras were allowed into Melwood. He was the unremarkable servant who had been at the club for 35 years as player, odd-job man, physio, trainer, talent-spotter, coach and assistant manager who had chosen to stay firmly below the radar.

Yet ultimately that was the key to his potential, which Liverpool's board knew only too well. This canny old owl had soaked in all of that knowledge and experience and knew the blueprint for staying successful. So why go searching for a shining managerial star when there was gold glinting in front of your eyes?

As for all of those stellar names mentioned above, including

Shankly, when it came to the one thing fans pined for, filling the trophy cabinet, Paisley eventually left them trailing in his wake, retiring as the most successful coach in English football history, having led the Reds to six league Championships, three European Cups, one UEFA Cup and three League Cups.

As with most things in football his appointment made sense in hindsight. Paisley was a kind of Shankly-plus. All the great man's strengths and weaknesses had been observed with a laser-like precision and on top he had his own individual genius.

Both he and Shankly had seen the good times and the bad, as player and coach. They were both fighters, one a Royal Air Force middleweight boxer, the other a Royal Artillery gunner.

They were both extremely loyal men who never dreamt of moving on for more money despite being among the best managers in the world and earning relatively little during their time at Anfield.

Both hailed from a mining community where the seam was drying up and hard times were on the way for themselves and their brothers unless they found an escape in football. Unlike Shankly's household there may have been little talk of socialism in Paisley's Hetton-le-Hole home but the sense of communal responsibility was a given. He, too, grew up to scorn elitism and foster a sense of collectivism in the workplace.

Both had little truck with players who demanded bigger wages when their profile rose through international recognition. To these pit-town products who had lived through the Great Depression and the General Strike, football was a lucky escape from lesser-paid manual labour. A passport out of poverty. And they resented any player who had forgotten their humble roots. Which some could argue takes the admirable notion of remembering where you came from to extremes as they were effectively doing the management's dirty work for them.

But it meant they instilled the values of respect and solidarity which had been bred into them into their players, and it resonated in such a radical, working-class city as Liverpool.

Management at first proved tough for Paisley as he was perceived to be on a hiding to nothing. If the team continued to pick up silverware people would say it was all down to the fine, young team Shankly had created. If standards slipped, as they did in Paisley's first trophyless season in charge, the new guy would be the fall guy.

But Paisley was very much his own man, a horse-racing lover who backed his instincts, and when that came to the basics of football he was peerless. He could spot a talent almost as quickly as he could detect an injury or fillet the tactics of an opponent.

He made world-class signings such as Kenny Dalglish, Alan Hansen, Graeme Souness and Ian Rush and made shrewd tactical changes such as converting Ray Kennedy from struggling striker to midfield star.

The quiet man just let his players do the talking and the trophy conveyor belt soon started up again. Although in private his dry humour could be as deadly as Shankly's. When Alan Kennedy missed a sitter on his 1978 debut, Paisley told him after the game that "they shot the wrong bloody Kennedy."

Brian Clough called him "as hard as nails and as canny as they come" and that certainly defined how he turned Liverpool into a European superpower.

Paisley realised the team's style and mentality needed changing if they were to deliver Shankly's dream of conquering the bloody world. He recognised the need for eleven players perfectly synchronised to a subtle, slow-slow-quick approach that beat the Continentals, as he called them, at their own game.

Consequently, he gave the fans more great European nights than Stella Artois. None more so than the second leg of the 1977 quarter-final against St Etienne.

Anfield had never been driven by such a collective will to succeed. The fans, so close to the pitch they could see the hairs quivering in their French opponents' nostrils, created a terrifying wall of ear-splitting passion.

When David Fairclough waltzed past two defenders and scored the winner, 26,000 Kopites were sucked towards the goal by a giant Hoover of emotion. One journalist described it as a mass human trampoline. And that is how it felt.

A few months later in Rome, the Trevi Fountain and Spanish Steps were awash with red flags that told the tale of the journey to the European Cup final against Borussia Moenchen-gladbach: 'Joey ate the frogs legs, made the Swiss roll, now he's munching Gladbach.' They were indeed munched. Paisley, on his first return to Rome since entering it in a tank as a great liberator, stayed sober that night to savour every moment of his emotional triumph.

But in Liverpool, they partied hard for days on end. In the hot summer of 1977 the rest of Britain rolled out the barrel to celebrate the Queen's Silver Jubilee but the red half of Merseyside declared independence and raised toasts to Paisley's Kings of Europe.

It was just the beginning of their domination. A sublime chip from Kenny Dalglish was enough to see off Bruges the following year at Anfield South (Wembley). And in 1981 Real Madrid were put in their place in Paris thanks to a trademark smash from Alan Kennedy, allowing the first Scouse captain Phil Thompson to raise the cup above his head (it would later end up in the boot of a Cortina outside a Kirkby pub, but that's another story.)

By the early 80s, thanks to Paisley's quiet revolution Liverpool weren't just standing head and shoulders above the rest of Europe, they were standing head-and-shoulders at the peak of Mont Blanc.

And the city and its people badly needed it, because economically, it was on its arse. The port faced the wrong way – to the old routes of Empire, not east to Europe – manufacturing industries were decimated as companies either closed or relocated to more central locations, inward investment shrank, men were told at 40 they would never work again and kids left school with little hope of a decent job unless they got out of town.

In the first five years of that decade, as Thatcherite policies bit hard, Liverpool lost 50,000 jobs, unemployment stood at 25 per cent, the population was plummeting, it had riots in Toxteth and elected a Militant council with a brief to declare war on Westminster. For their part, the Tory government contemplated adopting a policy of decline. Allowing a port that was known earlier that century as The Second City of Empire to slide off the map.

As the city took an unprecedented image-battering, Liverpool FC's European domination was a beacon of pride and defiance. It said we are still a centre of European excellence, a major player on the global stage, no matter how much you want to demoralise us or mismanage us into insignificance.

And pulling the strings and pushing them on to greater

heights was the flat-capped genius who ruled with a low-pitched ruthlessness.

Unlike Shankly, Paisley was openly prepared from the beginning of his reign to be hated by his own men for making the toughest of calls. He had no time for sentimentality and would drop players, and end careers, without warning or explanation. Hence his nickname among some of them – The Rat – which referenced him being a Desert Rat in World War II, but more importantly a dislike of what they perceived to be his callousness.

But the best players loved and admired him without question. "When you talk of the greats you think of Sir Matt Busby, Jock Stein and Shanks, and if he is not among them, he should be above them because none of them achieved what he did in the domestic game," said Emlyn Hughes.

"I don't think anybody who came into contact with Bob could have anything but total respect for his honesty and integrity," said Kevin Keegan.

"I learned more about football from him than anyone else," said Graeme Souness.

Paisley trusted few people in football outside his own inner sanctum and had no time for wooing the media, preferring to play on his own stereotype and keep journalists at arm's length with few, often indecipherable words.

So I had little expectation of a positive response when I wrote to him in 1989, six years after his retirement, asking if I could interview him for a series I was doing for the *Liverpool Daily Post* on the 30th anniversary of Shankly's arrival at Anfield. But to my eternal gratitude, he wrote back, inviting me to his Woolton home for a chat, on the grounds that the least he owed his great friend Bill was a few words on how he changed the world for everyone who loved Liverpool.

Bob was a few months short of his 71st birthday and living in the same Woolton semi he had been in for decades with his devoted wife Jessie.

She ushered me into the front room where he was sitting watching the racing. He wore a patterned-jumper that zipped up at the front, a striped tie underneath, black slacks, slippers and Brylcreemed hair he kept patting down unconsciously.

He smiled shyly, got up to shake my hand uncomfortably, muttered about switching the telly off then, with a limp he'd carried for 40 years after a bad ankle injury playing for Liverpool, hobbled over to do it manually.

It was like visiting your mate's house and finding his grandad had moved in.

The room was pure working-class but with a thicker shag pile to the carpet, which was testament to the fact he'd earned a few bob more than his coal-mining father. Not that he was showing it.

On every spare surface – the mantelpiece, coffee table, top of the telly – were school photos of grandchildren still in their cardboard frames, and knick-knacks brought back from family holidays, carrying the name of the resort above a view of the beach. As with every grandad, the gas fire was turned up way too high.

I thought to myself that here was the most accomplished manager in the history of British football, a man who gave 44 years unbroken service to the country's most successful club, yet he could be any pensioner in any house in the land.

Looking back I wasn't sure if that said more about the way

that football had gone, how men whose talent would struggle to be described as mediocre lived like film stars, or if it said more about Bob Paisley. Probably the latter. Because he was normality personified. The most uncomplicated, honest and modest of men. But nobody's fool.

Jessie went to make us some tea and Bob sank back in his armchair and said "so you want to talk about Bill then, because we'll have to keep it to that." Before adding with his trademark chuckle, "I can't be getting into no more trouble."

He was referring to the fact that he had stopped doing interviews two years earlier after being quoted in the *Sunday Express* saying the First Division was worse than in his day, and John Aldridge wasn't fit to lace Ian Rush's boots. From the boardroom to the terraces, Anfield was taken aback. It was wildly out of character that Paisley would be so outspoken and appear so bitter.

His family claimed he had been conned and misquoted but the reporter stuck by his story. Paisley just seemed perplexed by it all, apologising, but claiming he couldn't remember what he had or hadn't said. It was the first public sign that all wasn't well.

The sad truth was he was in the early stages of Alzheimer's Disease, and just over a year after our meeting it would be officially diagnosed. I was having a deep privilege bestowed on me. The great man had stopped giving interviews but felt it only right that he should contribute to a series about Shankly. It turned out to be one of the last times he would be capable of sharing his memories in public with any real lucidity.

When Jessie brought the tea in she was nervous, concerned about her husband's state of mind and what he might not realise he was saying. But equally worried that I might suss he wasn't the full shilling. I half expected her to sit in with us, so concerned were the family that I might be out to turn him over. She left, reminding him in a semi-serious way to be on his best behaviour, looking at me and nodding knowingly back at him, as if to say, "we're trusting you here son, don't let us down."

There was no chance of that. How could I contemplate it when I was there to talk about Shankly with the man who knew him best?

When he started talking, the doubts kicked in. The interview didn't seem to be going anywhere. He appeared to be struggling with the most basic questions, mumbling back in broken sentences, looking away, coming back at them after a few seconds. Going off on disjointed tangents.

He'd drift into asides, chuckle to himself, or just end a sentence with the phrase "the doings." Always mentioning "the doings." As in "so-and-so could put it in the doings (the goal)" or "the other fella, now he had the doings."

The longer I spoke to him the more I understood his speech patterns and realised there was something profound behind most of what he had to say. When I played the tape back and edited out the "erms, ahs, likes and ya knows" I'd never heard such clear footballing logic. There was a clinical authority to his thoughts. It felt like I'd captured pearls of wisdom.

How did he react when he heard Shankly was calling it a day? "I tried harder than anyone to get him to stay. I'd say to him 'Bill, what are you going to do with yourself if you retire?' You see, he was a real loner. He didn't knock about with anyone.

"Nessie begged me to get him to change his mind and I did. I went on my hands and knees and told him he couldn't pack it in because it would kill him. And sad to say, it did."

What convinced him to take the job once Shankly had gone? "I asked the players whether I should and they said 'yes.' So I thought, 'well, a new fella wouldn't know how it worked round here, not properly. So I thought, go on then, I'd best do it.'"

There was an aura about him, a calm serenity that was almost saint-like.

How would he sum up his relationship with Shankly? "In all the years we worked together, seeing a thousand Liverpool games, we never once had an argument. We may have disagreed but we'd just have our say and that was it. No arguing. Because I always gave Bill a straight answer and he could take that from those he respected."

I asked him what Shankly's weaknesses were, which revealed more about his own astute strengths: "If I had one criticism of Bill, it was that he didn't break up the 1960s team quicker. He was content with what he'd done and kept faith with the players. He was a very loyal man but I thought what was more important than staying loyal to players who were getting past it, was us getting back to winning ways again."

Paisley had a ruthlessness Shanks didn't possess. And which the wider footballing world underestimated to its great cost. He understood that Shankly's human failings had kept Liverpool in the wilderness for seven years and it convinced him there was no room for sentiment in the modern game.

I asked him the big one about why Shankly went, hoping I might strike lucky and the unarguable truth would be laid bare. But he just shrugged. I pointed out that he must surely have his own private theory and that it would be a shame not to share it. And he relented.

"If I was pushed I'd say maybe he was frightened of having

another lean spell. He'd built a second great side and I think at the back of his mind he may have been afraid of failure. I think he'd made up his mind to go at the top like a class boxer. Because more than anything Bill was a boxer at heart."

I'd heard dozens of theories put forward as to why Shankly retired, even asked him myself, but none struck me as being as close to the truth as Bob Paisley's. Because no-one knew Shankly better than his old lieutenant. Including, possibly Shankly himself.

Jessie popped her head in, and asked if he was behaving himself. I just grinned nervously. She said she was nipping out to work, that she had a bit of a part-time job but I could stay as long as I wanted. But I could sense Bob was getting a bit twitchy and wanted the horse-racing back on his telly and said I was more or less finished.

I took one last look around the simply-furnished, semi-detached front-room and asked Bob if he thought his time at the very peak of football should have made him a richer man, especially when he read how much today's top managers were earning. He looked at me quizzically, giggled and waved his hand dismissively, before turning the racing back on: "I never moaned about what they paid me then, so why should I moan now? Besides, there's more to being rich than having money."

As I left, Jessie asked how it had gone and I told her "fine." But what I wanted to say was it felt like I'd been in the presence of humility yet I'd never felt more humbled.

Bob stood at the front door as Jessie and I left, looking about as uncomfortable as his slippers-and-tie combo, and waved me off. I felt privileged to have been granted that audience.

There, above that zipped-up jumper on that suburban

doorstep, was the greatest of football brains who did something nobody else could have done. Taken Shankly's exceptional work to another level.

He was the great moderniser who decided there was no room for a traditional burly centre-half like Ron Yeats or Larry Lloyd in a team that wanted to win the European Cup, so employed ball-playing central defenders like Phil Thompson, Alan Hansen and Mark Lawrenson.

Here was the innovator who perfected the split-strikers role, with Dalglish behind Rush, way before others saw how vital that was to unlocking defences. The thinker who masterminded the strategy that would elevate Liverpool from an English giant to a global one.

There stood the most successful manager in English football history at the door of his ordinary semi, watching his wife go off to work. This is what you get when you labour all your life for love not money, I thought. Afternoons in front of the telly watching the racing with photos of your grandkids to keep you company. A life like everybody else's.

There are many quotes that ensure Bill Shankly was elevated to the status of Anfield's all-time sage. But two of the most telling utterances on how Liverpool maintained their supremacy for so long, I heard from Paisley's mouth that day.

When he was judging players and had to separate the diamonds from the dross, one thought was uppermost: "The first few yards are in the head." When asked to define the Liverpool Way, he replied, "If you're lost in a fog, you stick together. That way you don't get lost. If Liverpool has a secret, that's it."

Bob's Alzheimer's became so bad in the mid-90s that he had to be put into a nursing home. When he died in 1996 Jessie said he had been so ill towards the end he couldn't remember being manager of Liverpool, let alone any of the three European Cups or six league titles he had won.

Her revelation has haunted me ever since. That most loyal of servants had given Liverpool supporters so much pleasure as a player, coach and manager over five decades.

So many great signings, so many inspired decisions, so many glorious victories, so many fabulous nights of celebration, which will stay with us to our dying day. Yet he had lost all memory of those moments. A crueller, more undeserving fate is hard to imagine.

When he died in February 1996 a profound sadness was shared among Liverpool fans, made deeper by the fact the club which averaged more than two trophies a season under Bob's management were in their sixth season without a proper title challenge. English football mourned the loss of its most successful manager with an overriding sense of regret that he had not received anything like the due recognition he deserved for his remarkable haul of trophies.

In death, as in life, he was overshadowed by Shankly. In the sporting tributes, outpourings of praise were qualified with the rider that he inherited a great side and a great system from his great friend. Unlike with Shankly's death, the news made little impact outside the sports pages, except for one leader in *The Independent*, headlined 'Hero of Post-war Britain.' It nailed it:

Bob Paisley was the personification of a post-war ideal. He was a working-class man who made good, but whom extraordinary success failed to corrupt or sour.

The ordinary soldier who fought through Africa and Italy was a perfect mix of the true experiences of a whole generation together with the Boys' Own fantasy of sporting triumph.

His obvious and most remarked traits were loyalty, quietness and doggedness. But what these sheltered was the keen intelligence without which he could not possibly have become the most successful club manager in British soccer history.

Paisley's Liverpool were not Revie's talented but unloved Leeds team, nor the dour technicians of George Graham's Arsenal. They were the marriage of individual brilliance with commitment to team and plan; the elegance of Dalglish and Hansen welded to the determination of Souness. When they beat the best that Europe had to offer it was not with the long-ball game, or with unfair tackling, but with the same insistence on technique and tactics that many lament is now missing from the British game.

Bob Paisley stands for all those hundreds of thousands of his generation whose intelligence and loyalty achieved much, but whose attributes went largely unrecorded and underestimated.

And who did not mind.

Over the years many Liverpool fans have written to me asking for support in their campaign to get posthumous knighthoods for Bill Shankly and Bob Paisley. It rankles deeply with many Kopites that three Manchester United legends – Matt Busby, Alex Ferguson and Bobby Charlton – were knighted, when Shankly and Paisley had to make do with an OBE each.

I'd tell them that I knew where their anger was coming from because in 1974, as a 16-year-old, I wrote to my MP, Harold Wilson, telling him I was disgusted that Shankly had been snubbed in the New Years Honours List yet again, despite becoming the first manager to win the English title and a

European trophy in the same season. And demanded he did something about it. His secretary wrote back reminding me that Harold was no longer in Downing Street, so he was a bit stymied. To be fair to Harold, he put him on his first list when he was back in power.

But I grew to hate the honours system. Especially when it came to handing medals to popular celebrities like footballers to disguise the corrupt back-scratching that was going on.

And I'd heard first-hand how the corruption worked. In 1999, Labour spin doctor Alastair Campbell had become so pally with party supporter Alex Ferguson, he was his guest at the Champions League final in Barcelona, and sat with the family.

After Manchester United's dramatic victory Campbell put in motion a plan, agreed with Tony Blair, to offer him a knighthood on the spot. But he couldn't get through to him in the ensuing mayhem, so asked his wife to tell him the offer was there but he needed to answer immediately in order for Labour to grab a slice of the swathes of positive publicity that followed United's Treble-clinching comeback.

Fergie agreed and the knighthood was his. No wonder he famously uttered that night in the Nou Camp: "Football. Bloody hell." As Campbell later told me, the quick-thinking coup was "a very New Labour honour".

As was Geoff Hurst's knighthood in the first Queen's Birthday Honours List Tony Blair had control of in June 1998. Which was leaked on the day the 1998 World Cup kicked off, a tournament which had captured the nation's imagination, following the near-miss of Euro 96. More football camouflage to disguise all the dodgy honours being dished out.

It's why I am glad neither Shankly's nor Paisley's memories

were tarnished with a knighthood. I would hate to have seen these two proud working-class men who built football teams that were the antithesis of elitism, who believed with every fibre of their being in the notions of equality and collectivism, on their knees bowing before inherited wealth.

The only titles they sought were the ones they put in the Anfield trophy cabinet. The only honours list they cared about was on the inside of the match-day programme.

I wrote to Shankly after Wilson's secretary informed me there was nothing Harold could do about the Honours System snub but would bear him in mind if he got back into power. I told Shanks that I was on a mission to get him a knighthood and wouldn't rest until he had one. On the opposite page, you can see his reply.

If any piece of writing is going in my coffin, it is that one. Its sincerity, humility and honesty sum the man up to perfection

Because of what they did and who they were, the names of Shankly and Paisley are guaranteed to reverberate forever. They don't need letters added to them to tell the world of the deep and lasting impact they had on a city and its people. Their records show that. Their statues outside Anfield show that. The love and respect they earned show that.

The warm smiles on the faces of Liverpool fans whenever their name is mentioned glitters far brighter than any Establishment bauble ever could.

The honour was very much ours.

LIVERPOOL FOOTBALL CLUB
AND ATHLETIC GROUNDS CO. LTD.

ANFIELD ROAD LIVERPOOL L4 0TH
051-263 2361/2

January 21st 1974.

B.Reade Esq.,
32,Acadia Ave,
Huyton,
Liverpool.
L36-5TW

Dear Brian,
      Received your letter,also the one you received from Mr.Harold Wilson,,thanks very much indeed.

      It is very good of you to write on my behalf.I appreciate it.However Brian I am not really disappointed about not being recognised.The people who dish out honours are not my people,my people go to Anfield.If I can make you all happy,then that is my greatest ambition.

        Very sincerely,,

           Bill Shankly.

MANAGER : W. SHANKLY SECRETARY : P. B. ROBINSON

9

THE
LAW-CHANGER

DOREEN
LAWRENCE

COURT 16, THE OLD BAILEY, LONDON — *January 2012*

SHE took the verdict with the grace and dignity we had come to expect.

When, finally, the lead juror spoke the word that released Doreen Lawrence from almost two decades of unfathomable pain, I could see no emotion on her face, despite sitting only a few yards away.

As 'guilty' followed the name Gary Dobson, her head jolted back slightly, as though dodging a blow, her chest gave a slight heave and her narrowing eyes wrestled with the enormity of that single, two-syllable word.

She stared hard at the jury foreman, her placid features locked in concentration, awaiting the verdict on David Norris. When 'guilty' again fell from his lips, a small tear rolled from her right eye.

Rubbing it away, she gazed at the Old Bailey ceiling, as if trying to connect with her precious son, Stephen, to tell him what she had always promised: That she would never rest until this day arrived.

Next to Doreen, her youngest son Stuart grabbed her left hand and squeezed it hard. His resemblance to his brother was a haunting snap-shot of how Stephen may have looked had he reached 37.

Six seats away, Neville Lawrence held his head in his hands, his big shoulders and chest vibrating in time to sobs that came from somewhere deep inside. The weight of his burden had been released. The realisation was dawning on him that finally someone would pay for spilling his son's blood over a south London pavement back in 1993.

Spilling it simply for being black.

I counted ten seconds between the foreman being asked if he had a verdict on Dobson, what that verdict was, and the word "guilty" being uttered. Ten seconds. As long as the frenzied attack that killed Stephen Lawrence at that Eltham bus stop.

But in between was 18 years and eight months of torment his family should not have had to endure.

In the dock, Dobson and Norris, two of the five racists who had launched that murderous assault on Stephen, at first stared impassively. Then Dobson shook his head and Norris nodded, as though recognising fate had finally caught up with him. With thinning hair, pale-faced and deep, dark bags under their eyes, they looked at least a decade older than their mid-thirties. After half a lifetime spent living the most heinous of lies, maybe that was visible justice.

Justice Treacy had warned the court he wanted no show of emotion when the verdicts came in. It was a tough ask.

For the killers' relatives in the public gallery who gasped and muttered "he's innocent" and "he did not kill that man." For Dobson himself, who yelled, "You have condemned an innocent man here. I hope you can live with yourselves." And for the rest of us gathered in the Old Bailey's Court 16.

Because this was a punch-the-air moment for every decent-minded person in Britain. A moment we had waited half a generation to enjoy after being forced to watch arrogant, violent bigots swagger around the streets of south London, wallowing in their infamy and flaunting their contempt at our inability to take away their liberty.

But this moment did not belong to us. It belonged to Doreen Lawrence.

This petite Jamaican woman who came to England, aged nine, to seek a better life but who, four decades later, sent her son back to the island to be buried in a family plot, was finally having her day in court.

The formidable battler, who forced politicians to launch the Macpherson inquiry which labelled the Metropolitan Police "institutionally racist" and became a campaigner for victims of racially motivated crime, finally won justice for her beloved son – justice for a well-mannered, educated young man with a bright future as an architect, slain simply because his assailants objected to him having a different coloured skin to theirs.

As his killers were taken down, Doreen glanced up at the dock above her, without catching a glimpse of them. She had been studying their features throughout the trial and afterwards explained why: "I wanted to see their faces once they had been found guilty because for years they thought they had got away with it.

"I think I was trying to see remorse, but they showed nothing to say they were sorry. Sometimes when you are young you do things and have some regrets later. But they didn't show any regrets at all.

"I could see that Norris still had the same blasé way as before. He came in as Jack the Lad. His demeanour hadn't changed from the first time I saw him. Dobson was a bit different. I think he understood the seriousness of it. Every day he came in he was trying not to look around. He didn't want to have eye contact with anybody, whereas Norris didn't seem to mind."

The Lawrences had sat in the Old Bailey court for seven weeks, praying for the eight men and four women of the jury to end a personal hell that had lasted almost a thousand weeks.

They had sat a few yards away from the men who, behind protective glass, had lied and lied throughout that time about their role in Stephen's murder.

"I ain't no racist and I ain't the murderer," said Dobson, after police surveillance tapes were played which destroyed the first part of that statement as it showed he viewed blacks and Asians as lower than vermin.

The Lawrences had been forced to listen in court to Norris claiming he did not know where he was on that night of April 22, 1993.

They had heard him trot out the standard denials: the fibres on the clothing weren't his, he wasn't racist, just an angry young man. They had heard his mother produce, for the first time, an alibi that he was at home when the murder happened. Fiction after fiction after fiction.

They had heard arguments about ruined evidence, which reminded them how criminally negligent the police had been in the initial investigation.

They had seen Duwayne Brooks, Stephen's best friend since their first day together at secondary school, who was with him at the time of the murder, break down in tears as he re-lived the pain of that night.

They had heard how a group of white strangers shouted, "What, what nigger?" before one of them ran into Stephen with a foot-long knife and, in Duwayne's words, went "wham, just like that". And how the 18-year-old staggered for 130 yards with blood gushing from his shoulder, before falling and dying on a pavement as drivers sped past on a busy road, unseeing or uncaring.

Stephen's murder was one of those watershed junctures in our nation's history, when we stop and ask, "What has happened to us that we could allow something so shocking in our midst."

It was the first time many had asked themselves a question which, decades later, would become a global mantra in the fight against systemic racism: Do black lives matter?

It wasn't just the murder that horrified those who cherished justice but the appalling investigation of it and the cruel aftermath. The Stephen Lawrence story became a stain on the British nation.

How could the initial reaction of a police force be not to catch the five youths whose names were being handed to them by dozens of local sources, but to ask Doreen and Neville Lawrence what a black youth was doing at a bus stop, miles away from home, at 10pm?

How could we allow parents to live with the awful truth that their son was not just killed by racist thugs for being black but treated as a criminal by a racist police force for being black? Parents who saw their marriage torn apart by the strain of trying to cope with their burden.

But finally, that January afternoon inside the Old Bailey, we saw a form of justice, even though the Lawrences would have to fight on to try to convict the rest of the gang involved in their son's murder.

When Neville, the mild-mannered, retired carpenter who now lived back in Jamaica left the court, he and his ex-wife Doreen made no connection. But he was hugged by weeping well-wishers and finally, after almost two decades of internalised anguish, a smile began to spread across his broad face. It was an acutely poignant moment to witness.

In terms of raw emotion, it took me back to hearing the speech

Doreen gave at Stephen's inquest: "When my son was murdered he was investigated as a criminal. His crime was waiting for a bus to take him home. Our crime is living in a country where the justice system supports racist murders against innocent people.

"But still we followed all the steps open to us and one by one the doors slammed in our face."

At last, on that cold January day, the Establishment opened a door, and a shaft of light crept back into their shattered hearts.

GROSVENOR HOTEL, LONDON — October 2012

I next saw Doreen nine months later at the *Daily Mirror*'s Pride of Britain awards where she received a Lifetime Achievement Award from actor Idris Elba, who told her, to a standing ovation from a 1,000-strong audience: "You have changed Britain for life."

Indeed she had. Without her dogged pursuit of the truth about how, and why, her son was killed at that Eltham bus stop, and why his killers were allowed to escape justice for so long, there would have been no proper police investigation, no national outrage about the inadequacies of the criminal justice system, no Macpherson inquiry, no Race Relations Amendment Act, no focus on institutional bigotry that dogs this country.

The overdue recognition was coming her way. Three months earlier I'd sat in the London Stadium and watched in admiration as she carried the flag at the opening ceremony of the 2012 Olympic Games along with UN Secretary General Ban-Ki Moon and Muhammad Ali, before a global TV audience of billions.

What an achievement that was for this quiet, working-class immigrant from rural Jamaica. Typically, she had been unsure whether to accept the honour offered by the ceremony organisers, believing she felt she was just another justice campaigner fighting for the truth. She felt she was nothing special because if the police had done their job on the night her son was murdered no-one, outside her friends and family, would ever have heard of her.

But after much soul-searching she concluded that if she carried that flag she would be striking a blow for all the other ordinary mothers and every other black person in Britain, as proof that they are centre-stage in society, not merely on the periphery of it.

It was at a previous Pride of Britain ceremony a decade earlier that I first met Doreen, as I hosted a table for the *Mirror* and she was seated next to me.

Such was her shy and modest demeanour it was impossible to conceive she would become such a vehicle for change in Britain that she would end up sitting in the House of Lords.

I didn't really know how far to go when asking about Stephen. I had spent a decade knowing and working with the Hillsborough mothers and would speak freely and openly to them about the events, inquiring about how they were feeling and asking intimate questions about the sons and daughters they lost in the football stadium disaster. But I'd grown to know them, as a Liverpudlian we were from similar backgrounds, fighting the same fight. But how could a white, middle-aged journalist bond with someone like Doreen Lawrence?

I told her of the Hillsborough mothers, their fight, and the parallels with hers and she was very interested, asking probing questions, eager to learn. There were many similarities between the two: the bigotry they faced when fighting for the truth about their children's deaths, the brick wall they kept running into whenever they took on the Establishment, campaigners smeared as being trouble-making lefties, the mother's love that was driving them on to eventual victory and an apology from the Prime Minister. And the certain belief that had it been their son who had caused the deaths, unlike those responsible, they would be behind bars.

When I told her that I was bowled over with how those mothers dealt with senior figures in authority she shrugged and replied in her softly-spoken voice, "Those figures you're talking about are just ordinary people like us who've been given titles so why should we feel we're on a different level to them?" Margaret Aspinall, who like Doreen also lost an 18-year-old son, gave the same answer after I'd seen her taking down Home Secretaries and Chief Constables over the Hillsborough cover-up.

Doreen was guarded when talking about her own fight for justice, the events of that fateful night and the systemic bigotry that led to her son being killed.

She would later write in her 2006 autobiography, And Still I Rise, that "journalists say they know little about me and this is true. Apart from my close family and some friends I am unsure who to trust, so I am very careful about speaking about my own life and I do not want to come across as if I am constantly mournful or aggressive."

Her reticence, when it came to race issues, was no surprise. Six years after Stephen's murder I spent a day on the estate where his killers were raised and witnessed most people unwilling to talk about the hate that was in evidence all around them.

ELTHAM, SOUTH LONDON — February 1999

I tried to find the memorial to Stephen at the spot on Well Hall Road where he fell and died but it was a hard task.

After asking for directions from three people I eventually discovered it, a simple grey marble paving slab with the words: 'IN MEMORY OF STEPHEN LAWRENCE 13.9.1974–22.4.1993. MAY HE REST IN PEACE'.

Next to it lay a lone, dying bunch of cheap flowers. It looked like a pauper's grave.

Twice in the previous year the plaque had been attacked by racist vandals. On one occasion it was daubed with paint and an attempt made to chisel out the name.

The second time it was so badly damaged by a hammer it had to be replaced.

Elly Witte, a Dutch woman in her 40s who lived in Eltham with her black partner, told me that, if anything, the racism had worsened in the years since his death.

How a friend of hers, white but married to a black man, was forced out of her home after a barrage of attacks and abuse.

Elly said, "I would never move away because of the racism. I would never let them win. When I am out with my husband we get treated differently because I am white and he is black. It is ridiculous because I am the foreigner.

"I fear for my daughter because she is of mixed race. This sounds bad but she is lucky because she is not black, but half-black. How sad is it that I should have to say that?"

I attempted to persuade Asian shop-owners to talk about the terror they faced but none would go on the record for fear of reprisals. It was understandable. In 1997 there had been 143 serious racist attacks recorded in Eltham, in 1998 that had climbed above 150. But they were just the reported ones. Only a small percentage of victims go forward and, when they do, police only manage a 10 per cent clear-up rate.

And the statistics failed to show the pain behind all the incidences of arson, smashed shop windows, faeces and blazing rubbish pushed through letterboxes.

One young Asian man who overheard me asking a shop-owner for some examples of racism in Eltham told me to go to the Brook Estate and look at the graffiti. So I did. It was hard to miss it.

I spotted a group of boys no older than eight playing football. They had white faces, cropped hair, were decked out in top class Nike and Reebok gear and as they whacked a ball against a garage door chanted "Shea-rer" whenever they hit the goal.

A typical Saturday morning sight back then on council estates the length of Britain. But something caught my eye about that goal.

No matter what angle the ball was struck it hit a swastika. There were 17 of them daubed on the garage next to the words 'PURE NAZI.' And below was a huge Union Jack with the letters NF scrawled at its heart.

After a while the lads took a rest from being Alan Shearer. The biggest one slumped against a grey electricity control box, his eyes sweeping around for a subject to kill the boredom. They went full circle then focused on the jumbled mass of graffiti below his arm. He started to read it slowly, taking in every word. These words:

'I stabbed Stephen Lawrence.'

'I hate niggers like Aaron.'

His eyes began to roam around the box and he mouthed the slogans slowly in a self-conscious whisper, as though he were reading to his teacher:

'Kill coons at birth.'

'I will kill every coon in the world.'

And then, getting the hang of the vocabulary, he read faster and out loud: 'Niggers should be hanged by the balls.'

'If they're brown knock them down. If they're black stab them in the back.'

Silence. He looked away bored, then strode impassively back to the game of football without flinching.

There was no look of puzzlement at what he had just read. No confusion or discomfort. He understood it. He breathed it. He lived it.

This was Eltham's Brook Estate. The breeding ground of four of the five men accused of stabbing Stephen Lawrence to death as he waited for a bus a short walk away.

Five products of a twisted philosophy drummed into them from birth: "If they're black, stab them in the back." Written on walls, signs, bins and playgrounds all over the estate by authors who defiantly sign themselves "Eltham Boyz."

A way of life passed down from father to son. You see the link emerge in the fading graffiti sprayed 30 years ago on the walls of the old railway bridges around the estate, written by the last generation of Eltham Boyz. In three-foot high letters: 'SKINHEADS.'

Middle-aged dads who were once shaven-headed boot boys with a penchant for Paki-bashing.

Lads whose fathers had moved to Eltham in the 1960s to escape the black migration into south London. Lads who married into their own, shed the Doc Martens and braces, had kids and passed on the benefit of their "wisdom."

And on and on the poison spreads. Give me the father and I'll give you the son who will give you the son who will abuse, persecute and even kill another human being for committing the heinous crime of not being white.

What chance does that eight-year-old have when he reads that the big lads on the estate wish they had stabbed Stephen Lawrence?

What chance do any of us have, I asked, when six years after Stephen's murder little had changed in Eltham? There may have been more awareness and racism may have been discussed more openly but underneath the surface the ugly boil still festered.

And who among us, I wrote, could say that Eltham was radically different from parts of our own towns or cities? Because what was so ominous about spending a day there is how ordinary it was. What was so chilling was that despite large numbers of Caribbean immigrants coming to British cities since the late-1940s, attacks on them for not being white had only increased.

In the summer of 2020, at the height of Black Lives Matter protests on the streets of the UK, YouGov did an extensive poll of black, Asian and minority ethnic Britons (BAME) to discover how racism affected their lives.

More than half said their career development had either directly suffered or they'd had assumptions made about their ability, based on their race. The poll also revealed that 50 per cent of black people claimed to have been racially abused in the workplace, which was virtually the same proportion who claimed to have been abused in the street. So it came as no surprise that two-thirds of black people polled believed there was still a "great deal of racism" prevalent in the UK.

It was an indictment on this country, showing as it did, how little had fundamentally changed from the bigotry endured by the post-war Windrush generation who arrived from the Caribbean to find signs in some landlords' windows saying, 'No blacks, no dogs, no Irish.'

Interestingly, in her autobiography, Doreen Lawrence said that when she started at her south London primary school, as an immigrant in the early-60s, she couldn't recall anyone treating her badly or being racist towards her, despite being the only black child in her class. In her secondary school, in New Cross, she was bullied in her first year, but by a group of black girls.

She felt she had possibly been passed over for promotion in her first clerical job yet, apart from that, she had not been aware of any prejudice towards her because of the colour of her skin.

'But nothing, not childhood or school, or my experience at work, prepared me for what happened when I thought my life had settled into happiness and middle age,' she wrote, referring to her son's murder.

Doreen Delceita Graham was born in Clarendon, a rural part of southern Jamaica, in October 1952. Although she had a difficult childhood with her mother emigrating to England without her when she was only two years old, Doreen felt such a belonging to her birthplace she chose the title Baroness of Clarendon when elevated to the Lords in 2013.

Her father left home when she was a toddler and she had no

recollection of her mother, Ruby, until she was reunited with her, in London, aged nine, in 1962. Prior to that she was brought up by her grandmother and aunt.

She left school with four CSEs and found a job as a clerk in NatWest bank's clearing house in London's Moorgate. When she was 17 she met Neville, who was a decade older than her, and married him two years later against her mother's wishes.

They were living in a small flat in Brockley when Stephen was born in 1974, but eventually moved to a house in Woolwich, where the family of five (Doreen had two more children, Stuart and Georgina) lived happily until murder tore them apart on that fateful night of April 22, 1993.

Stephen had spent that day at school in Blackheath and afterwards visited shops in Lewisham before taking a bus to an uncle's house in Grove Park, where he met his mate Duwayne and played video games until leaving around 10pm.

They took a bus to Well Hall Road where they had to change to take a different route home. The two stood apart as they looked out for a bus and at one point Duwayne called out to ask whether Stephen could see one coming.

From across the road one member of a group of five white youths shouted, "What, what nigger" then ran as one to engulf Stephen. He was forced to the ground, then stabbed twice, to a depth of five inches in the right collarbone and the left shoulder, severing arteries and penetrating a lung.

Duwayne ran and yelled at Stephen to follow him as the attackers fled. Stephen ran but soon collapsed on to the pavement where he lay bleeding to death.

Duwayne called an ambulance while an off-duty police officer stopped his car and covered Stephen with a blanket.

Doctors told Doreen at the Brook General Hospital that there had been nothing they could do for Stephen when he arrived. Only one police officer was present, who never spoke to them, and no officer offered to take them home after receiving news of their son's death. When Doreen got back to the house she went upstairs and laid on her bed staring at the darkness, unable to take in the enormity of what she had just been told. Even though she had seen his corpse, "I was still hoping that he would wake up, that the phone was about to ring and someone would say it had all been a mistake and then the front door would open."

The indifferent attitude of the police to Stephen's murder only poured a ton of salt on the rawest of wounds. Detectives repeatedly told the Lawrences that their failure to make arrests was due to a "wall of silence" surrounding his murder. But a later inquiry revealed that within hours of Stephen's death informants had given the police the names of the five prime suspects – Gary Dobson, brothers Neil and Jamie Acourt, Luke Knight and David Norris – who had all been previously involved in racist knife attacks in Eltham.

Doreen had naively believed at first that the police would do everything in their power to catch the killers but she soon realised they weren't doing anything. "People were ringing us at the house with information every day and we passed it on. But when we asked police what they were doing with it, they wouldn't tell us. They kept on saying, 'You don't understand, this is the way we operate.'

"They implied that we couldn't be asking such intelligent questions for ourselves. We must have been prompted by someone else."

Which was another example of overt racism. The Met were

convinced that radical black forces were using Doreen and Neville Lawrence to instigate their own anti-police agenda. Evidence would later come to light that the Lawrence justice campaign had been infiltrated, spied on and smeared by the Met police.

Fifteen days after Stephen's murder, the Acourt brothers and Dobson were arrested. Norris turned himself in and Knight was arrested weeks later. Neil Acourt and Knight were charged with murder but the charges were dropped on July 29 due to "insufficient evidence."

In September 1994, the Lawrences brought out a private prosecution against all five suspects but the Crown Prosecution Service dropped charges against Jamie Acourt and Norris, again due to insufficient evidence. When the trial went ahead, in April 1996, the three remaining suspects were acquitted of murder after the judge ruled that the identification evidence given by Duwayne Brooks was unreliable.

As Doreen sensed the judge was about to direct the jury to return not guilty verdicts she collapsed in court and had to be taken out of the back door of the Old Bailey in a wheelchair. It was her lowest point since the murder and she doubted whether she could take much more.

Something else on the brink of collapse was her marriage. In the months after Stephen's death Neville withdrew into a shell, taking refuge alone in his room, gripped by depression. The couple physically and emotionally grew apart and separated in 1998 with Neville eventually returning alone to Jamaica.

Neville later admitted that the couple never again touched one another after the night of the murder and Doreen claimed their marriage died along with Stephen.

She admitted around the time of their 1999 divorce that, as a mother, it was harder for her to let go of Stephen: "I gave birth to him, I nurtured him, I was there when he cried. Nobody has the right to take his life and not to do something about it. Part of me is angry that I've been forced into this position. I do want to get on with my life but events keep on throwing up new information. In the end, that's what you react to."

At the February 1997 inquest into Stephen's death the five suspects refused to answer any questions that were put to them, claiming privilege against self-incrimination. Their arrogant, dismissive stance worked against them and after only half-an-hour's deliberation the jury returned a verdict of unlawful killing "in a completely unprovoked racist attack by five white youths."

The following day *The Daily Mail* ran a front-page headline which said 'MURDERERS' in two-inch high letters above photos of the infamous five. *The Mail* directly accused them of killing Stephen writing, 'if we are wrong, let them sue.'

They never did.

At this point, Labour was months away from winning the General Election and keen to pick up support from all quarters. Doreen met Shadow Home Secretary Jack Straw who promised if Labour won power he would look again at the case, but fell short of promising an inquiry. A month after the landslide victory she met new Home Secretary Straw who tried to fob her off with a report. The Hillsborough Families had trodden the exact same route.

A furious Doreen, who sensed a report would merely give recommendations but have no teeth, dug her heels in and told him plainly, "That is not what I want. That will never give me what I want." After the meeting was over she pleaded with him to give her something more substantial such as a proper judicial inquiry. Unlike with the Hillsborough families, Straw relented.

Retired judge Sir William Macpherson chaired the inquiry and after hearing from 80-plus witnesses and reading 100,000 pages of documents over two years, he produced a report which concluded that the investigation into Stephen's killing had been 'marred by a combination of professional incompetence, institutional racism and a failure of leadership.'

Specific Met officers were named and the entire force was criticised. Seventy recommendations designed to show 'zero tolerance' for racism in society were made, comprising measures not just to transform the attitude of the police towards race relations and improve accountability, but also to force the civil service, NHS, judiciary and other public bodies to respond and change.

Some 67 of the report's recommendations led to specific changes in practice, or the law, within two years of its publication. They included the introduction of detailed targets for the recruitment, retention and promotion of black and Asian officers as well as the creation of the Independent Police Complaints Commission with the power to appoint its own investigators.

The report was 350 pages long but two incendiary words leapt off the page which would trigger fierce debate in Britain for years to come: The labelling of the country's largest police force as 'institutionally racist.'

The Met's Chief Commissioner John Stevens stated in 2001 that his force was in crisis because of that label and there was a vicious backlash from the right. Tory leader at the time, William

Hague, called it a "weapon of the liberal elite" with which to beat the police. Most right-wing newspapers decried it as the very essence of 'political correctness gone mad' and police officers claimed it meant they could no longer stop a black man on the street. Doreen Lawrence hit back in a speech by telling police that nobody was asking them to stop doing their job, just to do it properly, and with respect.

Twenty years on from his 1999 report Macpherson said he had recognised there was a problem within the force, which was "worse than individual acts of racism" and he stood by all of his recommendations. He said the report allowed police to take a step in the right direction but believed there was "obviously a great deal more to be done."

However, there was something else contained in that report which probably gave the Lawrence family more satisfaction than making the police force that bungled Stephen's murder face the reality of being racist to its core: The abolition of the Double Jeopardy rule which stated that people could not be tried for the same crime twice. Scrapping it meant it was possible to subject an acquitted murder suspect to a second trial if 'fresh and viable' new evidence later came to light.

That ruling would eventually lead to Gary Dobson and David Norris being convicted in 2012 for Stephen's murder, allowing Doreen to finally have her day in court.

It was astonishing that a woman not born in this country and from an ethnic minority whose needs had been marginalised should change the legal and cultural fabric of Britain so profoundly.

In 2019 Cressida Dick, the Met's Commissioner, hailed the Macpherson report, which came about through Doreen

Lawrence's unerring determination, "the most important thing that's happened in my service as it defined my generation of policing."

Typically, Doreen was modest about her achievement and sceptical about its power to defeat racism. 'When people say 'you changed policing in this country' I feel a chill because it sounds as though we're all right now and it is so easy to find reasons not to keep a close eye on what those with the power in our society do. It is easy to criminalise whole groups of people and not to take seriously what is done to them by others,' she wrote in her autobiography. It was spot-on.

When it emerged that Prime Minister David Cameron's chief policy adviser Oliver Letwin had told Margaret Thatcher there was no point giving financial assistance to black unemployed youths after the 1985 inner-city riots, because it would only end up being blown on the "disco and drug trade" you realised how deep casual bigotry ran.

Especially when Cameron's Old Etonian successor as Prime Minister, Boris Johnson, referred to Africans as "picaninnies with watermelon smiles."

And when the Duke and Duchess of Sussex told Oprah Winfrey in a TV interview in March 2021 that questions about the darkness of their baby's skin colour had been raised by a senior Royal, it was clear that racism resided in the hearts and minds of those at the very top of the British Establishment.

In the autumn of 2018 Doreen decided to do what she called "her last TV interview" on ITV's Loose Women, saying that after a quarter of a century of campaigning it was time to say "enough" and move on to the next chapter of her life.

When asked what had kept her going over the previous 25

years, she said, "My other two children and also knowing that Stephen had a life and I needed to fight for him. That's what I've been doing – his name, his legacy, what we've achieved over the years with the Trust – those are all the positive things, that's what's kept me going.

"Stephen didn't have a voice, I was his voice, but I didn't allow it to sort of swallow me up. If you do that you never move forward."

It was pointed out that Neville had recently said he could forgive Stephen's killers and Doreen was asked if she could ever do the same. "It's very difficult to forgive somebody who's never admitted they've done anything wrong. Unless they come up in front of me or I need to talk about it, I don't focus on them at all. I just think they're not there," she replied.

"My focus has always been looking forward, how do I make sure my children are ok? I've got grandchildren now, they're what's important to me. Twenty-five years is a long time to be out campaigning. I've not really lived my life in the way I would have liked to. I'm always being asked some question; I'm always being asked to do something. I just think I would like to be cheerful now. It's time to move on and think about me and my family and my grandchildren, so I can spend more time on positive things."

In July 2020, Doreen announced she was leaving the foundation she had set up to focus on creating a national Stephen Lawrence Day, every April 22, something she believed had become more necessary with the advent of the Black Lives Matter movement.

Writing in the *Daily Mirror* she said she wanted 'to bring all the forces of good together, all the support I have received over

27 years into a day for all marginalised people who have suffered disadvantage or prejudice.'

She hailed it 'a day for everyone with a cause which deserves justice. And a day of celebration of what we have achieved. Are we going back to the bad old days when it took a fight to get justice for a boy killed for doing nothing wrong? No. We are not.

'People kept asking me to say something about the Black Lives Matter movement and the protests after George Floyd was murdered by police in America. But I've always believed in action rather than words, so I was busy building a new organisation which will say, loudly and clearly on a UK national day for everyone, that black lives matter.

'Black lives always matter, of course, and we'll hold events, activities and build relationships which will shout this loudly across the whole year, every year.

'That will be more effective than a few quotes from me stating the obvious that I detest and deplore the waste of innocent black lives, of any young life, any injustice.

'Next April, Stephen Lawrence Day will allow thousands of people, from the very young to the very old, families and friends to show the world that black lives matter by attending our national events.

'And this won't be an improvised protest, it will be an official Day, a nationwide expression against injustice and cruelty; a celebration of tolerance and diversity.

'It will be a day for all disadvantaged sections of society, for everyone who has suffered prejudice or injustice.'

In the years that followed Stephen's death, random people who knew him would tell Doreen stories about her son that she had never heard before. A teacher told how he had acted as an informal mentor to younger pupils and the local chemist described how he would often call into the shop for a chat on his way home from school. She had always seen him as an extrovert but a picture emerged of someone who, on the quiet, cared deeply about others and was modest with it.

Stephen never sought deification. He was just a decent, ordinary teenager trying to do his best as he made his way through a complex and unforgiving world.

"When I go to schools, I say to young people, 'Stephen was never perfect, don't think he had this perfect life. He was just like anybody else.'"

But his mother wasn't.

Thanks to the Macpherson Report that her will forced on to this country's statute books, she introduced an explosive phrase to the British psyche: 'Institutional racism.'

A phrase that made millions of people, and most institutions, think differently. It's what Black Lives Matter was all about.

And Doreen Lawrence had ensured, decades before that movement took to our streets, that her son's life definitely did.

THE FIGHTER

10

JACK JONES

EBRO VALLEY, CATALONIA — *April 2017*

WHEN you reach Hill 481 at Gandesa, the two things that strike you are how steep and how bleak it is. Standing on the brow of the hill that British volunteers had nicknamed The Pimple and surveying the rugged terrain that stretches as far as the eye can see, the still and lifeless landscape feels like a place that time forgot.

It's hard to imagine that at night, in the late-1930s, this part of Catalonia, which saw the longest and bloodiest of battles in the Spanish Civil War, would have been hit with so much shelling, strafing and gunfire it would have looked as though a Biblical-scale blizzard of fireflies had descended.

Ernest Hemingway observed that when "the sudden thunder of their loads" was dropped by Hitler's Luftwaffe and Mussolini's Regia Aeronautica "the dust hung like a yellow fog all down the Ebro Valley."

As I tried to manoeuvre through thick bushes, clay-like soil and stubborn mounds of rock, my boot crunched on rotting reminders of the last time there was human activity here: rusted sardine tins, fragments of mines and grenades, the base of a metal water container, a bullet.

I picked the bullet up and stared at it then let my eyes drift back up to the crest of the hill where Franco's men fired their machine guns from concrete pillar-boxes on that August day in 1938 when International Brigade volunteer Jack Jones was shot. And I wondered if it was a similar sniper's bullet to the one that shattered his shoulder and ended his personal stand against the fascist takeover of Europe by sending him back to Lime Street station.

It was up Hill 481 that Jones repeatedly charged with the 15th International Brigade to take the heavily-fortified summit from Franco's fascists in the hope of capturing the Ebro Valley and turning the tide in the bloody civil war. But it was a virtually impossible task due to the superior numbers and weaponry of the enemy plus the sophisticated air support from Germany and Italy.

As Jones, parched from a lack of water and the searing Spanish summer heat, intermittently crawled then sprinted up the hill with his primitive rifle into ferocious fire, his comrades were falling all around him. Imagine being a 25-year-old from Liverpool barely trained in the art of warfare, facing that, I thought.

Imagine the fear in the pit of your stomach and the piss and the shit in your ragged trousers as you heard young men scream like babies, saw their faces blown off and knew you would probably soon be falling on to this piece of scrubland, 1,300 miles from home, and left to bleed to death.

All because of your principles.

Back in the 1930s, following the Wall Street Crash and the Great Depression, many were seduced into believing that fascism was a way out of their problems. The focus of the creed of hate in Britain was Oswald Mosley and his Blackshirts.

Jack, a committed internationalist and socialist, instinctively joined up with like-minded anti-fascists to break up Mosley's meetings across the North West. They were always thrown out, most of the time violently, and left unconscious on the street. As Jack put it, "I often ended up with a thick head. We'd be lifted out of seats by burly heavies thrown out on to the street then beaten up with knuckle-dusters as the police looked on."

As a Liverpool dockworker, Jones had learned first-hand from sailors on Spanish ships about the dire situation back home where General Francisco Franco was attempting to overthrow the left-wing Popular Front government through a military coup. It resulted in a civil war which lasted three years, cost more than half-a-million lives and turned Spain into a brutal dictatorship until Franco's death in 1975.

Despite an internationally agreed non-aggression pact, Hitler's Germany and Mussolini's Italy entered the conflict on the side of their fellow fascists, using it as a training exercise for World War II.

Rallying to the Republic's cause, an estimated 59,000 volunteers from 50 different countries formed into International Brigades, with 15,000 of them dying in combat. From Britain, 2,300 men and women from all classes and backgrounds went incognito to Spain, with more than 500 of them laying down their lives.

In late 1936, when the Republicans suffered heavy casualties, Jones volunteered to go but was told by his union, the Transport and General Workers, that he was of better use back home in Liverpool where he had set up and was chairing Aid Spain meetings. He badgered them to let him travel to Spain, growing increasingly impatient with, and critical of, the lack of support from unions and the Labour Party who backed the Tory government's non-intervention policy.

Eventually they agreed, with TGWU General Secretary Ernest Bevin giving him a letter of solidarity to hand to the leader of the Spanish trade unions.

He left Britain undercover and headed to Paris where he met up with fellow volunteers to be taken by coach to the Pyrenees.

There they posed as tourists and crossed the mountains surreptitiously on foot, avoiding the French police.

Once at Barcelona he handed over the letter and headed out to the Aragon front with a trade union battalion to taste war.

I first interviewed Jack for the *Liverpool Echo* in 1992, inside London's Transport House, where every day the then 79-year-old retired TGWU leader would head to plot a better deal for pensioners, and asked him to share personal memories of that war. At first, like all old soldiers, he was reticent. Then I reminded him how outspoken he'd been about the recently ended first Iraq War and the need for generations like mine to understand the horrors of conflict.

I told him that had I been a young man in Liverpool in the 1930s I'd have probably been alongside him scrapping with Mosley's Blackshirts on the streets and would like to think I'd have given up my job and gone to fight for the noble cause of defeating Franco.

He laughed and said he'd like to "disabuse me" of any romantic notions I had that war was noble.

He told of how hard and impersonal the reality of armed conflict turned him. How he eventually found himself burying fallen friends without any show of emotion. How he and another volunteer came across one of their own who lay dead on the battlefield and his first thought was to look over his gear to find if he had any supplies. And when he found an unopened tin of corned beef he and his famished comrade sat down, under heavy fire, and "ate like kings."

After fighting at the Aragon front, Jack's leadership skills were noted and he was promoted to political commissar of the Major Attlee company of the 15th International Brigade. "My job was basically to revive the spirits of the men. To tell them what was happening back home, how the war was going and how I saw the prospects for action," he said.

These were civilians of all trades; dockers and journalists, accountants and scaffolders, and they had to learn about the military and its way of life as they went along, with little food in their bellies, sometimes going days without water, in clothes not much better than rags, possessing the poorest of kit.

In a later interview, when I was at the *Mirror*, I asked Jack if he remembered killing anyone and he shrugged and replied, "Well I fired a lot, a hell of a lot, in their direction, so it's possible. But I couldn't say for certain. Especially with the archaic Russian-made rifles we had, which weren't the most accurate. Put it this way, many of my friends and comrades were killed and I'm sure the same fate befell men on the other side."

He told me that in the heat of battle you don't think about death even though people all around you are being killed because you are overcome with a kind of numbness that is impossible to describe.

"Your instinct is self-preservation while at the same time trying to take out the enemy. It's hard to stay calm and detached because the adrenaline pumping through you is overwhelming. Everything around you is almost a blur."

In his autobiography, Union Man, Jack wrote about the terror he felt in the moments leading up to being hit on that August day in 1938: 'The closer you got to the summit, the more it felt like you were entering hell. Everything was thrown at you. Machine-gun fire, shells, grenades, snipers' bullets. I was firing with my rifle, trying to take cover where possible, with the bullets whizzing over me and shells blasting on the ground, when all of a sudden my shoulder and right arm went numb. I knew I'd been hit because blood was scuffing everywhere and I couldn't lift my rifle. There was shrapnel in my leg and I was in such a terrible mess I could do nothing but lie where I was. I thought I was a goner.'

Next to him was a dead comrade and Jack could hear the screams of others, some begging to be put out of their misery, one crying for his mother. He waited until dark then crawled to the bottom of The Pimple in excruciating pain. He was eventually taken with other injured men to a field hospital, set up in a cave, and remembered: "It was like an abattoir, there was blood on the floor and the stench of blood in the air."

Eventually he was taken to a proper hospital in Barcelona before being sent back home to Liverpool. Typically, the first thing he did on his return was urge people through public speeches to come to the aid of the desperate people in Catalonia. He told the Liverpool Trades Council and the Labour Party that, "the children of Spain are dying of malnutrition and men and women at the front and in the factories are on the brink of starvation. We must send a food ship."

He pestered business for money and supplies, organised flag days, appealed to trade unions and co-operative guilds, brought in the Catholic and Anglican bishops of Liverpool and convinced the Mersey Docks And Harbour Board to waive their shipping fees. Lancashire farmers sent a massive amount of spuds. The ship sailed, much to the relief of the starving Spanish people, and Jack earned the nickname Councillor 'Potato' Jones after the Welsh sea captain who broke through Franco's blockade. Jack was like Bob Geldof, almost half a century before Live Aid was thought of, feeding strangers faraway who were starving.

When Jack looked back, decades later, he was filled with admiration for his comrades, those courageous young idealists who gave everything, without question, for their principles.

Men and women, who, in Britain, were disowned by the press and politicians for confronting a Hitler-backed army when that is exactly what they should have been doing. Men and women, who, because they weren't taking the King's shilling were never given any official recognition for their brave stand against the fascist takeover of Europe, years before governments were forced to agree with them and follow suit.

"Many amazing young men who would have been leaders in their different walks of life were killed at a very early age, for simply believing in democracy," Jack told me in a sorrowful tone. But was it all worth it?

"Going to fight in Spain was important from a point of principle by establishing the ideal of internationalism but the price was extremely heavy. Win or lose, the world needs to see individual courage in the face of oppression. Man needs to show sincerity. In Spain it was demonstrated by so many in full measure. Even unto death."

In 2017 I visited the hill where Jack was shot as part of a documentary I was making with Hurricane Films about his life, called Unsung Hero. For years I'd been badgering Hurricane's directors, Roy Boulter and Sol Papadopoulos, to make the film because, to me, James Larkin Jones was one of the greatest modern Britons.

The truest of working-class heroes who fought relentlessly, until he was 96, to steer future generations away from the squalor and inequality he was born into.

A hero who devoted his life to taking on the four greatest evils of the 20th century: want, fascism, worker exploitation and pensioner neglect. And took them on with such conviction in a 1977 Gallup Poll 54 per cent of the British people said they saw him as the most powerful man in Britain.

But that label was used against him by his right-wing enemies who portrayed him at best as a grasping militant, and at worst as a threat to national security. All because he fought to win working-class people a better life.

When he died, in 2009, the Labour movement realised it had lost a unique figure. Tony Benn remarked of Jack that, "Everything he said, he felt. Everything he said, he believed. He was one of the finest men I've ever met."

To meet him was a privilege because he was an irrepressible force of nature. A man whose heart was filled with compassion, who had a spirit made of steel and a brain as sharp as a razor. A man who, unlike the vast majority of today's politicians and public figures, didn't draw lessons from history, he delivered them.

I'd interviewed him a couple of times, and spoken to him occasionally on the phone, and one story in particular, from the 1992 meeting, resonated. A story that summed up how long and how passionately he'd been fighting the good fight. And how, compared to him so many of the politicians who had been feted at Westminster, were pygmies.

"There was a myth put about by propagandists on the right that we were a rag-bag shower of ne'er do well communists and anarchists who went to Spain to bring down democracy," he told me. "But the opposite was true. I went there to fight on the side of a democratically elected Popular Front government against a military coup.

"When that government fell, a junior minister called Portillo sought asylum in Britain. Today his son, Michael Portillo, sits in the Treasury making cuts that hit the elderly.

"I bumped into him recently in the Commons and I told him that his father would be ashamed of him for treating like dirt a generation of working-class people who fought for his family's freedom, and paid through their taxes for his education and his upbringing.

"And here's my point. More than half a century after fighting on behalf of the father for what is right, I'm fighting against the son for the same thing. That's how mad the world is under these Tories. And that's what keeps me fighting.

"Because when I see the way my country is run under people like Portillo, I am reminded of what Gandhi said in the 1930s when asked what he thought about civilisation in Britain. 'Yes,' he said. 'I think it would be a good idea.'"

Jack's early life reads like the Monty Python Yorkshiremen sketch. He was born in 1913 in a street by the Garston docks, full of tuberculosis and rat-infested slums where big families slept on bare boards with coats for blankets.

His mother had originally been married to a seaman, with whom she had had a daughter and two sons. After he died she went through a horrendous time fending for her family until she married a docker. She then had two more sons, of whom James (or Jack as he was always known) was the younger.

When Jack's father went to fight in the Dockers' Battalion during the First World War his mum had to rent out the front room to a lodger. The alternative was the workhouse.

As a young boy, Jack recalls being so hungry he would beg for sandwiches off men finishing their shifts on the nearby docks.

"I guess that's what you would call poverty," is how he modestly put it.

At school Jack was more interested in football than study, though one of his brothers involved him in the Sea Scouts and even persuaded him to take an interest in a religious Sunday School. But he soon rejected Christian dogma, preferring to join a Socialist Sunday School.

"Many working-class kids at the time didn't stand a chance of getting past the elementary age of school," Jack told me, decades later.

"We were thrown out at 14 and told to start at the bottom. The higher up the class system you went, the better were the education and the opportunities, through inherited privilege and contacts. And that was seen as the way it should be. And although it's a lot easier today for a bright working-class kid to get a good education and a decent job, the tenets of that haven't really changed," he said.

I knew where he was coming from. My own dad, Reg, was a bright lad who passed the 11-plus in the 1930s in a school not far from where Jack grew up. It took him to a Jesuits' Grammar School where he excelled, gaining nine O Levels. He showed a great talent for art and wanted to go on to be an architect, but being the eldest son of four boys whose dad was a docker and whose mother was a school cleaner, he had no chance. Any hope of training to enter a profession like the children from richer families was an unattainable pipe-dream and he was made to leave school at 15 and put wages on the family table. Eighty years later for some families, that's still the same sad story.

The lamentable living conditions, the grotesque inequality and the collectivist politics Jack inherited meant he was politically formed when he was a young boy. His life-long hatred of racism and fascism was partly inspired by seeing his mother helped by an elderly Jewish shopkeeper who gave her the food to keep her kids alive. He also learned a passion for workers' rights from infancy, at the knees of his father, a friend of legendary Liverpudlian trade unionist James Larkin, whom Jack was named after.

By the 1926 General Strike Jack had become fascinated with left-wing orators, read The Ragged Trousered Philanthropists, witnessed the employer backlash against trade unionists and shared in the sense of betrayal when the strike was called off. It also instilled in him a loathing of scabs.

Shortly afterwards he was apprenticed to a firm making components for shipbuilders Harland & Wolff. He was paid five shillings a week to work in appalling conditions which made him active in the TGWU, his father's union, becoming a branch delegate at the age of 17. By then he had already been secretary of his Labour Party ward for two years.

When the firm went bankrupt, he followed his father into the docks, and immediately began to organise, starting the fightback against the casual labour system we know today as zero-hours contracts. Another early and enduring campaign was for safety at work, originally inspired by the sight of injured dockers being taken away on handcarts for the knackers' yard. While barely a man, he was standing up to naked capitalist exploitation by taking industrial action.

He discovered, though, that "to speak your mind in the union then was like walking on glass". His puritanical instincts were particularly offended by the TGWU area secretary, Harry Pugh, who wore a bowler hat, sported a flower in his buttonhole, smoked a cigar and found union jobs for his family. He was the type of corrupt autocrat that inspired Jack to campaign for grass-roots democracy.

To prepare himself for future responsibilities, Jack read Marx and Engels, and applied himself to Ruskin College correspondence courses on industrial law and workmen's compensation. In 1934 he took part in the National Hunger March to London.

He moved into local politics attempting to eradicate the poverty he saw all around him, and aged 23, working the docks by day and canvassing at night, he became Liverpool's youngest city councillor when he was elected to the Croxteth ward.

That was despite early traumatic meetings where he was roughed-up by women in shawls in a Protestant area of North Liverpool for being a "Fenian bastard."

He started to make his mark alongside the fabled Labour figure Bessie Braddock on the Public Assistance Committee, where he fought to get more money for the poor. But when a different battleground emerged on the horizon, he went off to fight for the marginalised in Spain.

On his return, as well as organising aid for the people he'd left behind, Jack married Evelyn Taylor, whose first husband George was a fellow volunteer and friend of Jack's who had been killed in Spain. Jack and Evelyn, who had two boys – Jack Jnr and Michael – were ideologically joined at the hip and remained the closest of soulmates throughout their lives.

According to Jack the younger, his mother was even more left-wing than his dad. She was the idealist while he had learned to become more of a pragmatist. There is a clip of Evelyn doing a rare TV interview, which we used in Unsung Hero, that sums up her left-wing ideology.

"In the 1930s there were people without coal to put on their fires and we lived on an island built on coal. How stupid is that?" she said. "Ships full of bananas would come into the Mersey docks and because there was no sale for them, instead of distributing them to the people, they used to take them up the bar of the river and dump them overboard. How much more stupid can society be?

"It's such a pity that people put so much value on money as if money is wealth. Shelley said, and incidentally he wrote before Marx, that there's no real wealth but the labour of man. Were the mountains made of gold or the valleys of silver the earth would be not one grain of corn the richer. No single comfort would be added to the human race." Then speaking of her husband she said, "Socialism was Jack's religion. I know very few people who have devoted themselves so wholeheartedly to the cause."

In 1939 Jack was handed his "perfect challenge": TGWU's Coventry District Organiser. Due to the burgeoning motor industry the West Midlands became the new Workshop of Britain, but was woefully under-unionised. Jones had to overcome innumerable obstacles to unionise the factories including apathetic and frightened workers, old school management and the return of an old foe, the German Luftwaffe.

During the Great Blitz of 1940 there were 57 German air raids on Coventry, culminating on November 14, 1940, when more than 600 people were killed and much of the city centre reduced to rubble. Jack and his family survived by sheltering in the cellar of their house as the rest of the building was destroyed.

Jones helped see the city through these critical times without ever relaxing his aim for better working conditions. He was on decent terms with some of the bosses, such as Sir John Black, the chairman of Standard Motors, but never let them off the hook. When Black offered him the post of Labour Director at Standard, cleverly seeking to turn him from poacher to gamekeeper, he turned him down with a fury.

"Illegitimi non carborundum," he told his union colleagues. "Never let the bastards grind you down."

The workload was immense and the battle uphill, but he cracked it through a new and untried method, which he stayed loyal to all of his life. Gaining shop steward recognition from the management and racking up rank-and-file membership. No-one did more than Jones to recruit new members and build mass trade unionism after the War.

He also cut landmark deals with big employers which completely changed working-class lives. The "Coventry rate" that Jack negotiated gave TGWU members the highest wages in the country for shop floor workers. In 1946, an agreement he made with Standard Motors broke new ground by introducing a five-day week of 42.5 hours. The following year it came into force nationally, meaning for the first time ever, the working class of this country enjoyed a full weekend off.

In 1951, another agreement with Standard established two weeks' paid holiday. He also persuaded bosses to allow shop stewards to go on courses in company time and would go on to help usher in ACAS and The Health and Safety at Work Act.

By 1955, he had built up TGWU membership in Coventry to 40,000 and was made secretary for the entire Midlands region, at the head of 250,000 members.

His skills of persuasion, oratory and tenacity singled him out as a star of the Labour movement. In 1963 he was made assistant general secretary of the TGWU and moved to London.

And his power base widened in 1964 when he was elected to the Labour Party's National Executive Committee but his vocal opposition to some of Harold Wilson's government's economic policies saw him voted off it three years later.

In truth he was never much interested in power outside the union movement and when in 1968 he was elected TGWU General Secretary by a majority of 520,000 to 28,000, he'd reached the peak of his aspirations.

The next ten years marked the high point of Jack's public life, and by no coincidence, trade union power in Britain. So influential had Jack's persona become, he was perceived by the nation to be manipulating Prime Ministers Ted Heath, Harold Wilson and James Callaghan, and effectively running the country.

At the 1977 Labour Conference he chastised some Labour leaders for buying "grand country houses" and secured backing for a move to abolish the House of Lords.

He fought against every attempt to bring in anti-union legislation, maintained his hatred of racism by denouncing 200 London dockers who marched in support of Enoch Powell's 1968 Rivers of Blood speech and was an early advocate for women's rights, winning equal pay for them in the aircraft building industry.

TUC General Secretary Frances O'Grady told us when making Unsung Hero: "I think of Jack as a feminist. He respected women. He was famed for setting very high standards for officers in the way they treated women. That's one of the reasons that many ordinary people genuinely believed that he was the best Prime Minister we never had."

Not everyone on the left was enamoured with him though, and

his introduction of The Social Contract, which was an attempt to keep an embattled Labour government in power, led to fierce opposition from many in the trade union movement who viewed it as nothing more than an attempt to keep down wages.

To be fair, he got it from all sides. Which is never a bad indicator of your worth. The hard left called him (in Jack's words) a "bastard, traitor and a scab" accusing him of being too much in bed with Downing Street.

The centre accused him of bringing down Wilson's 1970 government through his refusal to accept legal restraints on unions.

The right attacked him for forcing Callaghan to give in to union demands, which led to the Winter of Discontent, and eventually 13 years of Thatcherism, despite the fact that Jack had retired from the leadership of the TGWU the previous year.

Meanwhile, the spooks at M15 were even leaking that Jack was in the pay of the KGB.

A story was circulated that Soviet spy Oleg Gordievsky paid him £200 for sensitive information about the government, the Labour Party and prominent trades union figures who could potentially be recruited for the KGB.

Jack always staunchly denied the charge, describing it as "a slur and an outrage". His son Mick called them the words of a consummate liar who was stooping low to sell a book. "The idea that my dad was slipped a few hundred quid for information is ridiculous. He would never take money for anything like that. He twice turned down the offer of being in the House of Lords and was offered endless directorships of companies. He could have feathered his nest over and over. We could have been living in a mansion," said Mick.

One of Jack's veteran trade union colleagues, Rodney Bickerstaffe, put it a different way when we interviewed him for Unsung Hero: "We used to call him 'Incorruptible Jack' because he couldn't be bought. He used to tell us 'never do deals for favours.'

"His only concern was to improve the lot of the ordinary man, which he worked for solidly week after week, year after year, decade after decade. He had a conviction throughout his whole life that workers had more knowledge about jobs than the bosses and that they should have a proper say in how their companies were run.

"He had this phrase he used all the time – 'keep on keeping on.' He knew nothing would ever be perfect but you had to keep on trying.

"There are a few people in the world, who, when you're with them, you believe there's something extraordinarily special about them, and Jack was undoubtedly one of those people," said Bickerstaffe.

As Jack neared retirement in 1978, Jim Callaghan offered him a seat in the Lords but he turned it down flat, saying he wanted to devote the rest of his life fighting for "those too old to work, too young to die."

The TGWU staff collected £10,000 as a retirement present. He put every penny towards the establishment of a Retired Members' Association, which became the forerunner of the National Pensioners Convention; the first ever nationally coordinated body to fight for the rights of the elderly. Jack was made chairman and eventually Honorary Life President.

In truth he'd been fighting for better pensions throughout his working life, way before any other union leader or politician broached the issue. He constantly pushed ministers to give OAPs pay rises, persuaded Labour to bring in cheap public transport for the elderly, and Ted Heath to give them a £10 Christmas bonus, which they still receive today. He also argued passionately against the Blair government's opposition for the restoration of the link between pensions and average earnings.

His retirement was spent in a Dulwich council house with Evelyn, using his free bus pass every day, to go to work, unpaid, at TGWU central London headquarters as chairman of the Convention. There he organised marches, increased its membership and profile and badgered politicians on all sides for a better deal for the elderly.

He was always there to answer the phone if you needed a chat, a quote for a story or advice. I rang him in May 2002, after landing an exclusive sit-down interview in 10 Downing Street with Tony Blair, to mark his fifth anniversary as Prime Minister.

I knew it was going to be a tough one, because the *Mirror* were slaughtering him at the time over his post 9/11 poodle-like obedience to warmonger George Bush.

The point of these interviews, especially with someone like Alastair Campbell pulling the strings, is they want to get a pre-prepared policy line out. In this case it was a new law and order diktat. But I wanted to try to find out from Blair why he thought so much of the optimism he'd taken into number 10 in 1997 had evaporated. Why, to misquote D:Ream, after 18 years of Tory rule, things hadn't got better.

So I rang Jack, who was then 89, and on his own after his beloved Evelyn had died a few years earlier, to ask his advice.

"Well, he'll answer whatever you put to him in typical legalise because first and foremost he's a barrister," he said. "But he'll also charm you because he's very persuasive. That's how he got to the top.

"He's no doubt agreed to do it in Downing Street because he thinks it will intimidate you sitting in the seat of power in front of the country's most powerful man. And it can be intimidating in there at first. But remember it's just another room and he's just another man. But very skilled at presentation.

"He'll just want to tell you what he wants you to hear. Your only hope of getting him to say something he doesn't want to, is to catch him off guard."

I told Jack that I thought I should go down the McCarthyist line of questioning, and ask him, "are you now, or have you ever been, a socialist?"

The veteran of many a confrontation with Prime Ministers laughed and said, "good luck but he'll shoot you down with a polished answer that makes him look good and makes you wonder why you ever asked it." He was spot-on.

When I put that to Blair he replied, "I've never pretended to be an old-style Scargill-like socialist because I don't believe in it. The idea that I promised to come into power and lead a red-blooded socialist revolution à la 1917 then turned it into a moderate government is not true. I spent my entire adult political life hearing people say: 'Ah yes, the Labour Party. My heart says 'yes' but my head says 'no.'"

During that phone call with Jack we spoke about socialism and whether, following the triumph of New Labour, it was now doomed as a mainstream political philosophy. When I asked him if he thought the best we could hope for in government was One Nation Toryism with a social conscience, I could feel an angry wince at the other end of the line.

"Never lose faith in socialism son, because it's the only way humans will get a better future. This every-man-for-himself philosophy can only lead to destruction. The right's obsession with extreme free marketeering is a conception, and we saw it perfectly illustrated under Thatcher, that only sows the seeds of division, hatred and inequality."

When we interviewed Dennis Skinner for our film he put into words why he felt Jack had stayed a committed socialist all of his life: "It's in your bones or it ain't. And I think his world was all about representing people at the bottom of the pile and trying to make their lives better.

"In the 1930s, as a young man, he had the inclination to fight against Franco and that was no small deal. Guys like him were thin on the ground. They had to be totally committed and they took part in battles in which a lot of them died and were injured.

"And so Jack Jones, long before he became that sterling figure at the head of Britain's biggest union, had proved beyond doubt, his commitment to his class."

Jack Jones wasn't faultless. He could be impatient, hectoring and those he disapproved of claimed that his extreme self-confidence bordered on arrogance. His puritanical sense of certainty in his beliefs tended to exclude any compromise. Jones saw issues in black and white. He divided the world between the virtuous "those who work" and the evil "those who make money." His hot temper left him contemptuous of anyone who doubted his intentions. There were those who say he garnered too much power. They cite graffiti that went up during the 1974 General Election which said, "Vote Jack Jones: Cut out the middle-man."

But his record, both on paper and from the mouths of those

who knew him, points to a giant of a man, who remembered the poverty and inequality he was born into, and who fought with every ounce of strength he possessed to raise future generations away from such a fate.

International solidarity among the workers of all creeds and races was at the core of his beliefs. He was an unashamed crusading socialist, dedicated to the collectivist ideal of Each for All and All for Each. A formidable figure who managed to bend both Labour and Conservative administrations to his agenda.

More than any other individual, he changed the unions from the centralised bureaucracies they had become in the 1950s, leading the shop stewards' movement which forced union leaders to respond to their members.

Jones saw himself as the workers' tribune, deriving his authority directly from the workers on the shop floor. Time and again he would tell politicians, employers and fellow union leaders who wanted him to go over the heads of his members to agree a quick settlement, "No union man has the right to change a worker's life without asking him first."

His story is not only one of the most inspirational of the last century but in these times of obscene wealth disparities, of unchecked worker exploitation, of the rise of the fascist right, of assaults on our public services, the lessons it teaches us are as relevant as they've ever been.

The last time I saw him was in 2003, in The Casa in Liverpool. They had invited Jack back home to celebrate his 90th birthday, taking the Garston Mud Man on a coach trip around his old haunts, then throwing a party for him.

He was on great form, as sharp as a pin throughout: pointing at faces on 70-year-old photos and giving potted biographies of old friends and comrades. I asked him how he was feeling and he replied, "as good as can be expected when your body's this old." When I told him, as many others had that day, that his brain seemed as good as ever, he said, "That's because I keep it ticking over all the time. The secret to life is keeping on using your brain as I'm doing with the Pensioners' Convention. And the best way to use your brain is to use it for helping those who can't help themselves."

In the 1970s Liverpool's most famous son sent a slogan around the world called 'Power to the People.' Jack Jones, had been living it for the previous half-century and carried on doing so until in 2009, when he died, aged 96, in the Peckham care home which now bears his name.

Few Britons of his, or any, generation did more to turn that slogan into an everyday reality.

Which is why, to me, he will always be my city's greatest son.

II

THE

NOURISHERS

IAN
BYRNE
DAVE
KELLY

GOODISON PARK — December 2018

THE inevitable yell turned a few heads and triggered laughter from the huddled masses heading down Goodison Road.

"Eh, Readey, have you finally seen the light and binned the Red shite, then?"

Standing in Everton Football Club's car-park as a known member of the opposite tribe had left me a sitting duck. It wasn't the first time. In the summer of 1999, when I was 41, I was ordered, by the *Mirror* editor, to go there and hold aloft an Everton scarf as part of a spoof feature aimed at proving that miracles can happen.

While the photographer urged me to look less like I'd impaled my ball-sack on a metal spike, two middle-aged men walked past and gawped at us.

"Who's he?" said one. "Looks like a new signing," said the other. "They're really taking the piss now. Have you seen the age of that grey-haired old bastard?" the first one exclaimed. And off the cursing pair trundled.

This time though, the mood was far more upbeat. It was a Monday night, two weeks before Christmas, and for some of the poorest, hungriest families in north Liverpool, Santa was coming early.

The pre-match fanzone was buzzing as Evertonians warmed to the prospect of that night's game with Watford. Hands were shaken, burgers scoffed, pints passed between mates, replica shirts bought for excited kids as goals from previous matches were beamed on to a big screen to heighten anticipation.

But to the side of that screen something was happening which, despite being a testament to the generosity and solidarity of the football fans, shamed the sixth-richest economy in the world.

Match-goers were handing over bulging shopping bags containing UHT milk, long-life fruit juice, tins of meat and veg, packets of soup, pasta and noodles in the hope it would stave off hunger in the working-class communities close to the home of their beloved football club.

Few of the thousands of fans streaming down Goodison Road gave the trestle tables that were weighed down with emergency supplies a second glance, because they had seen them there, and on the other side of Stanley Park outside Anfield, on every match day since 2015, thanks to a partnership between the two supporter groups, called Fans Supporting Foodbanks (FSF).

In 2015, two Unite the Union organisers Dave Kelly and Ian Byrne (now a Labour MP for Liverpool West Derby) were at a community meeting near Liverpool's Anfield ground, when they spotted what they thought was a long queue outside a bingo hall. It was, in fact, for a foodbank.

When they approached they were invited inside and were gobsmacked to see supplies that were so depleted, a bag of pasta was being split and divided into sweet bags for distribution.

The grimness of the scene, and the fact it had become both widespread and acceptable, reminded Byrne of old black-and-white footage of soup kitchens during the Great Depression of the 1930s.

When he expressed his shock at how little food there was, he was told that demand was far outstripping supply. "I came away from it quite traumatised that my class was facing such an appalling situation," he said.

The two were also fan activists. Byrne was with Liverpool's

Spirit of Shankly and Kelly with Everton's Blue Union, and had worked together on the Football Supporters' Federation's successful Twenty's Plenty initiative, which capped the cost of Premier League away tickets. They tossed around ideas about how to address the desperate lack of food, and along with fellow Evertonian Robbie Daniels decided they needed to take joint action on the grounds that poverty was a curse regardless of the football team you support.

And so their slogan 'Hunger Doesn't Wear Club Colours' was born.

They asked Liverpool City Council to donate some wheelie-bins, which they placed outside the Albert Pub next door to Anfield and the Winslow Hotel opposite Goodison on successive weekends, and through clever use of social media enjoyed a tremendous response from the off.

But they realised they needed to get closer to the grounds to maximise their weekly take so Byrne and Kelly approached key figures at both clubs to persuade them to let them set up their collection points on the grounds' footprints.

The clubs didn't just agree, they gave access to their official social media channels and websites, and sent emails to all season ticket holders informing them how and where to donate food. They were up and running.

They got the backing of the Football Supporters' Association, and other fan groups (including Newcastle, Celtic, Huddersfield, West Ham, Manchester United, Aston Villa, Doncaster and Sunderland) followed suit, and set up their own matchday collections. The concept even spread to Ireland.

They had no paid workers but simply relied on the generosity and time of fellow supporters to make it work. And it did work.

Before Covid struck, forcing all fans to stay at home, the Anfield and Goodison matchday foodbanks were providing almost a third of the city's emergency food supply.

Their work was vital because the numbers were frightening. As I stood helping with the collections that night outside Goodison, 2,000 people in just Anfield and Everton alone, including 755 children, were reliant on free food.

I asked Dave Kelly what his motivation was and he replied, "Our only reason for existing is to do everything we can to ensure that the warehouses are full across the city.

"Unfortunately, we have a humanitarian crisis in every town and city in the UK. I would love to never stand outside a stadium collecting food ever again, but until things change we will continue doing so.

"And by the way, this isn't charity. It's solidarity, it's about working-class communities showing unity and helping each other in their hour of need."

I told him he must draw great satisfaction from his humanitarian efforts and he frowned and replied, "Well, personally, I sleep easier at night knowing for a fact that fewer children are going to bed hungry. So that will do for me."

A few weeks earlier they had rebranded the meeting of Liverpool and Everton at Anfield the Universal Credit derby, and 2.2 tonnes of foods and toiletries were collected in three hours before kick-off. That meant North Liverpool Foodbank had an extra 158 emergency three-day food parcels, providing more than 6,300 meals for families in crisis. Which made a massive difference to the poorest families, especially in the run-up to Christmas.

As we took bags off the fans and sorted them into pallets to be driven to the foodbank warehouse, I asked Ian Byrne if he could envisage a time when they didn't need to beg fans to turn up to games with bags of food. He shrugged his shoulders, sighed and answered, "We have a poverty epidemic on our streets, due to government policies, and football fans have become a safety net. Which is bizarre when you stop and think about it.

"We don't want to have to ask supporters to turn up for matches with food donations but it just keeps getting worse. Surely it's the government's responsibility to look after its citizens, not football fans.

"The day we can close up foodbanks will be a great one for our city but people are slipping through the gaps and we can't stand by and do nothing. We're just a sticking plaster but we are doing what we can."

The fans I spoke to were delighted to have the chance to show solidarity with the poorest of the club's neighbours, as Leanne Dillon from Whiston remarked handing over a shopping bag "these guys are real heroes. But it's a disgrace that in this day and age people are having to use foodbanks."

Richard Robinson along with his wife Karen, from Huyton, told me they had donated at every game for the past three seasons. "Collecting food at matches to feed people is an embarrassment to this nation but thankfully we have people like these who are doing it."

"I've heard all this guff about some recipients abusing the system but I don't buy into it. There are people out there in genuine need and if you can afford to help you should. We used to pay to park the car, now we park it on the street a bit further away and spend the money on food," added 61-year-old Richard.

As someone who had been going to football grounds since the mid-60s, witnessing such scenes of mass generosity was extremely moving. It was obvious that the working-class communities which surrounded old Victorian stadiums like Goodison Park had much less back then and that Liverpool had gone through harder times in the 1980s when mass unemployment blighted the city. Yet here in 2018, was the humiliating sight of fans being asked not just to support their football club, but also people who needed to eat, in the streets that surround it.

English football fans had been vilified since the 1970s when hooliganism was rife among travelling supporters, especially whenever the national side played abroad and European towns and cities were ransacked.

And the so-called English Disease was still rearing its ugly head. Two months before I was collecting food outside Goodison, England fans had created carnage in the beautiful Spanish city of Seville. It was the usual script. Drunken inadequates had annexed a square, put up their flags of St George, downed an endless supply of strong lager, sang their boorish songs about not surrendering to the IRA, how they would "rather be a Paki than a Spic." They even delighted in chanting, "Fuck the Pope" to casual passers-by in a devout Catholic country. Nice.

It's still the same when they follow England to Germany and sing about the RAF killing their pilots or in France and Belgium when they give it "if it wasn't for the British you'd be Krauts."

And it always spirals towards the same depressing conclusion: Riot police wading in, dozens of drunks being violently scattered, then whining to cameras about how they were victimised.

Around the same time that Seville was being ransacked, the

self-styled Democratic Football Lads' Alliance had their own ugly clashes with police in London, as they protested "returning jihadists, AWOL migrants, rape gangs and groomers".

They were basically a bunch of neo-fascists looking to recruit white football followers the way the National Front had done in the 1980s when they leafleted outside grounds. They were Nazis hijacking the most tribal and working-class of sports to spread a vile ideology, tarring the overwhelming majority of decent fans with the same rancid brush.

What a contrast with what Dave Kelly and Ian Byrne were doing: uniting communities, not just by nourishing bodies, but enlightening minds to the fact that football-lovers have more in common with each other than that which divides them.

During the 2018 World Cup the pair approached Liverpool's Muslim leaders, who agreed to set up foodbanks in the Abdullah Quilliam mosque during screenings of evening games, inviting fans of all races and religions to come together to watch football while helping the hungry.

After dozens of people turned up to watch the Russia v Egypt match, in which local hero Mo Salah scored, Mumin Khan, CEO of the Abdullah Quilliam Society, said, "It's amazing that Muslims and non-Muslims were sitting down to watch the World Cup cheering on Mo Salah. It was a fantastic occasion. Throughout the rest of the World Cup we will be screening all the matches and we are open to the public to come and watch them. It's a chance to get to know each other."

Word of what FSF were doing in Merseyside soon spread, with fans across the country adopting similar foodbank schemes, often with guidance from Dave and Ian. Newcastle United supporters set up a foodbank in February 2017 and within two years it was responsible for a third of all donations across the city.

An FSF conference in Liverpool's St George's Hall in October 2018 was attended by delegates from more than 50 clubs. Their purpose was to celebrate the effectiveness of fan activism, to share ideas on how to improve what they do, and how to roll out their scheme at every club in the land.

The pair had done something remarkable. They had wired into the fact that football has a unique power which makes it the perfect platform to do good in the local community. They challenged the status quo, questioning whether you had to accept the diktats from politicians above and let the poor go without or if you could get off your arse and fight back. They had asked if tribalism really had to be the most crucial part of a fan's identity. They were saying to everyone who watches football that they have the power to change things in society.

By the time the 2020 pandemic struck, FSF had been present at 233 consecutive games at Goodison and Anfield and were collecting around a tonne of food per game. They had put food poverty and foodbanks on the national agenda and shown that the much-maligned football fan could be a catalyst for good. And they inspired those who play it to do the same.

While self-publicising tycoons like Richard Branson, who never cease to bang on about the wealth they spread, were treating loyal workers like unwanted tax demands during the beginning of the Covid lockdown, football stepped up to the plate.

Clubs embarrassed by the poverty on their doorsteps were using their community arms to send deliveries to the vulnerable and holding breakfast clubs for kids, with players and ex-players doing their bit.

Liverpool's Jordan Henderson founded the Players Together initiative which encouraged his fellow pros to donate to the NHS. Wolves manager Nuno Espírito Santo gave £250,000 to the Feed Our Pack project which supported foodbanks in the city. Gary Neville and Ryan Giggs handed their hotels over to the NHS, Joe Cole donated £25,000 to support health staff and Chelsea's Reece James donated £10,000 to The Felix Project, which supplies 400 frontline charities and 120 schools in the poorest areas of London.

Liverpool, Manchester City and Manchester United players dug deep for local foodbanks. Wilfried Zaha handed his rental properties to the NHS, Pep Guardiola donated a million euros for medical supplies in Spain and the community branches of clubs joined in the effort.

Raheem Sterling said he was "done talking" and announced a foundation to push kids from deprived backgrounds up the social-mobility ladder so those at the bottom can see "there is something better to England."

Ahead of the Goodison derby, Liverpool and Everton marked five years of Fans Supporting Foodbanks by emblazoning their logo on the players' pre-match warm-up tops.

And thanks to a remarkable 22-year-old called Marcus Rashford, football's crusade to feed the poor had moved on from a couple of purple wheelie bins outside pubs in Liverpool 4 to the epicentre of power in Westminster SW1.

His campaign started in March 2020 when schools were closed as part of lockdown measures. According to his representative Kelly Hogarth, "Marcus's reflex response was 'what are the kids going to eat?'" He contacted food waste charity FareShare, which distributes meals to 11,000 voluntary and community groups, to offer a sizeable cash donation. However, after speaking to him and sensing his passion, CEO Lindsay Boswell persuaded the Manchester United striker to get on board and help deliver cooked food to children who were no longer receiving their free school meals. "In previous years, the best we might have got is £200,000 of donations from the general public," Boswell said. "Within a week of Marcus's involvement, we had half a million pounds, from people in 35 different countries."

By June the initiative had raised more than £20 million and the charity was reaching three million kids nationwide.

Rashford was making a fool out of Health Secretary Matt Hancock who, at one of his early Covid briefings argued that "millionaire footballers" needed to "take a pay cut and play their part." To his credit, the millionaire footballer chose to carry on making the Tory Cabinet look like incompetent and uncaring clowns.

He wrote an open letter to MPs, urging them to reverse a government decision not to provide free school meals to children from low-income backgrounds during the upcoming summer holidays. His eloquence and honesty leapt off the page and shamed the people in power. This is what he wrote:

To all MPs in Parliament,

In a week that would have opened UEFA Euro 2020, I wanted to reflect back to May 27th, 2016, when I stood in the middle of the Stadium of Light in Sunderland having just broken the record for the youngest player to score in his first senior international match. I watched the crowds waving their flags and fist-pumping the three lions on their shirts and I was overwhelmed with pride not only for myself, but for all of those who had helped me reach this moment and achieve my dream of playing for the England national team.

Understand: without the kindness and generosity of the community I had around me, there wouldn't be the Marcus Rashford you see today: a 22-year old Black man lucky enough to make a career playing a game I love.

My story to get here is all-too-familiar for families in England: my mum worked full-time, earning a minimum wage to make sure we always had a good evening meal on the table. But it was not enough. The system was not built for families like mine to succeed, regardless of how hard my mum worked.

As a family, we relied on breakfast clubs, free school meals, and the kind actions of neighbours and coaches. Foodbanks and soup kitchens were not alien to us; I recall very clearly our visits to Northern Moor to collect our Christmas dinners every year. It's only now that I really understand the enormous sacrifice my mum made in sending me away to live in digs aged 11, a decision no mother would ever make lightly.

This summer should have been filled with pride once more, parents and children waving their flags, but in reality Wembley Stadium could be filled more than twice with children who have had to skip meals during lockdown due to their families not being able to access food. (200,000 children according to Food Foundation estimates).

As their stomachs grumble, I wonder if those 200,000 children will ever be proud enough of their country to pull on the England national team shirt one day and sing the national anthem from the stands.

Ten years ago, I would have been one of those children, and you would never have heard my voice and seen my determination to become part of the solution.

As many of you know, as lockdown hit and schools were temporarily closed, I partnered with food distribution charity FareShare to help cover some of the free school meal deficit. Whilst the campaign is currently distributing three million meals a week to those most vulnerable across the UK, I recognise it's just not enough.

This is not about politics; this is about humanity. Looking at ourselves in the mirror and feeling like we did everything we could to protect those who can't, for whatever reason or circumstance, protect themselves. Political affiliations aside, can we not all agree that no child should be going to bed hungry?

Food poverty in England is a pandemic that could span generations if we don't course-correct now. Whilst 1.3 million children in England are registered for free school meals, one quarter of these children have not been given any support since the school closures were ordered.

We rely on parents, many of whom have seen their jobs evaporate due to Covid-19, to play substitute teacher during lockdown, hoping that their children are going to be focused enough to learn, with only a small percentage of their nutritional needs met during this period.

This is a system failure and without education, we're encouraging this cycle of hardship to continue. To put this pandemic into perspective, from 2018-2019, nine out of 30 children in any given classroom were living in poverty in the UK. This figure is expected to rise by an additional one million by 2022. In England today, 45 per cent of children in Black and minority ethnic groups are now in poverty. This is England in 2020.

I am asking you to listen to their parents' stories as I have received thousands of insights from people struggling. I have listened when fathers have told me they are struggling with depression, unable to sleep, worried sick about how they are going to support their families having lost their jobs unexpectedly, headteachers who are personally covering the cost of food packages for their vulnerable families after the school debit card has been maxed out; mothers who can't cover the cost of increased electricity and food bills during the lockdown, and parents who are sacrificing their own meals for their children. In 2020, it shouldn't be a case of one or the other.

I've read tweets over the last couple of weeks where some have placed blame on parents for having children they 'can't afford'. That same finger could have been pointed at my mum, yet I grew up in a loving and caring environment.

The man you see stood in front of you today is a product of her love and care. I have friends who are from middle-class backgrounds who have never experienced a small percentage of the love I have gotten from my mum: a single parent who would sacrifice everything she had for our happiness. THESE are the kind of parents we are talking about. Parents who work every hour of the day for a minimum wage, most of them working in hospitality, a sector which has been locked down for months.

During this pandemic, people are existing on a knife's edge: one missed bill is having a spiral effect, the anxiety and stress of knowing that poverty is the main driver of children ending up in care, a system that is designed to fail low-income families. Do you know how much courage it takes for a grown man to say, 'I can't cope' or 'I can't support my family'? Men, women, caregivers, are calling out for our help and we aren't listening.

I also received a tweet from an MP who told me 'this is why there is a benefit system'. Rest assured, I am fully aware of the Universal Credit scheme and I am fully aware that the majority of families applying are experiencing five-week delays. Universal Credit is simply not a short-term solution. I also know from talking to people that there is a two-child-per-family limit, meaning someone like my mum would only have been able to cover the cost of two of her five children.

In April 2020, 2.1 million people claimed unemployment-related benefits. This is an increase of 850,000 just since March 2020. As we approach the end of the furlough scheme and a period of mass unemployment, the problem of child poverty is only going to get worse.

Parents like mine would rely on kids' clubs over the summer break, providing a safe space and at least one meal, whilst they work. Today, parents do not have this as an option. If faced with unemployment, parents like mine would have been down at the job centre first thing Monday morning to find any work that enables them to support their families. Today, there are no jobs.

As a Black man from a low-income family in Wythenshawe, Manchester, I could have been just another statistic. Instead, due to the selfless actions of my mum, my family, my neighbours, and my coaches, the only stats I'm associated with are goals, appearances and caps. I would be doing myself, my family and my community an injustice if I didn't stand here today with my voice and my platform and ask you for help.

The Government has taken a 'whatever it takes' approach to the economy – I'm asking you today to extend that same thinking to protecting all vulnerable children across England. I encourage you to hear their pleas and find your humanity. Please reconsider your decision to cancel the food voucher scheme over the summer holiday period and guarantee the extension.

This is England in 2020, and this is an issue that needs urgent assistance. Please, while the eyes of the nation are on you, make the U-turn and make protecting the lives of some of our most vulnerable a top priority.

Yours sincerely, Marcus Rashford

He went public with his powerful letter and it struck a chord with a nation ignorant of the true level of deprivation endured by families on the wrong end of austerity. Fearing a backlash, a cowering Boris Johnson swiftly reversed his decision and vowed to provide free meals during the summer holidays. Rashford's strategy was seen by veterans of Westminster affairs as a political masterclass.

As a salute to their local hero a bedsheet was tied to a Welcome To Wythenshawe sign with these words daubed on it: 'Rashford 1, Boris 0'. It now hangs in the National Football Museum.

In September, he formed a Child Food Poverty Task Force in collaboration with major UK food brands, supermarkets and charities calling on Johnson for an expansion of free school meals and an extension of school holiday food support. He was told by Downing Street that it had already increased support to local authorities and Universal Credit.

Undaunted, Rashford started a petition calling for the government to offer free school meals in England during school holidays, which reached more than a million signatures by October, allowing Labour to call for a debate on his proposals. Unsurprisingly, Tory MPs were whipped to vote against the motion and it was defeated by a majority of 61.

As I watched that Commons debate it felt like travelling back to the dark days of the 1980s. To a time when little-known Tories who wanted to impress their heroine, Margaret Thatcher, would queue up to attack single mothers as feckless scroungers who were the biggest threat to British society and the economy. This time it was hungry kids.

Backbencher Brendan Clarke-Smith declared, "I do not believe in nationalising children" and called for everyone to "get back to the idea of taking responsibility". Ben Bradley dismissed it as an extended "freebies" scheme, and Paul Scully saw no value in it because kids "have been going hungry for years."

Had they tap-danced across the green benches holding pots of gruel and singing Food, Glorious Food from the musical Oliver! as an example of how things were in the good old days, I wouldn't have been surprised.

It took me back to trying to set up an interview with former Tory minister Edwina Currie in the late-90s, which she agreed to only on the condition I took her for an expensive meal at the Savoy Hotel. I did. And she filled her boots with the finest offerings on the menu telling me, as she saw my chin drop at her foie gras starter order, "you can claim it all back on expenses can't you?"

A few years later she was arguing that benefits claimants who asked for tins of beans from foodbanks to feed their families were parasites who'd spent all of their money on cigarettes and booze. Oh, the irony.

Rashford's response to his Commons defeat was typically cutting: "Have any of the people in government speaking about this had a life where they can literally afford to buy food and pay bills and that's it? I doubt that they have. The way they speak about it is so insensitive. For me, it's like they don't have a big enough understanding on the issue."

The Tories had badly misread the public mood once again and their callousness backfired. The majority of the nation were on Rashford's side and countless businesses, councils, charities and individuals showed solidarity with the footballer, offering free meals to struggling families over the school holidays.

Once again, Boris Johnson was shamed into doing an embarrassing U-turn, expanding free school meals throughout all school holidays in the coming year along with a £400 million Covid winter grant scheme to support vulnerable families in England.

The Wythenshawe flag was now out of date. Rashford had just fired in a second goal, but typically, he wasn't going over the top with the celebrations. "I'm happy we've got to this stage," he said after Johnson paid him the honour of a bootlicking phone call, "but I can't stop thinking about what the bigger picture looks like."

It became 3-0 in January 2021, when images emerged on Twitter of pathetic free school meal hampers that outsourcing firm Chartwells were delivering to some homes containing half-cut tomatoes, two carrots, slices of frozen bread, a tin of beans and some Frubes.

Rashford re-tweeted photos of the worst examples adding his own commentary: '3 days of food for 1 family ... Just not good enough' and 'Imagine we expect the children to engage in learning from home. Not to mention the parents who, at times have to teach them, who probably haven't eaten at all so their children can...We MUST do better. This is 2021'.

The images went viral, sparking national outrage with senior

Tories jumping in quickly to defuse the scandal. Chartwells were hauled in by the Department for Education, forced to issue apologies and pledge there would be no repeat. Labour MP Catherine McKinnell asked Boris Johnson in the Commons, "Why do children needing to eat keep taking the government by surprise? Is the Prime Minister not ashamed of being schooled on child hunger by a young footballer like Marcus Rashford?"

True to form, Johnson waffled incoherently with his head down, but later rang Rashford to apologise, hoping in vain to avert another PR disaster. Hat-trick scoring Rashford was turning into the Unofficial Leader of the Opposition.

The most compelling aspect of his remarkable crusade was that it came from a real place. The hunger he had endured as a child growing up with a single mum had been the motivating force for him to become a successful footballer. He wasn't putting something back for effect. The place he came from became a cause that drove him to the top of his profession so that he could become a voice for the dispossessed, helping to prevent other kids who had nothing from enduring the same misery he and his siblings had.

He knew all about hunger as a child. His father was not around to contribute a wage, leaving his mother Mel to struggle on alone as she attempted to feed her five children. Despite working as a cashier at a betting shop and having two cleaning jobs there were times when there was no bread in the house. Times when she would go without food to make sure her children had enough on their plate, telling the kids she had already eaten.

In a BBC documentary Rashford opened up on his family hardship: "When there wasn't any food, you'd just go to sleep.

The people that were closest to me knew about the situation me and my family were going through, but my team-mates and coaches didn't. It should never be normal to feel how I felt. When you get to the position I'm in now, I feel like if they are in need, and they don't have anyone fighting for them, I should be the one that does it really. I think in sport you have to have something behind you that is pushing you. When you come from a place of struggle and pain, a lot of the time it switches and it becomes your drive and motivation."

Mancunian street artist Akse painted a huge mural of Rashford on the wall of a Withington cafe. Accompanying it was this quote: 'Take pride in knowing that your struggle will play the biggest role in your purpose.'

Like Ian Byrne and Dave Kelly, Rashford had become a catalyst for change and transformed the lives of the marginalised. The three were simply working-class men who never forgot where they came from, who gave a voice to the voiceless in the face of a terminally deaf government.

Fans Supporting Foodbanks went from strength to strength during the pandemic. When the government failed to deliver enough Personal Protective Equipment (PPE) to carers and NHS staff, they distributed 5,000 visors to key workers in London, Manchester, Newcastle and Yorkshire. They also launched a mobile pantry service, the first of its kind in the UK, going into deprived communities that lacked supermarkets to offer fresh, nutritious food to families at very low prices.

Like Rashford, MP Byrne took the fight to end food poverty to the Houses of Parliament, campaigning for a Right To Food law to be passed, guaranteeing the legal right to food for everyone. His early day motion, which was supported by 59 MPs, stated that foodbanks were mere sticking plasters attempting to cover gaping wounds in the poorer parts of Britain and government intervention was urgently needed. He called for, among other things, a proper Living Wage, universal free school meals and the utilising of school kitchens to feed the elderly and vulnerable.

In January 2021, Liverpool declared itself the first Right to Food City in the UK with the council demanding access to food to be a legal right for all. Knowsley, Sefton, St Helens, Wirral, Halton, Greater Manchester, Rotherham, Brighton, Haringey, Newcastle and Portsmouth soon followed.

Fans Supporting Foodbanks launched a petition demanding the government implement this policy which drew 53,656 signatures. And the wider supporter base waded into the fight.

When the Premier League took the cynical step of charging £14.95 to watch extra games on top of their already pricey TV packages, a new slogan emerged from below: 'Feed the Needy not the Greedy'. Supporters were urged (with FSF at the forefront of the campaign) to snub pay-per-view and instead donate that £14.95 to foodbanks. The response was amazing. From Brighton, Crystal Palace and north London in the south, to Merseyside, Manchester, Leeds and Newcastle in the north, more than £300,000 was raised in a matter of weeks.

The Premier League was left looking cheap and out-of-touch and soon dropped the scheme completely. But football fans didn't stop there. When 1,700 university students in Manchester were confined to their flats, Everton's Blue Union, Liverpool's Spirit Of Shankly, the Manchester City Foodbank Support Group and the Manchester United Supporters' Trust took 3,000 pizzas to the students. Ancient differences were being discarded for the greater good.

When United visited Goodison Park in November there were no crowds, but fans put up this message on the big screen to honour Rashford: 'Thank you for sticking up for our kids who needed a voice, here on Merseyside and across the country.'

Spirit of Shankly chairman Joe Blott said, "I hope the next time United come to Anfield we can meet Marcus on arrival. Not just to welcome the coach but literally to carry him off it. What he has done transcends football rivalries. Yes, for 90 minutes, twice a year, let's sing and chant, but we are actually hued from the same stone. There's genuinely more that binds Liverpool and Manchester than divides us. Let's use the power of the fan, and the power of the footballer, to make a radical difference."

The FSF foodbank initiatives, Rashford's school meals crusade and the fans' Feed the Needy Not The Greedy campaign, added up to a watershed moment in English football and wider society. As Ian Byrne said, "It feels like a turning point for the nation's psyche."

Thanks to these principled stands during a time of cowardice among supposed leaders, footballers and fans went from national scapegoats to the country's conscience. They exposed those who ran the game and the country as lacking emotional intelligence at best, and being heartless charlatans at worst.

And they empowered each other. Now that supporters and players had found a voice and a way of getting it heard by uniting and organising from below, things may never be the same again. Suddenly fans and footballers, previously stereotyped as drunken yobs and bling-obsessed philanderers, were on the right side of history.

And the people they were shaming looked like the national pariahs.

THE LIFE SAVERS

12

Liz Glanister

Josephine Manini Peter

THE MOTHER MARYS

DIAMONDS IN THE MUD

BARCELONA — March 2003

MY taxi was forced to make a detour because Menlove Avenue was blocked due to a Japanese artist opening a semi-detached house for the National Trust.

When I finally arrived at the departure lounge of the airport that had been recently renamed after her dead husband, I heard Yoko Ono explain on TV why John Lennon's childhood home deserved to be a museum: "The spirit that changed the world profoundly has been remembered in this familiar place. He was a uniquely brilliant man," she said.

As the Barcelona-bound plane took off from John Lennon International Airport I looked down on the nearby council estate where the other half of that world-changing spirit was brought up. The one I was about to interview before another arena concert on a sold-out world tour.

The one whom Lennon's Hyacinth Bouquet-esque Aunt Mimi warned John away from, asking, "what are you doing with him … when he's from Speke?"

I wondered why the Beatle who couldn't have been more local to Liverpool's airport didn't even have a baggage carousel named after him. One who had put more back into his home city than the rest of the group put together.

The driving force behind Liverpool Institute For Performing Arts, who pumped £3 million of his own money into the project saving his old secondary school from decay in the hope it would give talented working-class Liverpool kids a leg-up in the creative world.

The one who wrote a classical oratorio about his home city

and contributed to two Number One singles to raise funds for the Hillsborough Families. The one who regularly came home, often incognito, to show his kids, his friends and partners, how proud he was of his roots.

The one who told *Playboy* magazine in 1984: "I've been around the world a few times and, in truth, I'd swear to God I've never met any people more soulful, more intelligent, more kind, more filled with common sense than the people I came from in Liverpool.

"I mean, the presidents, the prime ministers, I never met anyone half as nice as some of the people I know from Liverpool who are nothing, who do nothing.

"They're not important or famous. But they are smart, like my dad was smart. I mean, people who can just cut through problems like a hot knife through butter. The kind of people you need in life. Salt of the earth."

The Beatle who legend had harshly judged as being the cute one in more ways than one. The PR man. The money man. The one who wrote Silly Love Songs not Imagine. The one whose own genius has forever been shaded by an assassin's bullet.

"Olé-olé-olé-olé, Pauly, Pauly ..." More than 18,000 Spaniards screamed themselves hoarse for a third encore in the packed Barcelona sports arena. In the seats, the fans no longer left puddles but there was plenty of moisture in their eyes whenever McCartney went into a Beatles number that dragged them back to a better, more optimistic time.

On the floor, those who weren't alive when the group split screamed like ghosts of manic days past. Up on stage, the 60-year-old in a red T-shirt and jeans was being reborn. For most humans who were around in the 60s he was playing the lexicon of their lives. Potent reminders of who they were, who they loved and who they lost.

I'd been granted an audience with McCartney, an hour before he went on stage, and I'd love to say I unearthed some mind-blowing insights, but I'd be lying. The most complex of superstars had spent 40 years fending off attempts to get inside his head and pierce the shell he put around himself when he lost his mother as a 14-year-old. The charm, the mateyness, the dishing out of little nuggets of emotion were as prevalent in my piece as all the others written about him. But no gems were mined.

He told me that, after a few tough years following the death of his first wife, Linda, he felt like he was back in the land of the living. He spoke movingly of his love for his ex-bandmates who had passed away. About John and the bad blood that spilled out following the Beatles split: "We had our fall-outs over business. It was like a divorce and we bitched at each other. But, look, I'm the guy who knew him better than any other man. We slept together as teenagers, top-and-tailed in millions of hitch-hiking places.

"Thankfully we got to be good friends again before he died. It would have been really tough for me to deal with if we hadn't."

The most emotional part of our chat came when he described how George's death was a shattering blow: "It was different from my mum and John and Linda going, because their deaths were sudden and we knew George had been ill for a while.

"But it was very, very sad because I loved him so much. I'd just been through cancer with Linda and here I was going through it all again with a mate of 50 years. He wasn't my immediate family but he almost was. He'd always felt like my little brother. I knew George before I knew any of the others, before all that madness started, and I truly loved that man. I'm so proud to have known him."

He took a breath, looked wistfully at the ceiling and muttered "what a lovely boy" then carried on. "The last time I met him he was very sick and I held his hand for four hours. As I was doing it I was thinking, 'I've never held his hand before. Ever. This is not what two Scouse fellas do, no matter how well you know each other'.

"I kept thinking, 'he's going to smack me here and tell me to fuck off'. But he didn't. He just stroked my hand with his thumb and I thought, 'ah this is ok. This is life. It's tough, but it's lovely'. That's how it is. Lovely."

I asked him if, for someone who wants to come across as just an ordinary bloke, his huge wealth embarrassed him? (at the time he was worth an estimated £700 million although that was before he paid heavily for his worst mistake since The Frog Chorus – marrying Heather Mills).

"Not at all. When I left school I set out to get a job and earn good money if I could. I'm no different from anyone else. Some people think making all this money is uncool. I don't. I'm trying to do what I do to the very best of my ability. I'm not embarrassed if that means I earn loads. And the best thing about it is being able to help friends and relatives with health problems. That's the real buzz I get out of money."

I asked him about Bush and Blair invading Iraq, which had just happened, and whether he was against it, and he gave a typically diplomatic answer: "I'm a musician not a politician. So I'm not going to say our boys shouldn't be in there when they're laying their lives on the line. But yes, peace would definitely be preferable."

I imagined Lennon giving a much different answer were he alive. As in, "George Bush and his poodle Tony Blair are a pair of warmongering cretins who need taking out as badly as Saddam Hussein."

But that wasn't Paul McCartney. And that's the point. Since the Beatles had split in 1970 his every word, song, act, gesture and look was measured against the global peace icon and working-class hero he once wrote songs with. The straight family man with the catchy tunes versus the radical hippy with the revolutionary vision.

He was forever compared unfavourably with a dead saint he could never hope to out-sanctify. And it was unfair. Take the working-class hero bit. McCartney's first home was rented rooms in Anfield before the family moved to a council house in Speke in 1947 after his mother landed the job of resident midwife for the half-built estate. Eight years later they moved to another council house in nearby Allerton. And when his mum died of cancer, when he was 14, the wider family had to rally round to see them through financially after the loss of the main breadwinner.

John, on the other hand, despite being the son of a merchant seaman, grew up in his Aunt Mimi's elegant semi-detached home in a leafy suburb, and enjoyed a relatively middle-class upbringing. But he wrote the anthem about being a working-class hero, so that's how posterity has judged him.

These spurious comparisons don't need to exist.

Both Lennon and McCartney were one half of popular music's greatest song-writing team, a quarter of a 21st century cultural phenomenon.

The Beatles changed the world for so many working-class kids.

Prior to them, in Britain at least, people with provincial accents had to lose them to progress in virtually every professional field, including the arts. The successful Liverpudlian musical acts who came before them, such as Frankie Vaughan, Michael Holliday and Billy Fury were told to change their Scouse voice as it gave the impression they were dull and uneducated, and made to speak with a vague American twang. It was the same with actors like Rex Harrison and John Gregson who were told that unless they spoke with received BBC pronunciation they would struggle for work.

The Beatles turned the status quo on its head as they stormed the class barricades. They spoke as they wanted, dressed as they wanted, grew their hair as they wanted, mocked all forms of snobbery and refused to play before segregated audiences in southern American states, not giving a toss about how they were being perceived.

This brand of confidence, wit, originality and attitude had never before been seen in young men from such humble backgrounds. They turned black-and-white Britain into colour and helped to liberate working-class youth.

That's why I wanted to call this last chapter The World Changer, devoting it to the one Beatle I'd met. But I struggled to convince myself. On the one hand, McCartney helped transform opportunity in the 1960s by injecting a self-belief into fellow council house kids which hadn't existed before. And he stayed loyal to his roots. On the other hand, I wondered if the knight of the realm had become too rich and too Establishment to merit a place alongside the rest of the book's working-class heroes.

And then I thought back to a conversation we had after the interview in Barcelona, when I told him I'd come over quite emotional hearing him play My Love during that afternoon's soundcheck.

It was a song loved by my mum who had died suddenly the previous year, aged 74. It was one of those instant blasts of grief that comes from nowhere and blindsides you. And I told him it had left me choked. He seemed genuinely moved, telling me he was going to dedicate My Love to her in that night's show, and I should think of all the good things about her as he sang the words. I thanked him. And he replied, "You should never stop thinking about your mum, you know. I don't. Even though she went a long time ago. She's still here. They live through you and with you, our mums. Be proud of her."

And I realised, after being made aware of a serious health issue as I was about to write this chapter, that it shouldn't be about McCartney the world-changer but about the woman who produced him and whose spirit guided him through his difficult teenage years after her devastating death. The midwife whose job made them move to the south end of Liverpool where he would eventually meet John Lennon whom he would bond with over the shared grief of losing their beloved mum.

I realised the final chapter had to be devoted to nurses like her who brought us into this world and fought to keep us in it.

The Mother Marys. The ones who, in our hour of darkness were standing right in front of us, whispering words of wisdom.

LIVERPOOL ROYAL HOSPITAL — November 2020

I'm guessing I'm not the only person who believes that the three most dreaded words a doctor can say to you are "you've got cancer."

Neither do I doubt I'm the only one to feel that the worst time to hear them is in the middle of a devastating pandemic that has brought the country to its knees and stretched the National Health Service to breaking point.

But there I was, sitting in a small room inside Liverpool's Broadgreen Hospital discussing the options for dealing with a cancerous prostate that, until a fortnight earlier, I had no idea existed. When the surgeon told me there was a good chance he could whip it out in three weeks' time in the Royal Hospital, unless the Covid infections across Merseyside grew, the shock turned to disbelief.

How could that be possible when Liverpool was in the eye of the storm and the Royal had been turned into a virtual war zone, with dozens of deaths there every day?

Yet, three weeks after being floored by the deadly C-word, I was being wheeled towards an operating theatre in that dilapidated Royal which should have been completely rebuilt three years previously only for Carillion, the building firm which profited shamelessly from public sector contracts, to go bankrupt.

A five-strong team of anaesthetists and assistants put me under, before surgeons spent three hours removing my prostate, stitched me back up and left me to come around in a recovery room where, as I opened my hallucinating eyes, I found a sister holding my hand and telling me that all was fine.

I was moved to a ward in a Covid-free bubble of the hospital, where nurses set me up in a bed with a catheter and a drip and monitored me through the night until the day shift came in and began to get me mobile.

The cleaners and staff who brought meals and cups of tea, wearing full PPE, went out of their way to raise my spirits by cracking jokes despite being paid the minimum wage to work on the frontline of a war against a disease whose death toll was still mounting.

Throughout the day after the operation, with no visitors allowed to enter the hospital, nurses took time out of their meal breaks, and stayed on after their shifts, to talk to us recuperating patients. One of them asked me what I did for a living and I told her, in all sincerity, that like virtually every other job in the country right now, it paled into insignificance compared to what she and her colleagues were doing.

Walking every day into a building where they may pick up a killer disease knowing many of their colleagues had done so. Having a coffee with workmates, who then headed to the intensive care units where they would fight, for up to ten hours at a time, to stop people who were telling them, "I don't want to die yet" from drawing their last painful breath. Holding iPads to their faces so loved ones back home could say their final goodbyes via Zoom. Then going through the same heart-wrenching, mentally exhausting process day after day, with no respite, and no end in sight.

When I asked one nurse how she did it, she just smiled, and delivered these words of wisdom: "It's what we do," she said. Then asked if I needed any more painkillers as she plumped up my pillows.

The journalist in me kept asking them for stories about colleagues lost to Covid but they didn't want to go there. It was too close to home. As though to impart those details would be an act of disloyalty. Besides, one told me, you're not here to worry about what's going on in this place, but to concentrate on getting yourself out of it.

Yet nurses like them were losing their lives in hospitals across the country on a daily basis, especially in the early months when the deadly nature of the virus was not fully understood, and staff were disgracefully left short of vital protective equipment.

One name mentioned to me a couple of times by nurses at the Royal and Broadgreen was Liz Glanister. The much-loved 68-year-old had worked at Aintree Hospital and contacted the virus on the frontline, in early April, before dying in the Royal. One nurse I spoke to who knew her, and another who knew colleagues who had worked with her, described Liz as an exceptional person who had carried on after her retirement date, despite a lifetime in the NHS, because she felt a vocation to mentor younger staff.

Liverpool got to hear about this selfless grandmother whose work had touched tens of thousands of lives, and who had given her own in the cause of nursing, when the council lowered the flags at three of its most iconic buildings – the Town Hall, St George's Hall, and the Cunard Building – in her honour.

Mayor Joe Anderson spoke for his city when he said, "Words cannot express how much a debt of gratitude Liverpool owes to Liz Glanister. She gave everything she had to make a difference at such a crucial time. She was a hero in every sense of the word."

A Facebook page was set up inviting tributes from friends and colleagues. These were some of the responses: Nikita Healey wrote, 'I will never forget you, Liz, and how you welcomed me onto the ward on my first day. I would do anything to have a cuppa with you again and a little laugh. Look after her, God, she's so, so special'.

Vicky White wrote, 'Rest in Peace, Liz. Such a lovely lady who looked after my mum during her chemo'.

Anna Culshaw wrote, 'Liz was my chemo nurse, a beautiful soul. She will be a massive loss to her family and the NHS'. And Jane Green wrote, 'Liz may you rest in peace – you cared for so many in the years you nursed at Aintree'.

These were a few of the hundreds of tweets about her: 'A supernurse who made some of my darkest days while receiving chemotherapy brighten up with a joke and a hug' … 'She made you feel 10ft tall when leaving. A truly special nurse' … 'Gave her whole life to nursing, I'm so sorry for the way you have all been treated. On wards with insufficient protection and terrible guidance, despite this you all carry on'.

Her heartbroken family described the loss as "simply beyond words" and issued this request: "There are so many heroes out there, just like Liz, who are all putting their lives in danger to help save ours, so please help them to be the best they can be and stay inside."

Three days later, the words of Liz's family proved to be prophetic when Aintree Hospital announced that a second frontline worker had died after contracting coronavirus.

Barbara Moore was a patient discharge planner who ensured patients were able to leave the hospital with the right support. Chief nurse Dianne Brown hailed the 54-year-old, who had joined the hospital after spending most of her career as a care worker for people with disabilities, "an unsung hero" whose loss was an awful blow to everyone at Aintree.

"Many people don't think about the work of patient discharge planners when they think of a hospital. But Barbara's dedication to helping patients get safely out of hospital meant that people returned to their loved ones as soon and as simply as possible. She will be terribly missed," said Dianne.

The family statement showed how every single Covid death had a ripple effect that left scores of relatives devastated: "Barbara was a much-loved wife, mum, nan, sister, auntie, friend and beautiful person. She dedicated her life to caring for others and doted on her two beautiful children and grandchildren."

As would the passing of Janice Glassey a few weeks later. The mother-of-three had devoted 14 years to helping extremely ill patients with their end-of-life care, but the 66-year-old fell ill just 72 hours before she was due to retire and died a month later.

Janice was fit and full of life and engaged to be married when she became sick the day after Mother's Day and was taken to the intensive care unit of Whiston Hospital, before being transferred to Broadgreen, where she died.

Her daughter Kerri said she was loved by everyone. "Mum was very dedicated to her job, she would regularly cover people's shifts. She was so funny and had so much to look forward to.

"We are heartbroken. Mum was completely healthy. She was a bag of fun and used to love going shopping and for cocktails in Liverpool with her daughters and grand-daughters. She just wanted to live life and was so loving and giving."

Due to the vast number of foreign nurses who keep the NHS going, the pain caused by those who died on the job in Merseyside spread across the world.

Take the story I came across after reading an appeal on a GoFundMe page for donations to send the body of a "Fallen Hero" home to South Africa after she died in a Southport hospital.

Josephine Manini Peter, was born and raised in Tsakane, a

black township in Brakpan Springs, east Johannesburg, where she graduated in 1998 as a nurse. Four years later she responded to an NHS recruitment drive by moving to the UK.

The 55-year-old grandmother had worked in hospitals in Windsor and London, specialising in gynaecology and obstetrics before becoming a locum agency nurse and moving to Southport in February 2020. Two months later she contracted Covid and died in the hospital on April 18.

Manini left behind a husband, son, daughter, and grand-daughter. Her grown-up children had returned to South Africa and Manini was on the verge of moving back to her native country after devoting 18 years to the NHS. She had already started to ship her belongings to a house that was being built. It was her dream to spend retirement in her new home living near her family. But it wasn't to be.

Her husband, Thabo, said she was passionate and hard-working and always put others before herself. "She was my heroine," he said.

Cynthia Charles, a fellow nurse, described her long-time friend as "very kind, very outgoing, bubbly, you would have her on your guest list at a party. She was a wonderful human being with a passion for care.

"I have not been able to work for two days. I leave the house and turn around at the gate. We are just shocked, we are so worried about ourselves, thinking things like, 'should I go to work? If I do, will I come home in a coffin.' It makes you numb," she said.

The Fallen Hero GoFundMe page, set up by Cynthia, read: 'Manini was raised under harsh and vulnerable conditions of the South African apartheid regime, whereby she was whipped and humiliated. But her spirit was never broken. Her colleagues and South African friends are so shocked and devastated by her sudden and untimely passing. They are humbly appealing for a donation to cover repatriation and funeral costs on behalf of Manini's family'.

Her daughter Buhle gave this tribute to her mother who, she said, had the biggest heart and greatest capacity to love.

"My mama was full of so much love that it was incomprehensible. Her work ethic always inspired me and her fighting spirit was something so beautiful because it showed she would always persevere and push until she couldn't push any more. She was my hero. Her smile is permanently embedded in our minds."

Her body was never flown back to South Africa but her ashes were. The money raised from the GoFundMe page paid for a funeral and cremation which her children had to view via Skype in South Africa. "Watching that really hit me in the gut. It was unbelievable," said Buhle.

"She was at my side all my life and without her I wouldn't be the woman I am today. Having her taken from me has caused me so much unimaginable heartache.

"This beautiful woman whom I have the honour of calling my mother, was also my best friend and the root of my being. I can't describe how much I loved and adored her. She had the biggest heart and greatest capacity to love that it was difficult to comprehend that someone could love so much.

"All I want now is for my mother's life to be celebrated, as she so rightfully deserved, and for my dad to come home so we can be together as a family to remember her together. She was truly one of a kind and will continue to blossom in my heart and my family's hearts forever.

"Robala ka Kgotso, ma." (Which means, in Sesotho: Rest in Peace, ma).

The day after Manini died in Southport and Formby District Hospital another remarkable nurse in her 50s passed away over the Mersey in Birkenhead.

Julie Penfold, 53, was an Outpatients Health Care Assistant at Arrowe Park Hospital, where she also mentored trainee nurses and doctors. In a life devoted to giving, she had fostered more than 20 children and left behind two daughters, a son, an adopted daughter, two step-daughters, 11 grandchildren and her husband Nick. She also had a son and daughter who had sadly passed away.

Nick said that all she ever talked about when she was at school was being a nurse, describing her as someone who "never had a bad word to say about anybody and nothing was too much trouble for her. She was always checking on other people and looked after everyone. As a mentor, she loved training the younger ones and supported a lot of doctors. She was really well-loved. I was really proud of her.

"She was an exceptional woman."

Julie's brother, John Schofield, said after her funeral cortege had passed through the grounds of Arrowe Park where hundreds of staff gave her an emotional guard of honour: "She was a really beautiful woman who had angel wings. But you didn't see them. You just felt them. You felt her warmth when she was there."

They are just five tragic tales of nurses taken before their time who were local to me.

It is estimated that more than 250 NHS frontline staff caught Covid-19 and died in the first year of the pandemic, with that figure rising past 850 for the entire UK care sector. And few of those who survived as they went above and beyond the call of duty were left unscathed.

Gradually the heartbreaking stories of working in intensive care units came out. How nurses were being pressured by managers to free up beds of dead patients while still on the phone to a devastated relative, their visors steaming up through the heat of their tears. How they would put the phone down then whisper into the ear of the deceased the last words their loved one had spoken before taking off wedding bands and placing them in polythene bags.

Tales of how staff were suffering serious mental trauma, panic attacks and depression, many coming down with Post Traumatic Stress Disorder (PTSD), some even sectioned. By the time the second wave took hold in December 2020 the levels of sickness were at a record high, the knock-on effect pushing those who stayed and fought on the frontline, ever closer to burnout.

There was a perfect storm of ever-rising infection numbers, staff and bed shortages caused by austerity, lack of proper PPE, resignations, foreign nurses returning home and Covid wiping out the NHS workforce which pushed doctors and nurses to the brink. A senior doctor from North Yorkshire said it felt as if "we are the musicians aboard the Titanic continuing to play as the ship sinks and chaos reigns all around us".

A report came out in January 2021 which showed the number of doctors seeking psychiatric help through the British Medical Association (BMA) had doubled since the pandemic began and that nearly half of all staff working in intensive care units were likely to be suffering PTSD. In November 2020, a total of 371 doctors accessed the BMA's helpline. In December 2018, there had been only 132 calls.

In the summer of 2021, a mental health charity report claimed that 226 nurses and 79 paramedics had contemplated suicide due to the extreme trauma they faced working through the pandemic.

Dr David Wrigley, BMA deputy chair, claimed his members were being left "physically and mentally scarred" as a result of their experiences, adding that staff "will struggle to get back to the normal way of life" once the pandemic had passed.

Even soldiers on the frontline of war get relieved after a round of duty. Our NHS workers were just told to carry on, in ever-decreasing numbers, with no respite.

For some, there was anger, not just towards the government for its weak and inconsistent approach to tackling the disease, but Covid deniers who were calling it a hoax, the libertarians who saw lockdown as an attack on their freedoms, and people who flouted basic rules such as social distancing.

One NHS psychologist told *The Guardian* after there was an announcement that the weekly "clap for carers" was set to make a return, that many hospital staff were "raging" with one nurse telling her, "Fuck your clapping. Wear a fucking mask."

On January 13 I took a phone call from a lovely nurse called Michelle telling me that tests showed the surgeon had removed all of my cancer and I was free of the disease. I was so ecstatic I almost kissed the photo of Jacob Rees-Mogg in the open *Daily Mirror* on my desk. As Dennis Skinner told me when he was given the all-clear from bladder cancer: "Now that's happiness. You can't organise that."

I'd been lucky. To have been diagnosed with cancer, had it removed and given the all-clear within a few months in the middle of a winter when the NHS was under siege from Covid was nothing short of remarkable. All done with dedication, professionalism, love and humour.

We on the Left often get accused of over-romanticising the NHS and I admit it's far from perfect. But whenever myself, or my family, have been in need, it's been there to provide a peerless service. It's not the monarchy, the empire, the pomp and circumstance or the flag this country should be most proud of. It's the NHS. And its greatest asset is its workforce.

I wrote a column three months into the pandemic, when the majority of British people were standing outside their homes every Thursday clapping the carers, calling on the government to scrap the usual end-of-year Honours List and replace it with one which solely rewarded those who had helped the nation through its darkest peacetime days.

I wrote that if this country truly believed that NHS staff are the new heroes, it needed to prove it. Why not honour key workers who helped the country in its hour of need, I asked. Let's give posthumous orders of merit to the likes of Liz Glanister, Barbara Moore, Janice Glassey, Manini Peter and Julie Penfold, who had given their lives to save ours. And knighthoods and peerages to those deemed by their peers to have gone above and beyond the call of duty.

I wasn't alone. Indeed, the government let it be known as the New Year's list was about to be published that they had decided to honour their sacrifice and commitment in a year that "truly tested the resolve and determination of those on the frontline."

Yet when the 1,239 honours were announced, only 123 of them, a tenth of all, went to health and social care staff. And the majority were at the lower end of the scale, such as MBEs. The same medal that was awarded in that New Year's Honours List to the actress who plays Sally Webster in Coronation Street and the unremarkable singer Craig David.

Their recognition dropped way below the knighthoods that were being handed to tax exile racing driver Lewis Hamilton, cinematographer Roger Deakins and Tory MP Geoffrey Cox (who was forced to stand down from the parliamentary standards committee after failing to declare more than £400,000 in outside earnings) and the damehood given to actress Sheila Hancock.

It was left to comedian Ricky Gervais to sum up the outrageous insult to the medical profession, with these words: "There's nurses and doctors working 14-hour shifts. Give the honours to them, don't give them to some celebrity ponce for putting on a wig and saying some lines they got paid millions for."

You would have thought that a Prime Minister whose life was saved by NHS workers when he was admitted to intensive care with Covid would have grasped that point.

Or maybe not. For Boris Johnson to change the rules he would have had to break payback promises to friends, party donors and political cronies and that was never likely to happen. The chumocracy had to keep on being rewarded and the showbiz patsies had to take their gongs to create the headlines that would disguise the political chicanery.

Which hits at the heart of the twisted nature of heroism that keeps being perpetrated in Britain.

And if Sir Paul McCartney is half the man I think he is, knowing how much he treasures his mother, and his roots, I think he'd agree.

EPILOGUE

WHEN it became clear that Britain was leaving the European Union, I thought of my dear old nan and applied for an Irish passport.

There were many reasons for wanting to remain a citizen of Europe. The most attractive being to watch friends and family wait in long, foul-tempered queues at Spanish airports while I sauntered through customs and blew the froth off a freshly-pulled San Miguel in the arrivals bar, waiting for my sour-faced party to finally be allowed in with their blue passports.

To do so, I needed to gather the documents that proved she was born in the Republic.

Through an Irish agency, I learned the following. She was born Elizabeth Hobson in November, 1896, in Naas, County Kildare to Thomas Hobson, a Protestant housepainter from Dublin and Sarah McConville, a Catholic from Belfast. She was raised in her mother's faith. They moved to Dublin when she was young and she lived there until the end of the First World War when the family crossed the sea to Liverpool.

In 1921 she married my grandad, Victor Bartholomew, a private in the Scots Guards, in St Patrick's Church, Toxteth. By now she called herself Lilian (no doubt because she couldn't stand the royal connotations of Elizabeth) and worked as a waitress.

My grandad was born in London, the son of an Italian immigrant, Pietro Bartolomei, a plaster moulder who had moved to Liverpool to work on St George's Hall, anglicising the family name to Bartholomew along the way. According to the marriage certificate, my nan and grandad were living three doors down from each other in Park Street, Liverpool 8, before they married.

In 1927 they had their fourth of eight children, my mum Sheila, and were living in Walton before moving to Anfield and then Wavertree. My grandad was a docker by then, and my nan now called herself Lily. I'm guessing there was a foreign princess called Lilian knocking around that made her ditch that name.

I was ignorant of three-quarters of those facts before reading the passport documents, backing up my theory that most large working-class families know little about their immediate past because it's rarely spoken about. For my nan it was tough enough trying to get through the day without finding time to dwell on yesterday with one of her 26 grandkids. Which is a massive shame.

There was I, in 2016, applying for Irish citizenship, yet I'd never spoken about my family's history in that country to the woman whose birth qualified me for that status. Apart from laughing along as she told tales about the 'oul whoremaster' Churchill sending the Black and Tans over to rape nuns.

Even worse, the little she had told me about watching the Easter Rising exactly a century earlier from behind a fruit cart in O'Connell Street, I'd dismissed as a romantic figment of a wild imagination.

Yet the facts showed she probably was a first-hand witness

to a crucial moment in Irish and British history. By 1916, the Hobsons were living in Dublin and she was a 19-year-old waitress working in the city centre. So why wouldn't she, on a break or on her way home, have stopped to watch with incredulity the revolutionary scenes unfolding over six days outside the General Post Office?

I felt sad for not believing her or questioning her about everything she had seen and felt. I thought of the many times I'd walked down O'Connell Street on trips to Dublin and denied the family link to 1916.

Instead, I'd always felt a connection with the monument opposite the GPO building, dedicated to one of my city's most famous sons, James Larkin, who organised the 1905 Liverpool dock strike before moving to Ireland and single-handedly setting up the Irish Transport and General Workers Union.

Jack Jones's father was a union activist on Liverpool's docks alongside the legend they called Big Jim, and admired him so much he christened his son James Larkin Jones. His dad would regale young Jack with tales of his namesake's courage, leadership and inspirational oratory which Jones would later tell me "put me on the path to defending my class against the oppressors and the traitors."

The first woman to be elected to British parliament, Sinn Féin's Countess Markievicz, heard Larkin speak in 1913, the year Jack Jones was born, and wrote, 'I realised that I was in the presence of something that I had never come across before, some great primeval force rather than a man. A tornado, a storm-driven wave, the rush into life of spring, and the blasting breath of autumn, all seemed to emanate from the power that spoke. It seemed as if his personality caught up, assimilated, and threw back to the vast crowd that surrounded him every emotion that swayed them, every pain and joy that they had ever felt made articulate and sanctified. Only the great elemental force that is in all crowds had passed into his nature for ever.'

Three years after Larkin established the Irish TGWU, which by then was the country's largest union, he founded the Irish Labour Party and published a widely-read socialist newspaper called *The Irish Worker*. The Liverpudlian had become a genuine hero to Ireland's working-class.

But the finest of heroes are never forgotten and the man who used to organise rebellion on the shores of the Mersey was held in esteem by his own.

When Jimmy Nolan, leader of the sacked Liverpool dockers, announced their dispute was over in a letter to his members, he finished it by quoting Larkin: "Who is it speaks of defeat? I tell you a cause like ours is greater than defeat can know. It is the power of powers." That power lives on in The Casa, the monument to social justice that the sacked dockers left as their legacy.

Today, Big Jim's monument stands proudly opposite the GPO, close to where I'd like to think my nan watched the Easter Rising through the wheels of that fruit cart.

On the east face of the plinth is carved a quotation from playwright Sean O'Casey: 'He talked to the workers, spoke as only Jim Larkin could speak, not for an assignation with peace, dark obedience, or placid resignation, but trumpet-tongued of resistance to wrong, discontent with leering poverty, and defiance of any power strutting out to stand in the way of their march onward.'

On the front is an extract from one of Larkin's speeches, written in French, Irish and English, to emphasise that the human struggle for equality is a universal one:

"Les grands ne sont grands que parce que nous sommes à genoux: Levons-nous/Ní uasal aon uasal ach sinne bheith íseal: Éirímis/The great appear great because we are on our knees: Let us rise"

Next time I'm in Dublin I'm taking a bottle to that statue and toasting all the diamonds who rose from the mud.